Keys to College Success Compact

Carol Carter

Sarah Lyman Kravits

PEARSON

Boston   Columbus   Indianapolis   New York   San Francisco   Upper Saddle River
Amsterdam   Cape Town   Dubai   London   Madrid   Milan   Munich   Paris   Montréal   Toronto
Delhi   Mexico City   São Paulo   Sydney   Hong Kong   Seoul   Singapore   Taipei   Tokyo

Editor-in-Chief: Jodi McPherson
Acquisitions Editor: Katie Mahan
Editorial Assistant: Erin Carreiro
Senior Development Editor: Shannon Steed
Senior Managing Editor: Karen Wernholm
Senior Author Support/Technology Specialist: Joe Vetere
Executive Marketing Manager: Amy Judd
Senior Procurement Specialist: Roy Pickering
Image Manager: Rachel Youdelman
Text Design: John Wincek
Production Coordination and Illustration: Electronic Publishing Services Inc.
Composition and Illustration: Aptara, Inc.
Associate Director of Design, USHE EMSS/HSS/EDU: Andrea Nix
EMSS Program Design Lead: Heather Scott
Cover Design: Tamara Newnam
Cover Image: Pearson Education, Inc.

Credits and acknowledgments for material borrowed from other sources and reproduced, with permission, in this textbook appear on the appropriate page within text or on p. 152, which constitutes an extension of the copyright page.

Many of the designations by manufacturers and sellers to distinguish their products are claimed as trademarks. Where those designations appear in this book, and the publisher was aware of a trademark claim, the designations have been printed in initial caps or all caps.

Library of Congress Cataloging-in-Publication Data

Carter, Carol.
    Keys to college success compact/Carol J. Carter, LifeBound, LLC; Sarah Lyman Kravits,
Montclair State University.—First edition.
        pages cm
    ISBN 978-0-321-85742-2
    1. College student orientation—United States—Handbooks, manuals, etc.   2. Study skills—Handbooks, manuals, etc.   3. College students—United States—Life skills guides.   4. Career development—United States—Handbooks, manuals, etc.   I. Title.
    LB2343.32.C368 2015
    378.1'980973—dc23   2013030301

1 2 3 4 5 6 7 8 9 10—RRD-ROA—17   16   15   14   13

ISBN 10: 0-321-85742-9
ISBN 13: 978-0-321-85742-2

Carol Carter has spent her entire career in the business world, where she has a track record of success in corporate America, entrepreneurship, and non-profit. Her student success work is driven by firsthand knowledge of what employers expect and demand from today's graduates. As President of LifeBound, an academic and career coaching company, she drives the company's goal to help middle school and high school students become competitive in today's world, and she teaches study, interpersonal, and career skills to students as well as training and certifying adults in academic coaching skills. Carol speaks on educational topics nationally and internationally and is an expert blogger for the Huffington Post under "Impact," "College," and "Business." Carol is a co-author on many books for Pearson including the *Keys to Success* series as well as *Keys to Business Communication* and the *Career Tool Kit*. She has also published a series of books for K–12 students through LifeBound, including *Dollars and Sense: How To Be Smart About Money* and *Majoring In the Rest of Your Life: Career Secrets for College Students*.

Sarah Kravits teaches student success at Montclair State University and has been researching and writing about student success for over 15 years. As a parent of three children (ages 14, 12, and 8), a collaborator, a co-author, and an instructor, she lives the strategies for success she writes about, striving daily for goal achievement, productive teamwork, and integrity. Sarah is a co-author on the *Keys to Success* series, including *Keys to College Success*, *Keys to Community College Success*, *Keys to College Success Compact*, *Keys to Effective Learning*, *Keys to Online Learning*, and *Keys to Success Quick*. Sarah presents workshops and trainings on student success topics such as critical thinking, risk and reward, and time management at schools all over the country. Having attended the University of Virginia as a Jefferson Scholar, she continues to manifest the Jefferson Scholars Program goals of leadership, scholarship, and citizenship with her efforts to empower college students to succeed in school and in all aspects of their lives.

CONTENTS

LESSON 10   Information Literacy   112
Evaluating Sources Effectively

LESSON 11   Wellness and Stress Management   123
Staying Healthy in Mind and Body

KEYS TO COLLEGE SUCCESS COMPACT IS DIFFERENT
than any other text

Digital is Here. Students and instructors are engaging in more active learning and teaching. This requires a different kind of book. *Keys to College Success Compact* is developed specifically for one credit hour student success courses and/or those taught in blended and online environments, to address the needs and challenges of students as digital learners. It aligns with learning outcomes from both Student Success CourseConnect and MyStudentSuccessLab, designed as a standalone book or a print companion with one of these technologies.

Organized by learning outcome, both Student Success CourseConnect and MyStudentSuccessLab promote student engagement and help students "Start strong, Finish stronger" by building skills for *ongoing personal and professional development*. Student Success CourseConnect (www.pearson-learningsolutions.com/courseconnect) is one of many award-winning CourseConnect online courses designed by subject matter experts and credentialed instructional designers that supports a sequence of lessons, rich in content. *MyStudentSuccessLab* (www.mystudentsuccesslab.com) is an online solution with modules to support measurement using robust assessment with reporting capability, gradable activities, and professionalism topics.

Get Only What You Need. When students are taking (or instructors are teaching) 1 credit hour student success courses, it can be challenging to get through it all in the time available—and do so in an applied manner. There are many 'essentials' versions of books, but none offer the required 'application' piece—until now.

Keys to College Success Compact unlocks every student's potential to succeed in college, career, and life by challenging them to realize, "It's not just what you know . . . it's what you know **how to do.**" *Keys* sets the standard for connecting academic success to success beyond school, showing students how to apply strategies within college, career, and life.

This book offers *Keys*' tried-and-true emphasis on thinking skills and problem-solving, re-imagined with two goals in mind: One, a **risk and reward** framework that reflects the demands today's students face, and two, a focus on student experience specific to **1 credit or blended/online** with a more extensive research base and increased metacognition coverage.

Keys helps students take ownership, develop academic and transferable skills, and show the results of commitment and action so they are well equipped with the concentration, commitment, focus, and persistence necessary to succeed. When paired with *Student Success CourseConnect* or *MyStudentSuccessLab* as an online companion, it actively augments learning with activities, assessments, and extended thought-provoking exercises students need in order to understand how to apply concepts.

Keys to College Success Compact provides the established *Keys* set of tools for success—an understanding of how coursework connects to career and life goal achievement, and analytical, creative, and practical thinking coverage that empowers a range of cognitive ability. This program provides:

Personalized Learning with MyStudentSuccessLab. MyStudentSuccessLab (www.mystudentsuccesslab.com) **is a Learning Outcomes based technology that promotes student engagement through:**

- Full Course <u>Pre- and Post-Diagnostic</u> test based on Bloom's Taxonomy linked to key learning objectives in each topic.
- Each individual topic in the Learning Path offers a <u>Pre- and Post-Test</u> dedicated to that topic, an <u>Overview</u> of objectives to build vocabulary and repetition, access to <u>Video interviews</u> to learn about key issues 'by students, for students', <u>Practice</u> exercises to improve class prep and learning, and <u>Graded Activities</u> to build critical thinking skills and develop problem-solving abilities.
- <u>Student Resources</u> include Finish Strong 247 YouTube videos, Calculators, and Professionalism/Research & Writing/Student Success tools.
- <u>Three Student Inventories</u> are also available to increase self-awareness, and include *Golden Personality* (similar to Myers Briggs, gives insights on personal style), *ACES (Academic Competence Evaluation Scales)* (identifies at-risk), and *Thinking Styles* (shows how <u>they</u> make decisions).

College Connection to Career and Life Goals. Infused with **risk and reward**.

Risk and Reward Theme. To be rewarded with goal achievement in the fast-paced information age, students must take calculated, productive risks. The benefit of risks small (putting in the work your courses require) and large (aiming for a degree in a tough major, working toward a challenging career) is learning transferable skill building, persistence, and confidence. (Ex.—In every lesson)

Thinking Skills Coverage

- **Brain-based learning and metacognition.** The new edition cites research on building intelligence, the science of learning, the changes in the brain that happen when you remember, the cost of switch-tasking, brain development in adolescence and early adulthood, and more. This information builds student metacognition. (Ex.—Throughout the book as applicable, i.e., Lesson 1 (introduction), Lesson 5 (thinking), Lesson 7 (memory).
- **Successful Intelligence Framework.** Builds a comprehensive set of analytical, creative, practical thinking skills to empower students to strengthen their command of the problem solving process and take practical action. (Ex.—Introduced in Lesson 1; expounded upon in thinking lesson (Lesson 5); exercises *(Get Analytical, Get Creative, Get Practical)*.
- **In-lesson exercises focused on analytical (critical), creative, and practical thinking.** These exercises give readers a chance to apply an idea or skill to their personal needs and situations in a particular type of thinking. One of the following appears in each lesson. (Ex.—In each lesson, i.e., Lesson 2.)
  - *Get Analytical* builds analytical thinking skill
  - *Get Creative* builds creative thinking skill
  - *Get Practical* builds practical thinking skill
- **End-of-lesson exercises, each with a distinctive practical goal.** Exercises are targeted to develop a particular skill to have readers perform a lesson-related task that has specific personal value. (Ex.—End of lesson, i.e., Lesson 4.)
  - *Know It* builds critical thinking skill
  - *Write It* builds emotional intelligence and practical writing skill

Tailored to the 1-credit hour or Blended/Online Program experience. **Citations of groundbreaking work on motivation as well as current research on a variety of topics.** Citations add to credibility of author voice as they support ideas with research, provide the "why" behind the "what to do", and make the book relevant to today's students. They also reflect the substance of these topics to readers who may enter the course thinking it is "lightweight". (Ex.—Throughout the book, i.e., Citations of work by Robert Sternberg and Carol Dweck in Lesson 1.)

One last note: Many of our best suggestions come from you. Please contact your Pearson representative with questions or requests for resources or materials. Send suggestions for ways to improve *Keys to College Success* to Carol Carter at caroljcarter@lifebound.com or Sarah Kravits at kravitss@mail.montclair.edu. We look forward to hearing from you!

INSTRUCTOR
resources

Online Instructor's Manual. This manual provides a framework of ideas and suggestions for activities, journal writing, thought-provoking situations, and online implementation including MyStudentSuccessLab recommendations.

Online PowerPoint Presentation. A comprehensive set of PowerPoint slides that can be used by instructors for class presentations and also by students for lecture preview or review. The PowerPoint presentation includes summary slides with overview information for each lesson. These slides help students understand and review concepts within each lesson.

ACKNOWLEDGMENTS

The efforts of many have combined to make Keys to College Success Compact more than the sum of its parts. We earnestly thank:

Keys to College Success Compact Reviewers

Sheryl Bone, Kaplan University
Lyn Brown, Lamar Institute of Technology
Deidre Ann deLaughter, Gainesville State College
Kimberly Susan Forcier, University of Texas at San Antonio
Deb Holst, Metropolitan Community College
Janice Johnson, Missouri State—West Plains
Saundra Kay King, Ivy Tech Community College
John Paul Kowalczyk, University of Minnesota Duluth
Richard Marshall, Palm Beach State College
Carol Martinson, Polk State College
Donna Musselman, Santa Fe College
Jeffrey R. Pomeroy, Southwest Texas Junior College
Marie E. Provencio, California State University, Fresno
Mary Kay Scott-Garcia, Santa Fe College
Mary B. Silva, Modesto Junior College
Leigh Smith, Lamar Institute of Technology
Julie Stein, California State University, Easy Bay
Courtlann Thomas, Polk State College
Margaret Shannon Williamson, Dillard University
Jennifer Woltjen, Broome Community College

Reviewers for Previous Editions of Keys to Success Texts

Mary Adams, Northern Kentucky University
Peg Adams, Northern Kentucky University
Raishell Adams, Palm Beach Community College— Palm Beach Gardens
Veronica Allen, Texas Southern University
Fred Amador, Phoenix College
Angela A. Anderson, Texas Southern University
Robert Anderson, The College of New Jersey
Manual Aroz, Arizona State University
Dirk Baron, California State University—Bakersfield
Glenda Belote, Florida International University
Todd Benatovich, University of Texas at Arlington
John Bennett, Jr., University of Connecticut
Lynn Berkow, University of Alaska
Susan Bierster, Palm Beach Community College— Lake Worth
Ann Bingham-Newman, California State University—LA
Mary Bixby, University of Missouri–Columbia
Shawn Bixler, The University of Akron

Barbara Blandford, Education Enhancement Center at Lawrenceville, NJ
Jerry Bouchie, St. Cloud State University
D'Yonne Browder, Texas Southern University
Julia Brown, South Plains College
Mary Carstens, Wayne State College
Mona Casady, SW Missouri State University
Frederick Charles, Indiana University
Kobitta Chopra, Broward Community College
Christy Cheney, Valencia Community College—East Campus
Leslie Chilton, Arizona State University
Carrie Cokely, Curry College
Jim Coleman, Baltimore City Community College
Sara Connolly, Florida State University
Kara Craig, University of Southern Mississippi
Jacqueline Crossen-Sills, Massasoit Community College
Janet Cutshall, Sussex County Community College
Donna Dahlgren, Indiana University Southeast
Carolyn Darin, California State University—Northridge
Deryl Davis-Fulmer, Milwaukee Area Technical College
Valerie DeAngelis, Miami-Dade Community College
Joyce Annette Deaton, Jackson State Community College
Rita Delude, NH Community Technical College
Marianne Edwards, Georgia College and State University
Judy Elsley, Weber State University in Utah
Ray Emett, Salt Lake Community College
Jacqueline Fleming, Texas Southern University
Ann French, New Mexico State University
Patsy Frenchman, Santa Fe Community College
Rodolfo Frias, Santiago Canyon College
Ralph Gallo, Texas Southern University
Jean Gammon, Chattanooga State Technical Community College
Skye Gentile, California State University, Hayward
Bob Gibson, University of Nebraska—Omaha
Lewis Grey, Middle Tennessese State University
Jennifer Guyer-Wood, Minnesota State University
Sue Halter, Delgado Community College
Suzy Hampton, University of Montana
Karen Hardin, Mesa Community College
Patricia Hart, California State University, Fresno
Maureen Hurley, University of Missouri—Kansas City
Karen Iversen, Heald Colleges

Valerie Jefferson, Rock Valley College
Gary G. John, Richland College
Cynthia Johnson, Palm Beach Community College—Lake Worth
Elvira Johnson, Central Piedmont Community College
S. Renee Jones, Florida Community College at Jacksonville—North Campus
Georgia Kariotis, Oakton Community College
Laura Kauffman, Indian River Community College
Kathryn K. Kelly, St. Cloud State University
Cathy Keyler, Palm Beach Community College—Palm Beach Gardens
Quentin Kidd, Christopher Newport University
Nancy Kosmicke, Mesa State College
Patsy Krech, University of Memphis
Dana Kuehn, Florida Community College at Jacksonville—Deerwood Center
Noreen Lace, California State University—Northridge
Charlene Latimer, Daytona Beach Community College—Deland
Paul Lede, Texas Southern University
Lanita Legan, Texas State University
Linda Lemkau, North Idaho College
Kristina Leonard, Daytona Beach Community College—Flagler/Palm Coast
Christine A. Lottman, University of Cincinnati
Frank T. Lyman, Jr., University of Maryland
Judith Lynch, Kansas State University
Patricia A. Malinowski, Finger Lakes Community College
Marvin Marshak, University of Minnesota
Kathy Masters, Arkansas State University
Howard Masuda, California State University—Los Angeles
Antoinette McConnell, Northeastern Illinois University
Natalie McLellan, Holmes Community College
Caron Mellblom-Nishioka, California State University—Dominguez Hills
Jenny Middleton, Seminole Community College
Barnette Miller Moore, Indian River Community College
Gladys Montalvo, Palm Beach Community College
Rebecca Munro, Gonzaga University
Nanci C. Nielsen, University of New Mexico—Valencia Campus
Kimberly O'Connor, Community College of Baltimore City
Sue Palmer, Brevard Community College
Alan Pappas, Santa Fe Community College
Bobbie Parker, Alabama State University
Carolyn Patterson, Texas State Technical College—West Texas
Curtis Peters, Indiana University Southeast
Tom Peterson, Grand View University
Virginia Phares, DeVry of Atlanta
Brenda Prinzavalli, Beloit College

Margaret Quinn, University of Memphis
Corliss A. Rabb, Texas Southern University
Terry Rafter-Carles, Valencia Community College—Orlando
Jacqueline Robinson, Milwaukee Area Technical College
Eleanor Rosenfield, Rochester Institute of Technology
Robert Roth, California State University—Fullerton
Manuel Salgado, Elgin Community College
Jack E. Sallie Jr., Montgomery College
Rebecca Samberg, Housatonic Community College
Karyn L. Schulz, Community College of Baltimore County—Dundalk
Pamela Shaw, Broward Community County—South Campus
Tia Short, Boise State University
Jacqueline Simon, Education Enhancement Center at Lawrenceville, NJ
Carolyn Smith, University of Southern Indiana
Cheryl Spector, California State University—Northridge
Julie Stein, California State University
Rose Stewart-Fram, McLennan Community College
Joan Stottlemyer, Carroll College
Jill R. Strand, University of Minnesota—Duluth
Tracy Stuck, Lake Sumter Community College—Leesburg Campus
Toni M. Stroud, Texas Southern University
Karla Thompson, New Mexico State University
Cheri Tillman, Valdosta State University
Ione Turpin, Broward Community College
Thomas Tyson, SUNY Stony Brook
Joy Vaughan-Brown, Broward Community College
Arturo Vazquez, Elgin Community College
Eve Walden, Valencia Community College
Marsha Walden, Valdosta State University
Susannah Waldrop, University of South Carolina, Upstate
Rose Wassman, DeAnza College
Debbie Warfield, Seminole Community College
Ronald Weisberger, Bristol Community College
Jill Wilks, Southern Utah University
Angela Williams, The Citadel
Don Williams, Grand Valley State University
William Wilson, St. Cloud State University
Kim Winford, Blinn College
Tania Wittgenfeld, Rock Valley College
Michelle G. Wolf, Florida Southern College

■ Robert J. Sternberg, for his groundbreaking work on successful intelligence and for his gracious permission to use and adapt that work for this text.

■ Our Editor-in-Chief Jodi McPherson, for her commitment to the *Keys to Success* series and her vision of the relevance of risk and reward.

- Our Acquisitions Editor Katie Mahan, Senior Development Editor Shannon Steed, and Editorial Assistant Erin Carreiro for their dedication, creative ideas, and constant effort in moving us all toward the goal.

- Our production team for their patience, flexibility, and attention to detail, especially Image Manager Rachel Youdelman, Designer John Wincek, Designer Heather Scott, and Diana Neatrour and the team at Electronic Publishing Services Inc.

- Our marketing gurus for their continued support, especially Amy Judd, Executive Marketing Manager; Julie Hildebrand and the other national account managers who support career schools and alternative education on behalf of Pearson; and sales directors and content specialists.

- Charlotte Morrissey for her guidance, wisdom, and insight regarding college students, and for her ongoing and dedicated efforts on behalf of the *Keys* series.

- Greg Tobin, President of Higher Education English, Math, and Student Success, and Tim Bozik, CEO of U.S. Higher Education, for their support of the *Keys* series.

- The Pearson representatives and the management team led by Eric Severson, Executive Vice President, Higher Education Sales.

- The staff at LifeBound for their hard work and dedication: Maureen Breeze, Brittany Havey, Jim Hoops, Angelica Jestrovich, Kyle Kilroy, Michelle Stout, Noel Wilson, Jimmy Young.

- The students who helped us develop our ideas and improve the effectiveness of our materials: Thuyanh Astbury, University of Denver; Jacklynn Blanchard, University of Colorado Boulder; Liv Shehawk Bryan, Arapahoe Community College; Brandy Castner, Metropolitan State University of Denver; Mark Davis, Colorado State University; Grainne Griffiths, Tufts University; Jenna Jacobs, University of Minnesota; Jordan Jones, Metropolitan State University of Denver; Nicoll Laikola, Metropolitan State University of Denver; Jonathon Lasich, University of Colorado Denver; Natasha Malchow, Metropolitan State University of Denver; Sarah Martinez, Metropolitan State University of Denver; Dylan Mey, CEC with Denver Public Schools; Maddie Mey, Wheat Ridge High School; Claire Petras, University of Colorado Denver; Alivia Porpora, Regis University; Woody Roseland, Metropolitan State University of Denver; Trevor Scannell, Miami University Hamilton; Danny Starr, Fort Lewis University; Danielle Thomas, Central Michigan University; Michael Tyrrell-Ead, Golden High School; Jacob Voegele, Gonzaga University; Jeanette Young, School of Mines.

- Photographers Erin Neely and Michael Santiago for authentically representing the student perspective through their original contributions to the photo program.

- Dede DeLaughter, Manny Larenas, and Cheri Tillman for their input and sage advice.

- Our families and friends, who have encouraged us and put up with our commitments.

- Judy Block, who contributed research and writing to this book.

- Special thanks to Joyce Bishop, who created the learning preference assessments, contributed to the success of this book over the past fifteen years, and continues to support college students with her wisdom and insights.

Finally, for their ideas, opinions, and stories, we would like to thank all of the students and instructors with whom we work. Sarah would like to thank her students at Montclair State University who have granted her the privilege of sharing part of their journey through college, as well as the insightful instructors and advisors affiliated with the Center for Advising and Student Transitions. Carol would like to thank the people who have gone through her coaching trainings and who continue to strive to improve students' ability to succeed, including Barbara Gadis, Jennifer Gomez-Mejia, Vanessa Harris, Lynn Montrose, Lindsay Morlock, Lynn Troyka, Melissa Vito, and Kathy York. To all of our readers: We appreciate that, through reading this book, you give us the opportunity to learn and discover with you—in your classroom, in your home, on the bus, and wherever else learning takes place.

BREAKTHROUGH
To better results

Give your students what they need to succeed.

As an instructor, you want to help your students succeed in college. As a mentor, you want to make sure students reach their professional objectives. We share these goals, and we're committed to partnering with educators to ensure that each individual student succeeds—in college and beyond.

Simply put, Pearson creates technologies, content, and services that help students break through to better results. When a goal as important as education is at stake, no obstacle should be allowed to stand in the way.

The following pages detail some of our products and services designed to help your students succeed. These include:

- Pearson Course Redesign
- MyFoundationsLab for Student Success
- MyStudentSuccessLab
- CourseConnect™

- Custom Services
- Resources for Students
- Professional Development for Instructors

PEARSON

Pearson Course Redesign

Collect, measure, and interpret data to support efficacy.

Rethink the way you deliver instruction.

Pearson has successfully partnered with colleges and universities engaged in course redesign for over 10 years through workshops, Faculty Advisor programs, and online conferences. Here's how to get started!

- Visit our course redesign site at **www.pearsoncourseredesign.com** for information on getting started, a list of Pearson-sponsored course redesign events, and recordings of past course redesign events.

- Request to connect with a Faculty Advisor, a fellow instructor who is an expert in course redesign, by visiting **www.mystudentsuccesslab.com/community.**

- Join our Course Redesign Community at **www.community.pearson.com/courseredesign** and connect with colleagues around the country who are participating in course redesign projects.

Don't forget to measure the results of your course redesign!

Examples of data you may want to collect include:

- Improvement of homework grades, test averages, and pass rates over past semesters

- Correlation between time spent in an online product and final average in the course

- Success rate in the next level of the course

- Retention rate (i.e., percentage of students who drop, fail, or withdraw)

Need support for data collection and interpretation?

Ask your local Pearson representative how to connect with a member of Pearson's Efficacy Team.

MyFoundationsLab for Student Success

Prepare your students for college-level work in basic skills.

MyFoundationsLab®

Built on the success of MyMathLab, MyReadingLab, and MyWritingLab, **MyFoundationsLab** is a comprehensive online mastery-based resource for assessing and remediating college- and career-readiness skills in mathematics, reading, and writing. The system offers a rich environment of pre-built and customized assessments, personalized learning plans, and highly interactive activities that enable students to master skills at their own pace. Ideal for learners of various levels and ages, including those in placement test prep or transitional programs, MyFoundationsLab facilitates the skill development students need in order to be successful in college-level courses and careers.

New! MyFoundationsLab for Student Success

In response to market demand for more "non-cognitive" skills, Pearson now offers **MyFoundationsLab for Student Success**, which combines rich mathematics, reading, and writing content with the 19+ MyStudentSuccessLab modules that support ongoing personal and professional development. To see a complete list of content, visit **www.mystudentsuccesslab.com/mfl**.

If you're affiliated with boot camp programs, student orientation, a testing center, or simply interested in a self-paced, pre-course solution that helps students better prepare for college-level work in basic skills, contact your Pearson representative for more information.

"Students like learning at their own pace; they can go as fast or as slow as they need. MyFoundationsLab facilitates this structure; it's more driven by mastery learning, not by what the teacher says a student should be doing."

—Jennifer McLearen, Instructor,
Piedmont Virginia Community College

Data from January 2007 through June 2008 offers solid evidence of the success of MyFoundationsLab:

91% of students who retested in reading improved at least one course level

70% of students who retested in writing improved at least one course level

43% of students who retested in math improved at least one course level

MyStudentSuccessLab

Help students start strong and finish stronger.

MyStudentSuccessLab™

MyStudentSuccessLab helps students acquire the skills they need for ongoing personal and professional development. It is a learning-outcomes-based technology that helps students advance their knowledge and build critical skills for success. MyStudentSuccessLab's peer-led video interviews, interactive practice exercises, and activities foster the acquisition of academic, life, and professionalism skills.

Students have access to:

- Pre- and Post-Full Course Diagnostic Assessments linked to key learning objectives

- Pre- and Post-Tests dedicated to individual topics in the Learning Path

- An overview of objectives to build vocabulary and repetition

- Videos on key issues that are "by students, for students," conveniently organized by topic

- Practice exercises to improve class prep and learning

- Graded activities to build critical-thinking and problem-solving skills

- Student resources, including Finish Strong 24/7 YouTube videos, professionalism tools, research aids, writing help, and GPA, savings, budgeting, and retirement calculators

- Student Inventories designed to increase self-awareness, including Golden Personality and Thinking Styles

Topics and features include:

- College Transition
- Communication
- Critical Thinking
- Financial Literacy
- Goal Setting
- Information Literacy
- Interviewing
- Job Search Strategies
- Learning Preferences
- Listening and Taking Notes in Class
- Majors/Careers and Resumes
- Memory and Studying
- Problem Solving
- Reading and Annotating
- Self-Management Skills at Work
- Stress Management
- Teamwork
- Test Taking
- Time Management
- Workplace Communication
- Workplace Etiquette

Students utilizing MyStudentSuccessLab may purchase Pearson texts in a number of cost-saving formats—including **eTexts, loose-leaf Books à la Carte editions**, and more. Contact your Pearson representative for more information.

Assessment

Beyond the Pre- and Post-Full Course Diagnostic Assessments and Pre- and Post-Tests within each module, additional learning-outcome-based tests can be created using a secure testing engine, and may be printed or delivered online. These tests can be customized to accommodate specific teaching needs by editing individual questions or entire tests.

Reporting

Measurement matters—and is ongoing in nature. MyStudentSuccessLab lets you determine what data you need, set up your course accordingly, and collect data via reports. The high quality and volume of test questions allows for data comparison and measurement.

MyLabsPlus service is a teaching and learning environment that offers enhanced reporting features and analysis. With powerful administrative tools and dedicated support, MyLabsPlus offers an advanced suite of management resources for MyStudentSuccessLab.

Content and Functionality Training

Organized by topic, the **Instructor Implementation Guide** provides grading rubrics, suggestions for video use, and more to save time on course prep. Our **User Guide** and **"How do I…" YouTube videos** indicate how to use MyStudentSuccessLab, and show scenarios from getting started to utilizing the Gradebook.

Peer Support

The **Student Success Community** site is a place for you to connect with other educators to exchange ideas and advice on courses, content, and MyStudentSuccessLab. The site is filled with timely articles, discussions, video posts, and more. Join, share, and be inspired!
www.mystudentsuccesscommunity.com

The **Faculty Advisor Network** is Pearson's peer-to-peer mentoring program in which experienced MyStudentSuccessLab users share their best practices and expertise. Our Faculty Advisors are experienced in one-on-one phone and email coaching, webinars, presentations, and live training sessions. Contact your Pearson representative to connect with a Faculty Advisor or learn more about the Faculty Advisor Network.

Integration and Compliance

You can integrate our digital solutions with your learning management system in a variety of ways. For more information, or if documentation is needed for ADA compliance, contact your local Pearson representative.

CourseConnect™

Trust that your online course is the best in its class.

Designed by subject matter experts and credentialed instructional designers, **CourseConnect** offers award-winning customizable online courses that help students build skills for ongoing personal and professional development.

CourseConnect uses topic-based, interactive modules that follow a consistent learning path–from introduction, to presentation, to activity, to review. Its built-in tools–including user-specific pacing charts, personalized study guides, and interactive exercises– provide a student-centric learning experience that minimizes distractions and helps students stay on track and complete the course successfully. Features such as relevant video, audio, and activities, personalized (or editable) syllabi, discussion forum topics and questions, assignments, and quizzes are all easily accessible. CourseConnect is available in a variety of learning management systems and accommodates various term lengths as well as self-paced study. And, our compact textbook editions align to CourseConnect course outcomes.

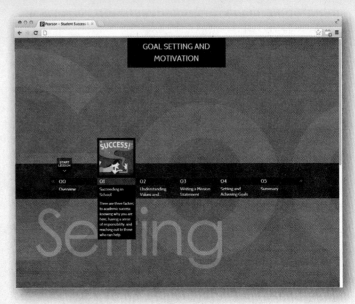

Choose from the following three course outlines ("Lesson Plans")

Student Success

- Goal Setting, Values, and Motivation
- Time Management
- Financial Literacy
- Creative Thinking, Critical Thinking, and Problem Solving
- Learning Preferences
- Listening and Note-Taking in Class
- Reading and Annotating
- Studying, Memory, and Test-Taking
- Communicating and Teamwork
- Information Literacy
- Staying Balanced: Stress Management
- Career Exploration

Career Success

- Planning Your Career Search
- Knowing Yourself: Explore the Right Career Path
- Knowing the Market: Find Your Career Match
- Preparing Yourself: Gain Skills and Experience Now
- Networking
- Targeting Your Search: Locate Positions, Ready Yourself
- Building a Portfolio: Your Resume and Beyond
- Preparing for Your Interview
- Giving a Great Interview
- Negotiating Job Offers, Ensuring Future Success

Professional Success

- Introducing Professionalism
- Workplace Goal Setting
- Workplace Ethics and Your Career
- Workplace Time Management
- Interpersonal Skills at Work
- Workplace Conflict Management
- Workplace Communications: Email and Presentations
- Effective Workplace Meetings
- Workplace Teams
- Customer Focus and You
- Understanding Human Resources
- Managing Career Growth and Change

Custom Services

Personalize instruction to best facilitate learning.

As the industry leader in custom publishing, we are committed to meeting your instructional needs by offering flexible and creative choices for course materials that will maximize learning and student engagement.

Pearson Custom Library

Using our online book-building system, create a custom book by selecting content from our course-specific collections that consist of chapters from Pearson Student Success and Career Development titles and carefully selected, copyright-cleared, third-party content and pedagogy. **www.pearsoncustomlibrary.com**

Custom Publications

In partnership with your Custom Field Editor, modify, adapt, and combine existing Pearson books by choosing content from across the curriculum and organizing it around your learning outcomes. As an alternative, you can work with your Editor to develop your original material and create a textbook that meets your course goals.

Custom Technology Solutions

Work with Pearson's trained professionals, in a truly consultative process, to create engaging learning solutions. From interactive learning tools, to eTexts, to custom websites and portals, we'll help you simplify your life as an instructor.

Online Education

Pearson offers online course content for online classes and hybrid courses. This online content can also be used to enhance traditional classroom courses. Our award-winning CourseConnect includes a fully developed syllabus, media-rich lecture presentations, audio lectures, a wide variety of assessments, discussion board questions, and a strong instructor resource package.

For more information on custom Student Success services, please visit **www.pearsonlearningsolutions.com** or call **800-777-6872**.

Resources for Students

Help students save and succeed throughout their college experience.

Books à la Carte Editions

The Books à la Carte (a.k.a. "Student Value" or "Loose Leaf") edition is a three-hole-punched, full-color version of the premium text that's available at 35% less than the traditional bound textbook. Students using MyStudentSuccessLab as part of their course materials can purchase a Books à la Carte edition at a special discount from within the MyLab course where "Click here to order" is denoted.

CourseSmart eTexbooks

CourseSmart eTextbooks offer a convenient, affordable alternative to printed texts. Students can save up to 50% off the price of a traditional text, and receive helpful search, note-taking, and printing tools.

Programs and Services

As the world's leading learning company, Pearson has pledged to help students succeed in college and reach their educational and career aspirations. We're so dedicated to this goal that we've created a unique set of programs and services that we call **Pearson Students**. Through this program, we offer undergraduate students opportunities to learn from, and interact with, each other and Pearson professionals through social media platforms, internships, part-time jobs, leadership endeavors, events, and awards. To learn more about our Pearson Students programs and meet our Pearson Students, visit **www.pearsonstudents.com**.

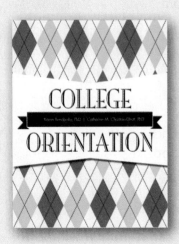

Orientation to College

In Bendersky's *College Orientation,* students learn how to adapt to college life and stay on track towards a degree—all while learning behaviors that promote achievement after graduation. This reference tool is written from an insider's point of view and has a distinct focus on promoting appropriate college conduct. It covers topics that help students navigate college while learning how to apply this knowledge in the workplace.

Help with Online Classes

Barrett's *Power Up: A Practical Student's Guide to Online Learning*, 2/e serves as a textbook for students of all backgrounds who are new to online learning, and as a reference for instructors who are also novices in the area or who need insight into the perspective of such students.

Effective Communication with Professors

In Ellen Bremen's *Say This, NOT That to Your Professor*, an award-winning, tenured communication professor takes students "inside the faculty mind," and guides them to manage their classroom experience with confidence. This book aims to facilitate improved relationships with professors, better grades, and an amazing college experience.

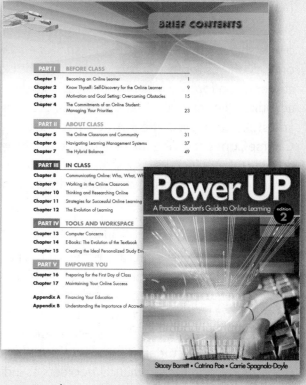

Power UP
A Practical Student's Guide to Online Learning   edition 2

Stacey Barrett • Catrina Poe • Carrie Spagnola-Doyle

Expert Advice

Our consumer-flavored *IDentity* series booklets are written by national subject-matter experts, such as personal finance specialist, author, and TV personality, Farnoosh Torabi. The authors of this series offer strategies and activities on topics such as careers, college success, financial literacy, financial responsibility, and more.

Quick Tips for Success

Our *Success Tips* series provides one-page "quick tips" on six topics essential to college or career success. The *Success Tips* series includes MyStudentSuccessLab, Time Management, Resources All Around You, Now You're Thinking, Maintaining Your Financial Sanity, and Building Your Professional Image. The *Success Tips for Professionalism* series includes Create Your Personal Brand, Civility Paves the Way Toward Success, Succeeding in Your Diverse World, Building Your Professional Image, Get Things Done with Virtual Teams, and Get Ready for Workplace Success.

Professional Development for Instructors

Augment your teaching with engaging resources.

Foster Ownership

Student dynamics have changed, so how are you helping students take ownership of their education? Megan Stone's *Ownership* series offers online courses for instructors, and printed booklets for students, on four key areas of professional development: accountability, critical thinking, effective planning, and study strategies. The instructor courses, in our CourseConnect online format, include teaching methods, activities, coaching tips, assessments, animations, and video. Online courses and printed booklets are available together or separately.

Promote Active Learning

Infuse student success into any program with our *Engaging Activities* series. Written and compiled by National Student Success Institute (NSSI®) co-founders Amy Baldwin, Steve Piscitelli, and Robert Sherfield, the material provides educators strategies, procedural information, and activities they can use with students immediately. Amy, Steve, and Robb developed these practical booklets as indispensable, hands-on resources for educators who want to empower teachers, professional development coordinators, coaches, and administrators to actively engage their classes.

Address Diverse Populations

Support various student populations that require specific strategies to succeed. Choose from an array of booklets that align with the needs of adult learners, digital learners, first-generation learners, international learners, English language learners, student athletes, and more.

Create Consistency

Instructional resources lend a common foundation for support. We offer **online Instructor's Manuals** that provide a framework of ideas and suggestions for online and in-class activities and journal writing assignments. We also offer comprehensive **online PowerPoint presentations** that can be used by instructors for class presentations, and by students to preview lecture material and review concepts within each chapter.

The Rewards of College

TAKING RISKS THAT MOVE YOU TOWARD SUCCESS

IN THIS LESSON YOU WILL LEARN HOW THE THINKING SKILLS OF SUCCESSFUL INTELLIGENCE— ANALYTICAL, CREATIVE, AND PRACTICAL THINKING—CAN HELP YOU ACHIEVE YOUR GOALS. YOU WILL LEARN HOW CALCULATED RISKS CAN BRING YOU REWARDS AS YOU CONNECT WITH RESOURCES, NAVIGATE COLLEGE CULTURE, BUILD INTEGRITY AND EMOTIONAL INTELLIGENCE, AND CREATE A GROWTH MINDSET.

52%

Notes +

Today   Mar 10   8:01 AM

Working through this lesson will help you to:

- Explain three keys to academic success   P. 4
- Analyze the relationship between values, motivation, and academic success   P. 8
- Write a personal mission statement   P. 9
- Analyze the characteristics of SMART goals   PP. 9–10

WHY IS COLLEGE A RISK,
and what reward does it offer?

What comes to mind when you think about risk? Cliff diving, perhaps, or buying shares of stock in a volatile company, or serving in the combat division of the military? Perhaps the word conjures up images of substance abuse, unsafe sex, or breaking the law. Whether you tend to think of deliberate risks calculated to bring reward (like the stock purchase) or problematic, not-so-deliberate risks that often come as a byproduct of a choice (like drinking too much), one thing is fairly certain: Most people would not include "going to college" on a list of risks.

College is often seen as a risk-free, safe choice that increases your chances of career stability. However, striving for a degree in higher education is one of the most risk-filled and potentially rewarding actions you will take in your lifetime. To follow this path, you risk your most valuable resources—time, money, and yourself. Only with this risk come the rewards essential to your success. Skills, intelligence, motivation, employment, growth, and advancement can be yours, but only as a result of hard work, dedication, and focus.

MyStudentSuccessLab
(www.mystudentsuccesslab.com) is an online solution designed to help you "Start Strong, Finish Stronger" by building skills for ongoing personal and professional development.

Begin your transition to college by looking at the present—the culture of college, what you can expect, and what college expects of you. As you read, keep in mind that the reward you earn from college depends on the risk you take.

The Culture of College

In high school, students learn all kinds of information but don't often put it to work. The result? They tend to forget much of it. College instruction and learning give you the opportunity to take things to a new, more meaningful level. What are some key elements of college culture?

Independent learning. College offers the reward of freedom and independence in exchange for the risk of functioning without much guidance. Instructors expect you to take note of and remember key syllabus deadlines, keep up with reading, attend class, complete assignments and projects, and more without much guidance.

Fast pace. College courses move faster, with more papers, homework, reading, and projects than you probably had in high school or on the job. Although demanding, the pace can also energize and motivate you, especially if you did not feel inspired by high school assignments.

Challenging work. Although challenging, college-level work can reward you with enormous opportunity to learn and grow. College texts often have more words per page, higher-level terminology, and more abstract ideas compared to high school texts. In addition, college often involves complex assignments, challenging research papers, group projects, lab work, and tests.

More out-of-class time to manage. The freedom of your schedule requires strong time management skills. On days when your classes end early, start late, or don't meet at all, you will need to use open blocks of time effectively as you juggle responsibilities, including perhaps a job and family.

Diverse culture. Typically, you will encounter different ideas and diverse people in college. Your fellow students may differ from you in age, life experience, ethnicity, political mindset, family obligations, values, and much more. Also, if you commute to school or take hybrid or fully online courses, or attend class with others who commute or e-commute, you may find it challenging to connect with fellow students.

Higher-level thinking. You'll need to risk moving beyond recall. Instead of just summarizing and taking the ideas of others at face value, you will interpret, evaluate, generate new ideas, and apply what you know to new situations (more on thinking skills later in this lesson).

College offers a range of resources to help you academically, financially, socially, and emotionally. Your end of the bargain is to seek out the resources you need.

Connect with People

Learning about who can help you, and reaching out to those people, will help you become more successful in college and beyond.

Faculty and staff

Faculty and staff are among the most valuable—but underused—sources of help. As a recent survey shows, only 25% of students asked a teacher for advice outside of class at any time during the term.[1] Instructors can help you learn more, and more efficiently.

Mentors

A *mentor*, defined as a wise and trusted guide, is a person with qualities you admire who takes a particular interest in your growth. A mentor can come to you as part of an organized program, but more often students find a mentor in a casual way, discovering a teacher, administrator, more experienced student, supervisor, or other person who offers advice and support. Think about the people who guide you every day. If someone stands out to you, seek that person's advice. You may find a true mentor who can help you through the ups and downs of college life.

Connect with Technology and Written Resources

The booklets, papers, and emails you get at the start of college and every term often have key information. Keep them at the ready. Here's how to put these resources to use.

Class and course information

Your syllabus is one of your most important resources. The syllabus tells you everything you need to know about your course—when to read chapters and materials, dates of exams and due dates for assignments, how your final grade is calculated, and more. Make use of it by writing key dates in your calendar, spotting time crunches, and getting a sense of how much time you need to set aside to study. Keep it handy, or bookmark or print it if it is online, so you can refer to it throughout the term.

Also, consult your student handbook and course catalog for information about school procedures and policies—registration, requirements for majors, transferring, and so on. These publications are most likely available both in hard copy and on your school's website.

Technology

You will be expected to connect to your college's network and use the network for a variety of purposes, including research and communication. How can you make the most of it?

- *Get started right away.* Register for an email account and connect to the college network. If your school uses a learning management system (LMS), such as Blackboard, make sure you are signed up. In addition, register your cell phone number with the school so you can get emergency alerts.
- *Use the system.* Communicate with instructors and fellow students using your school email and/or LMS.
- *Save and protect your work.* Save electronic work periodically onto a primary or backup hard drive, CD, or flash drive. Use antivirus software if your system needs it.
- *Stay on task.* During study time, try to limit Internet surfing, texting, cruising Facebook, and playing computer games (and avoid these activities entirely during class time for an online course).

It also pays to use email etiquette when communicating with instructors, rather than sending the same kinds of emails that you would send to your friends.

What You Can Gain from College

Studies show the following benefits of a college education:[2]

- *Increased income.* College graduates earn, on average, around $20,000 more per year than those with a high school diploma.
- *Increased chances of finding and keeping a job.* The unemployment rate for college graduates is less than half that of high school graduates.

Getting through the day-to-day activities of college demands basic computer know-how, as well as an understanding of the school's research and communication technology.

- *Better health.* With the knowledge and increased self-awareness that college often brings, both college graduates and their children are more likely to stay healthy.
- *More money for the future.* College graduates, on average, put away more money in savings.
- *Broader thinking.* College graduates tend to be more open minded and less prejudiced. They generally have more understanding of cultures and more knowledge of the world.
- *Better decision making.* As consumers, college graduates tend to think more carefully and comprehensively about the pros and cons of a purchase before diving in.

Now that you have an overview of the college experience, think more broadly about how your thinking skills can set you up for success in your college experience and beyond.

WHAT SKILLS AND ATTITUDES *can help you succeed?*

How can you successfully shift to college-level work? First, know that you can grow as a thinker. Research by psychologists such as Robert Sternberg, Carol Dweck, and others suggests that intelligence is not fixed; people have the capacity to *increase* intelligence as they learn.[3] In other words, the risk of effort and focus can produce the reward of greater brain power. Research shows that when you are learning through questioning, answering, and action, your brain and nerve cells (neurons) are forming new connections (synapses) among one another by growing new branches (dendrites).[4] These increased connections enable the brain to do and learn more.

Next, explore the types of thinking that make that growth happen.

The Three Thinking Skills of Successful Intelligence

How can you take productive risks that move you toward your important goals in college, work, and life? According to Sternberg, it takes three types of thinking: analytical (critical), creative, and practical. Together, he calls them *successful intelligence*.[5] What does each of the three thinking skills contribute to goal achievement?

- Commonly known as *critical thinking*, analytical thinking starts with engaging with information through asking questions and then involves analyzing and evaluating information, often to work through a problem or decision. It often involves comparing, contrasting, and cause-and-effect thinking.
- Creative thinking involves generating new and different ideas and approaches to problems, and, often, viewing the world in ways that disregard convention. It can involve imagining and considering different perspectives. Creative thinking also means taking information that you already know and thinking about it in a new way.
- Practical thinking refers to putting what you've learned into action to solve a problem or make a decision. Practical thinking often means learning from experience and emotional intelligence (explained later in the lesson), enabling you to work effectively with others and to accomplish goals despite obstacles.

Together, these abilities move you toward a goal. Read on to explore more skills and attitudes that can get you where you want to go.

The Growth Mindset

Although you cannot control what happens around you, you *can* control your attitude, or *mindset*. Based on years of research, Carol Dweck has determined that the perception that talent and intelligence can develop with effort—what she calls a *growth mindset*—promotes success. "This view creates a love of learning and resilience that is essential for great accomplishment," reports Dweck.[6]

By contrast, people with a *fixed mindset* believe that they have a set level of talent and intelligence, and they tend to work and risk less. "In one world [that of the fixed mindset], effort is a bad thing. It . . . means you're not smart or talented. If you were, you wouldn't need effort. In the other world [growth mindset], effort is what *makes* you smart or talented."[7]

For example, two students do poorly on an anatomy midterm. One blames the time of day of the test and says she is horrible in science, while the other feels that she didn't put in enough study time. The first student couldn't change the material or the class time, of course, and didn't see the value of changing her study plan (no risk or extra effort). As you may expect, she did poorly on the final. The second student put in more study time after the midterm (risk and increased effort) and improved her grade on the final as a result. This student knows that the risk of focused effort brings valuable reward.

You don't have to be born with a growth mindset; you can build one. "You have a choice," says Dweck. "Mindsets are just beliefs. They're powerful beliefs, but they're just something in your mind, and you can change your mind."[8] Actions that may help you change your mind include being responsible, practicing academic integrity, and learning from failure.

Be responsible

A growth mindset encourages you to take responsible actions, building self-esteem in the process. If you know you can earn the reward of accomplishing something, you will be more likely to risk trying. Action and belief form an energizing cycle—the more you do, the more you believe you *can* do, which leads you to do more yet again.

Being a responsible student means taking the basic actions that form the building blocks of success (see Key 1.1).

Consider this example: Two students start the term feeling pretty confident. One works to get to class, keep up with assignments, and study regularly. The other attends class but does the minimum necessary outside of class. Although they have both spent

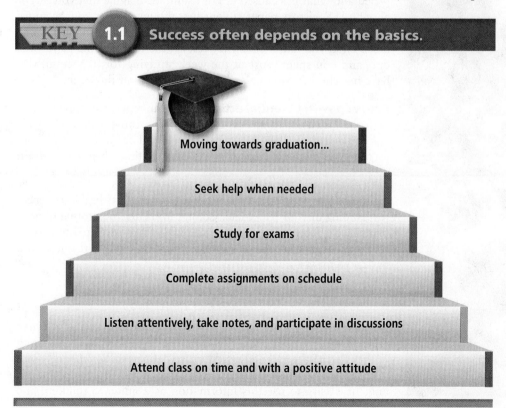

KEY 1.1 Success often depends on the basics.

Moving towards graduation...

Seek help when needed

Study for exams

Complete assignments on schedule

Listen attentively, take notes, and participate in discussions

Attend class on time and with a positive attitude

the same number of hours in class and the same amount of money, one student probably has profited far more from it, having built both knowledge and a growth mindset that will contribute to future learning.

Practice academic integrity

Choosing to act with *integrity*—by one definition, meaning that you are honest, trustworthy, fair, respectful, and responsible[9]—increases your self-esteem and earns respect from those around you. It gives you more of a chance to retain what you learn, and builds positive habits for life.

Despite the benefits, the principles of *academic integrity* (acting with integrity in your dealings with information and people as a college student) are frequently violated. In a recent survey, three of four undergraduate students admitted to cheating at least once during college.[10] If caught, you risk losing grade points, failing a course, or suspension or expulsion.

What does academic integrity have to do with a growth mindset? Well, first of all, being fair, honest, and responsible takes risk and effort. Second, and more important, academic integrity comes naturally to students who aim to grow and see struggle and failure as opportunities to learn. If you want the reward of learning, cheating won't help you earn it.

Read your school's code of honor or academic integrity policy in your student handbook or online. When you enrolled, you agreed to abide by it. Take a good look at the potential consequences of violating the policy. Measure these consequences against the risk of working hard to complete your degree with integrity. Which reward would you choose?

Learn from failure

Every single person experiences failures. What turns a failure into an opportunity is the determination to learn from the experience. Failure approached with a growth mindset can spark motivation, showing you what you can do better and driving you to improve. The next time something stops you in your tracks, try the following.

Analyze the situation realistically. Look carefully at what happened and what has caused it. For example, imagine that you forgot about a U.S. history paper. If your first thought is that your memory is useless, get yourself off that unproductive path by looking at some facts. First, you had a chemistry test on the day that the paper was due, and you spent most of the week studying for it. Second, you have not checked your calendar consistently over the week.

Come up with potential actions. You can request an appointment with the instructor to discuss the paper. You can set alarms in your planner and check due dates more regularly. If chemistry is a priority for you, you can accept that it's okay to put it first when time is short.

Take action and cope with consequences. Meet with your history instructor to discuss the situation, accepting there may be consequences for handing in your paper late. Commit to better monitoring of your planner, perhaps setting dates for individual tasks related to assignments and trying to complete papers a day before they are due so you have time for last-minute corrections.

Emotional Intelligence

Success in a diverse world depends on relationships, and effective relationships demand emotional intelligence. Psychologists John Mayer, Peter Salovey, and David Caruso define *emotional intelligence* (EI) as the ability to understand "one's own and others' emotions and the ability to use this information as a guide to thinking and

Emotional intelligence helps you build positive and productive relationships in and out of college.

get practical

USE EMOTIONAL INTELLIGENCE TO GET INVOLVED

Complete the following on paper or in digital format.

First, look in your student handbook at the resources and organizations your school offers. These may include some or all of the following:

Academic centers (reading, writing, etc.)	On-campus work opportunities
Academic organizations	Religious organizations
Adult education center	School publications
Arts clubs (music, drama, dance, etc.)	School TV/radio stations
Fraternities/sororities	Sports clubs
Groups for students with disabilities	Student associations
International student groups	Student government
Minority student groups	Volunteer groups

As you read the list, take note of how different organizations or activities make you feel. What interests you right away? What makes you turn the page? What scares you? What thoughts do your feelings raise—for example, why do you think you like or fear a particular activity? Is a positive outcome possible from trying something that scares you at first?

Taking this emotional intelligence feedback into consideration, risk trying some new experiences. List three offices or organizations you plan to explore this term. Then, using school publications or online resources, find and record the following information for each:

- Location

- Hours, or times of meetings

- What it offers

- Phone number, website, or email

Finally, when you have made contact, note what happened and whether you are considering getting involved.

behavior."[11] Emotional intelligence helps you *understand* what you and others feel and use that understanding to choose how to think and how to act. Look at Key 1.2 to see how you move through a set of skills, or abilities, when you use emotional intelligence.

You might think of emotional intelligence as thinking skills applied to relationships. Putting emotional intelligence to work means taking in and analyzing how you and others feel, creating new ways of thinking that these feelings inspire, and taking action in response—all with the purpose of achieving the best possible outcome. Given that you will interact with others in almost every aspect of school, work, and life, EI is a pretty important tool.

Research has indicated that:[12]

- Emotionally intelligent people are more competent in social situations.

- Managers in the workplace with high EI have more productive working relationships.

- Employees scoring high in EI were more likely to receive positive ratings and raises.

KEY 1.2 Take an emotionally intelligent approach.

PERCEIVING EMOTIONS
Recognizing how you and others feel

THINKING ABOUT EMOTIONS
Seeing what thoughts arise from the feelings you perceive, and how they affect your mindset

UNDERSTANDING EMOTIONS
Determining what the emotions involved in a situation tell you, and considering how you can adjust your mindset or direct your thinking in a productive way

MANAGING EMOTIONS
Using what you learn from your emotions and those of others to choose behavior and actions that move you toward positive outcomes

Source: Adapted from Mayer, John D., Peter Salovey, and David R. Caruso, "Emotional Intelligence: New Ability or Eclectic Traits?" *American Psychologist,* vol. 63, no. 6, pp. 505–507. September 2008.

Here's an example. Two students are part of a group you are working with on a project. One always gets her share of the job done but has no patience for anyone who misses a deadline. She is quick to criticize group members. The other is sometimes prepared, sometimes not, but responds thoughtfully to what is going on with the group. She makes up for it when she hasn't gotten everything done, and when she is on top of her tasks she helps others. Whom would you work with again? The bottom line is that more emotional intelligence means stronger relationships and more goal achievement.

HOW DO YOU SET
and achieve goals?

A *goal* is a dream with a deadline; it is a result you want to achieve. You may have goals in any area in your life. Here are just a few examples:

- *Fitness:* Improve eating habits; run 2 miles every other day.
- *School:* Decide on a major by June; get an A in chemistry.
- *Finances:* Save up enough money to buy a new laptop.

Setting meaningful, effective goals starts with focusing on what's important to you.

Establish Values

You make life choices based on your personal *values*—principles or qualities you consider important. The choice to pursue a degree, for example, may reflect how you value the personal and professional growth that come from a college education. If you like to be on time for classes, you may value punctuality. If you pay bills regularly and on time, you may value financial stability.

Values shape your most important goals by helping you to:

- *Understand what you want out of life.* Your most meaningful goals reflect what you value most.
- *Choose how to use your valuable time.* When your day-to-day activities align with what you think is most important to do, you gain greater fulfillment from them.
- *Find people who inspire you.* Spending time with people who share similar values helps you clarify how you want to live and provides support for your goals.

For example, the fact that you value education may have led you to college. This practical choice will help you build skills and persistence, choose a major and career direction, find meaningful friends and activities, and achieve learning goals.

Long-Term Goals

Long-term goals are goals that sit out on the horizon, at least six months to a year away. They're goals that you can imagine and maybe even visualize, but they're too far out for you to touch. These are goals that outline the rewards you want in a way that reflects who you are and what you value. The more you know about yourself, the better able you are to set and work toward meaningful long-term goals. Here are some examples of long-term goals for one student who loves reading books and enjoys writing:

1. Declare my major in Writing and Literature by the end of the year.
2. Work at an internship with a publisher my junior year.
3. Get a bachelor's degree in Writing and Literature in four years.
4. Get a master's in Fine Arts in Creative Writing in five years.
5. Find an editing job with a publisher.

Having a *personal mission* can help you anchor values and goals in a comprehensive view of what you want out of life. Think of a personal mission as your longest-term goal, within which all of your other long-term goals should fit. Defining your personal mission involves creating a *mission statement*, which Dr. Stephen Covey describes as a philosophy outlining what you want to be (character), the rewards you aim for (contributions and achievements), and the principles by which you live (values).[13] Begin to ponder what your personal mission statement would look like now. Because what you want out of life changes as you do, your personal mission should remain flexible and open to revision. Think of your mission as a road map for your personal journey. It can give meaning to your daily activities, promote responsibility, and encourage you to take risks that lead you toward the long-term rewards you've laid out.

Most long-term goals are far more achievable if you break them into smaller chunks. These chunks become short-term goals.

Short-Term Goals

A *short-term goal* is a step that moves you closer to a long-term goal. Short-term goals make your long-term goals seem clearer and easier to reach. Short-term goals last a few hours, days, weeks or months. For example, suppose you have a long-term goal of graduating and becoming a nurse. You may decide to set the following short-term goal with three smaller, supplemental short-term goals:

Short-term goal: Meet with a study group two hours a week to better understand the skeletal and muscular system.

- *By the end of today:* Call study partners and find out when they can meet.
- *One week from today:* Schedule each weekly meeting for the month.
- *Two weeks from today:* Hold the first meeting.

These short-term goals might not seem risky to you. However, any action that requires energy and subjects your work to scrutiny is a risk. The smallest ways in which you "put yourself out there" can lead you step by step to the greatest rewards.

Create SMART Goals

Setting a goal doesn't necessarily mean you'll achieve it. If you set SMART goals, however, you'll be more likely to succeed. *SMART* is an acronym for a list of qualities that make rewarding goals concrete and improve your chances of achieving them.

- *Specific.* Make your goal concrete by using as many details as possible. Focus on behaviors and events that are under your control and map out specific steps that will get you there.

- *Measurable.* Define your goal in a measurable way, and set up a system to evaluate your progress. This could mean keeping a journal, an alarm system on your phone or computer, or reporting to a friend. Don't leave progress up to chance.
- *Achievable.* To see if you have what it takes to achieve the goal, first see if it aligns with your hopes, interests, abilities, and values. Then, reflect on whether you have the skills or resources needed to make it happen. If you're missing something, plan out how to get it.
- *Realistic.* Make sure your risks are reasonable and calculated. Create specific deadlines that will help you stay on track without making you feel rushed. If the challenge or risk is too great and the timeline too short, you are likely to struggle.
- *Time frame linked.* All goals need a time frame so you have something to work toward. If a goal is a dream with a deadline, then without the deadline, your goal is only a dream.

Here is an example of a rather vague goal, followed by a more concrete SMART goal:

> *Original goal:* I will choose a major. (This goal leaves unanswered questions: When are you going to do this? How will you do it? Why do it? By contrast, SMART goals provide specific answers to these questions.)
>
> *SMART goal:* I will choose and declare a major this term. To make an educated decision about my academic path, I will speak with an academic advisor, meet with students in the major, and research possible career paths from it.

- *Specific.* By saying that you will "choose and declare a major" you are defining the nature of this task.
- *Measurable.* By adding the "and declare" to the goal, you're provide a way to measure the completion of it.
- *Achievable.* Including resources like academic advisors and research provides a way to move past obstacles you may encounter.
- *Realistic.* The wording of the goal solidifies it as an attainable action and emphasizes the benefits associated with completing the task.
- *Time frame:* You have set from now through the end of the term as your time frame.

Work toward Goals

Setting goals is only the start. The real risk is in working toward them, and the real reward is in reaching them. To do so, follow the basic steps in Key 1.3.

Of course, things don't always go as planned. Although you can't often control what roadblocks stop you in your tracks, you *can* control how you deal with them as you encounter them. What can you do if you get stuck?

- Continue to remind yourself of the benefits of your goal.
- Discuss your challenges with someone supportive or someone who can help you. Don't invite negative feedback from people who will drag you down.
- Replace your inner critic with your inner cheerleader. This means replacing negative self-talk with positive self-talk every day.

Get Ready to Risk

The willingness to take calculated risks, both large and small, is essential to your life success. In everything that you approach in life, a reward waits in exchange for your risk. Here are just a few examples of how to take action, earn rewards, and build your risk-taking habit while in college:

- Risk looking confused asking a question in class for the reward of greater understanding.
- Risk the awkwardness of reaching out to an instructor for the reward of a relationship that can deepen your academic experience and perhaps provide career guidance.
- Risk the hard work required to prepare honestly for a test, for the reward of learning you can use in higher-level courses or in the workplace.
- Risk saying no to a substance or action that brings a healthier reward, even if it costs you a friend or an affiliation.

Imagine you are sitting in class with your growth mindset, ready to learn. You are prepared to use analytical and creative skills to examine knowledge and come up with new ideas. You are motivated to use your practical skills to move toward your goals. Your emotional intelligence has prepared you to adjust to and work with all kinds of people. With focused and productive risks, you will find out just how much reward waits for you.

KEY 1.3 Work actively toward your goals.

- *Commit to the goal.* You need to believe 100% in the goal and feel a sense of energy and enthusiasm around it. Your commitment becomes the engine that drives you when times get tough.

- *Identify your resources.* Take stock of where you are today so you can identify the resources that can help you move forward, including books, websites, instructors, and other students.

- *Build your support team.* Find people who can both help you *and* hold you accountable. Share your goal with them so it becomes more concrete. However, make sure you choose supportive people who will not judge you harshly if progress is erratic or slow.

- *Make an action plan.* How do you plan to reach your goal? Brainstorm with your support team about ways to get to the finish line. A common way to create an action plan is to break up the goal into subgoals or milestones, and then map out the steps to achieve each milestone.

- *Identify deadlines and establish a timeline.* If you've created a SMART goal, you established an end date for accomplishing your goal. Now, work backward from that date and create a realistic time line that includes specific milestones and the steps to achieve them.

- *Track your progress and be accountable.* Set aside time to review how you're doing. Make adjustments to your plan if you need to.

- *Celebrate!* It's important to recognize your progress and accomplishments—you might even choose to reward yourself when you've achieved your goal.

RISK ACTION

FOR COLLEGE, CAREER, AND LIFE REWARDS

Complete the following on paper or in digital format.

KNOW IT *Think Critically*

Robert Sternberg found that people who reach their goals successfully share some characteristics that keep them motivated to persist.[14] The self-assessment below will help you measure your level of motivation right now.

1	2	3	4	5
Not at All Like Me	Somewhat Unlike Me	Not Sure	Somewhat Like Me	Definitely Like Me

Please highlight or circle the number that best represents your answer:

1. I am able to translate ideas into action.	1 2 3 4 5
2. I am able to maintain confidence in myself.	1 2 3 4 5
3. I can stay on track toward a goal.	1 2 3 4 5
4. I complete tasks and have good follow-through.	1 2 3 4 5
5. I avoid procrastination.	1 2 3 4 5
6. I accept responsibility when I make a mistake.	1 2 3 4 5
7. I independently take responsibility for tasks.	1 2 3 4 5
8. I work hard to overcome personal difficulties.	1 2 3 4 5
9. I create an environment that helps me to concentrate on my goals.	1 2 3 4 5
10. I can delay gratification to receive the benefits.	1 2 3 4 5

Choose one item that you rated a 5. Generate a list of how you demonstrate your motivation in this area. Then, choose one item that you rated a 1 or 2. Generate a list of ideas about how you might improve in this area.

WRITE IT *Communicate*

Define Your "College Self"

When you understand who you are as a student, you will be more able to seek out the support that will propel you toward your goals. Analyze and describe who you are as a college student. Include details such as student status (traditional/returning, full time/part time, and so on), whether you transferred, what your goals are for your college experience, family and work obligations, culture and ethnicity, lifestyle, fears, challenges, academic interests, and whatever else defines your "college self."

Time Management

BEING IN CONTROL OF YOUR SCHEDULE

THIS LESSON WILL HELP YOU UNDERSTAND YOURSELF AS A TIME MANAGER AND CHOOSE HOW TO BUILD A SCHEDULE THAT WORKS FOR YOU. YOU WILL LEARN HOW YOUR SHORT-TERM CHOICES ARE LINKED TO, AND CAN BUILD A BRIDGE TO, YOUR MOST IMPORTANT LONG-TERM GOALS.

52% 🔋

Notes +

Today   Mar 10 8:01 AM

Working through this lesson will help you to:

- Identify effective time-management strategies   PP. 13–15
- Explain the importance of prioritizing activities   PP. 15–16
- Explain the advantages and disadvantages of various
  time-management tools   P. 15
- Recommend strategies for avoiding time-management
  pitfalls   PP. 18–21

WHO ARE YOU AS
a time manager?

Everyone has 24 hours in a day, and 7 to 8 of those hours involve sleeping (or should, if you want to remain healthy and alert enough to achieve your goals). You can't manage how time passes, but you *can* manage how you use it. Making productive choices about how you spend your time gives you the best chance at the reward of accomplishing what is important to you.

The first step in time management is to investigate your personal relationship with time. The more you're aware of your own time-related behaviors, the better you can create a schedule that maximizes your strengths, minimizes your weaknesses, and reduces stress. Determine who you are as a time manager by exploring your preferences and assessing your needs.

Identify Your Preferences

People have unique body rhythms and habits that affect how they deal with time. Some people have lots of energy late at night. Others do their best work early in the

MyStudentSuccessLab
(www.mystudentsuccesslab.com) is an online solution designed to help you "Start Strong, Finish Stronger" by building skills for ongoing personal and professional development.

day. Some people are chronically late, while others get everything done with time to spare. The following steps will help you create a personal time "profile":

- *Identify your energy patterns.* At what time of day does your energy tend to peak? When do you tend to have the least energy?
- *Notice your on-time percentage.* Do you tend to be early, on time, or late? If you are early or late, by how many minutes are you normally off schedule? Do you set your clocks 5 or 10 minutes early to trick yourself into being on time?
- *Look at your stamina.* Do you focus more effectively if you have a long block of time in which to concentrate on a task? Or do you need regular breaks in order to perform effectively?
- *Evaluate the effects of your preferences.* Which of your time-related preferences are likely to have a positive impact on your success at school? Which are likely to cause problems? Which can you make adjustments for, and which will just require you to cope?
- *Establish an ideal schedule.* Describe an ideal schedule that illustrates your preferences. For example, one student studies better during the day and when he has a long block of time. His ideal schedule description might read: "Classes bunched together on Mondays, Wednesdays, and Fridays. Tuesdays and Thursdays free for studying and research. Study primarily during daytime hours."

Assess Your Needs

Of course, very few people are able to perfectly align their schedules to their profile and preferences. Your set of needs may or may not fit easily into your schedule. Needs include:

- Certain courses, for core requirements or for your major
- Work hours, if you have a job
- Family responsibilities, if you care for children, parents, or others

The goal is to consider your needs and your ideal schedule together, and come up with an option that fulfills your needs but also takes your preferences into account. Consider the student in the ideal schedule example. Looking to schedule next term's classes on Monday, Wednesday, and Friday, he finds that one class he has to take meets only on Tuesday and Thursday. He has a choice of 11 am and 4 pm, though, so he chooses 4 pm, giving him a bigger block of time to study and work prior to the class. Because his part-time job hours are all day on the weekends, he does have to put in some evening study hours, but he is glad that he has those Tuesday and Thursday daytime hours to use when he is most alert.

Finally, remember that you will have more control over some things than others. For example, a student who functions best late at night may not have much luck finding courses that meet after 10 pm (unless she attends one of several colleges that have begun to schedule late-night classes to handle an overload of students). However, her college may offer online coursework that she could complete on a more flexible schedule.

HOW CAN YOU SCHEDULE
and prioritize?

With your preferences and needs in mind, you are ready for the central time management strategy—creating and following a schedule. An effective schedule can help you gain control of your life in two ways: (1) It provides segments of time for goal-related tasks, and (2) it reminds you of tasks, events, due dates, responsibilities, and deadlines.

Choose a Planner

Your first step is to find the right planner for you, one that will help you achieve the control that a schedule can provide. Time-management expert Paul Timm says "rule number one in a thoughtful planning process is: use some form of a planner where you can write things down."[1]

There are two major types of planners. One is a book or notebook, showing either a day or a week at a glance, where you note your commitments. Some planners contain sections for monthly and yearly goals. The other type is an electronic planner or smartphone, such as an iPhone or iPod Touch, BlackBerry, or Sidekick. Basic functions allow you to schedule days and weeks, note due dates, make to-do lists, perform mathematical calculations, and create and store an address book. Because most smartphone calendars have companion programs on computers, you can usually back up your schedule on a computer and view it there.

Although electronic planners are handy and have a large data capacity, they cost more than the paper versions, and they can fail due to software or battery problems. Analyze your preferences and finances, and decide which tool will be most useful and reasonable for you. For example, a blank notebook, used consistently, may work as well as a top-of-the-line smartphone. You might also consider online calendars, such as Google Calendar, which can "communicate" with your phone or other electronic planning device.

Establish Priorities

Prioritizing—arranging or dealing with items according to importance—helps you focus the bulk of your energy and time on your most important tasks. Since many top-priority items (classes, work) occur at designated times, prioritizing helps you lock in these activities and schedule less-urgent tasks around them.

Whether it's a task or goal you're scheduling, here are some basic ways to assign priorities. Think about what results your risks might bring, and what may result from taking *no* risks.

- *Priority 1:* Crucial, high-reward items that you must do, usually at a specific time. They may include attending class, working at a job, picking up a child from day care, and paying bills.
- *Priority 2:* Important items that have some flexibility in scheduling. Examples include study time and exercising.
- *Priority 3:* These are less important items that offer low-key rewards. Examples include calling a friend or downloading songs onto your iPod.

Prioritizing isn't just for time management. You should also prioritize your long-term and short-term goals. Consider keeping high-priority long-term goals visible alongside your daily schedule so you can make sure your day-to-day activities move you ahead toward those goals. For instance, arriving at school a half hour early so you can meet with an advisor can be a step toward a long-term goal of deciding on a major.

Having structure in your schedule often helps you fit in fun activities. When you know you are on top of your responsibilities, you may enjoy your social time even more.

Build a Schedule

Scheduling and goal setting work hand in hand to get you where you want to go. The most clearly defined goal won't be achieved without being put into a time frame, and the most organized schedule won't accomplish much unless it is filled with tasks related to important goals.

Be detailed and methodical about building your schedule. Follow these steps:

1. *Enter Priority 1 items in your planner first.* This means class times and days for the term, including labs and other required commitments; work hours; and essential personal responsibilities such as health-related appointments or childcare.

2. *Enter key dates from your course syllabi.* When you get your syllabi for the term, enter all dates—test and quiz dates, due dates for assignments, presentation dates for projects, holidays and breaks—in your planner right away. This will give you a big picture view of responsibilities and help you prepare for crunch times. For example, if you see that you have three tests and a presentation all in one week later in the term, you may risk rearranging your schedule during the preceding week for the reward of extra study time.

3. *Enter dates of events and commitments.* Keep on top of your commitments by putting them in your schedule where you can see and plan for them. Include club and organizational meetings, events you need to attend for class or for other purposes, and personal commitments such as medical appointments, family events, work obligations, or important social events.

4. *Schedule Priority 2 items around existing items.* Once you have the essentials set, decide where you can put in study time, workouts, study group meetings, and other important but flexible items. Schedule class prep time—reading and studying, writing and working on assignments and projects—in the planner as you would any other activity. As a rule, you should schedule at least two hours of preparation for every hour of class—that is, if you take 12 credits, you'll spend 24 hours or more a week on course-related activities outside of class.

5. *Include Priority 3 items where possible.* Schedule these items, such as social time or doing errands, around the items already locked in.

When you are scheduling and evaluating the potential rewards of various tasks, keep in mind that *reward* does not necessarily equal *fun*. For example, you might consider spending an hour on Instagram more fun than studying for a test. However, the reward for working toward a good test grade may be more desirable than what you gain from posting and liking photos.

Link Tasks to Long-Term Goals

Linking day-to-day events in your planner to your values and long-term goals gives meaning to your efforts and keeps you motivated. For example, planning study time for an economics test will mean more to you if you link that time to your goal of being accepted into business school and your value of meaningful employment. If you were a student with a goal of entering business school, you might link these action steps for the next year to your goal:

- *This year.* Maintain my class standing while completing enough courses to meet curriculum requirements for business school.
- *This term.* Complete my economics class with a B average or higher.

- *This month.* Set up economics study group schedule to coincide with quizzes and tests.
- *This week.* Meet with study group; go over material for Friday's test.
- *Today.* Go over Chapter 3 in economics text.

You can then arrange a schedule that moves you in the direction of your goal. You can schedule activities that support your short-term goal of doing well on your economics test and enter them in your planner. In this situation, your motivation to do well in the course is your long-term goal of going to business school.

Another important way to link short-term tasks to a long-term goal is to schedule milestones toward major papers and assignments. If you know you have a huge project or research paper due at the end of the term, brainstorm a list of steps toward that goal—for example, research goals, different drafts, peer review—and set them up in your calendar.

Before each week begins, remind yourself of your long-term goals and what you can accomplish over the next seven days to move you closer to those goals. Every once in a while, take a hard look at your schedule to see if you are spending enough time on what you really value.

Make To-Do Lists

When you have a cluster of tasks to accomplish, you may find it useful to create a to-do list and check off the items as you complete them. A to-do list can be helpful during exam week, in anticipation of an especially busy day, for a long-term or complicated assignment, or when keyed to a special event. Some people keep a separate to-do list focused on low-priority tasks and refer to it when a bit of free time appears.

Use a code to prioritize items so that you address the most important ones first. Some people list items in priority order and number them. Some use letters and some use different-colored pens. Others use electronic planners, choosing different highlighting or font colors.

Finally, each time you complete a task, check it off your to-do list or delete it from your electronic scheduler. This physical action can enhance the feeling of confidence that comes from getting something done.

Manage Your Schedule

Use these strategies to make the most of your schedule:

- *Plan regularly.* Set aside a time each day to plan your schedule (right before bed, with your morning coffee, on your commute to or from school, or whatever time and situation works best for you). Check your schedule at regular intervals throughout the day or week. This reduces the chance that you will forget something important.
- *Use monthly and yearly calendars at home.* A standard monthly or yearly wall calendar is a great place to keep track of your major commitments. A wall calendar gives you the "big picture" overview you need.
- *Get ahead if you can.* If you can take the small risk of getting a task done ahead of time, get it done, and see how you appreciate the reward of avoiding pressure later. Focus on your growth mindset, reminding yourself that achievement requires persistent effort.
- *Schedule downtime.* It's easy to get so caught up in completing tasks that you forget to relax and breathe. Even a half-hour of downtime a day will refresh you and improve your productivity when you get back on task.
- *Schedule sleep.* Sleep-deprived bodies and minds have a hard time functioning, and research reports that one-quarter of all college students are chronically sleep-deprived.[2] Figure out how much sleep you need and do your best to get it. When you pull an all-nighter, make sure to play catch-up over the days that follow. With adequate rest, your mind is better able to function, which has a direct positive impact on your schoolwork.

One last overarching strategy: *Be flexible.* No matter how well you plan ahead, sudden changes can upset your plans. Although you may not be able to control all the events that occur in your life, you have some control over how you handle your response to them.

Small changes—the need to work an hour overtime at your after-school job, a meeting that runs late—can result in priority shifts that jumble your schedule. For changes that occur frequently, come up with a backup plan (or two) ahead of time. For sudden changes such as medical emergencies and car breakdowns, or serious changes such as failing a course, use problem-solving skills to help you through. Your ability to evaluate situations, come up with creative options, and put practical plans to work will help you manage changes.

Resources at your college can help you deal with change, as well as with any scheduling or time-management problem. Your academic advisor, counselor, dean, financial aid advisor, and instructors can provide ideas and assistance.

HOW CAN YOU
handle time traps?

Everyone experiences *time traps*—situations and activities that eat up time. With thought and focus, you can use your time in the most productive way possible. This doesn't mean *never* doing things like chatting on Facebook or watching Funny or Die videos. It means thinking ahead about risks—both the risk of being unproductive as well as the risk of prioritizing work over your social life—and what rewards may or may not come from them.

Some time traps are a part of daily life. See Key 2.1, which lists the ones students encounter often and offers ideas for how to handle them. Others are linked to choices

---

KEY 2.1 Take control of time wasters.

1. **Commute:** Although we cannot always control it, the time spent commuting from one place to another is staggering.
   Take Control: Use your time on a bus or train to do homework, study, read assignments, or work on your monthly budget.

2. **Fatigue:** Being tired can lead to below-quality work that you have to redo. Fatigue can also make you feel ready to quit altogether.
   Take Control: Determine a "stop" time for yourself. When your "stop" time comes, put down the book, turn off the computer and *go to bed.* During the day, when you can, take naps to recharge your battery.

3. **Confusion:** When you don't fully understand an assignment or problem, you may spend unintended amounts of time trying to figure it out.
   Take Control: The number one way to fight this is *to ask.* As the saying goes, ask early and ask often. Students who seek help show they want to learn.

4. **Preference and schedule mismatches:** When your schedule goes against who you are as a time manager, you can waste a lot of time trying to stay focused. For example, a night person who is consistently late to morning classes will spend extra time getting caught up on material he missed.
   Take Control: You aren't likely to get a perfect match, but take your preferences into account as much as you can when scheduling classes, work, and study time.

that people make. It can be risky to deliver the focus that your work may demand, but the reward is an education that can help you fulfill your most significant goals. Make productive choices by confronting procrastination, setting effective limits, and minimizing multitasking.

Confront Procrastination

It's human, and common for busy students, to leave difficult or undesirable tasks until later. However, if taken to the extreme, *procrastination*—the act of putting off a task until another time—can develop into a habit that causes serious problems. For example, procrastinators who don't get things done in the workplace may prevent others from doing their work, sabotage a work project, or even lose a promotion or a job because of it.

If procrastination can cause such major issues, why do it? One reason people procrastinate is to avoid the truth about what they can achieve. "As long as you procrastinate, you never have to confront the real limits of your ability, whatever those limits are,"[3] say procrastination experts Jane B. Burka and Lenora Yuen, authors of *Procrastination: Why You Do It and What to Do about It*. A fixed mindset is another factor, because it naturally leads to procrastination. "I can't do it," the person with the fixed mindset thinks, "so what's the point of trying?"

Here are some strategies that can help you avoid procrastination and its negative effects.

- *Analyze the effects.* What reward will remain out of reach if you continue to put off a task? Chances are you will benefit more in the long term by facing the task head-on.
- *Set reasonable goals.* Because unreasonable goals can immobilize, take manageable risks. If you concentrate on achieving one small step at a time, the task becomes less burdensome.
- *Get started whether you "feel like it" or not.* Break the paralysis of doing nothing by doing something, anything. Most people, once they start, find it easier to continue.
- *Ask for help.* Once you identify what's holding you up, find someone to help you face the task. Another person may come up with an innovative method to get you moving again.
- *Don't expect perfection.* People learn by starting at the beginning, making mistakes, and learning from them. Approach mistakes with a growth mindset, and you will experience learning and growth.
- *Acknowledge progress.* When you accomplish a task, celebrate with whatever feels like fun to you.

Set Effective Limits

Many people find it challenging to resist the pull of activities such as video games, YouTube surfing, and socializing virtually or in person. However, the fun stuff can run away with your time before you know it, preventing you from taking care of responsibilities and ultimately causing serious problems. Because technology is so much a part of modern life, it can seem risky to limit your exposure to it. However, controlling when and for how long you interface with technology will earn you the reward of its benefits minus the suffering from its drawbacks.

There is a saying that goes, "The river needs banks to flow." Within those banks—the reasonable limits that you set on activities that tend to eat up time—you can be the thriving, healthy river, flowing toward

Like a river flowing strongly between its banks, you can maximize your productivity if you set effective limits on time-draining activities.

get creative

THINK YOUR WAY OUT OF TIME TRAPS

Complete the following on paper or in digital format.

Different people get bogged down by different time traps. What are yours? Think of two common time traps that you encounter. For each, come up with two ways to manage it through action. Here's an example:

Time Trap: Texting

Action 1: Tell friend: "I'll call you in an hour. I need to finish this paper."

Action 2: Decide I will respond to my text messages after I've read two chapters.

1. Your turn: For each time trap of yours, name it and describe two possible responses.

2. Next, for each of the two time traps you identified, name which of the two responses will most help you to take control of the situation and why.

3. Finally, what did this exercise teach you about your personal time traps? Do you find yourself needing to be stricter with your time? Why, and how?

the goals most important to you. Without the banks, and without the limits, you (the river) can spill out all over, losing the power to head in any single direction.

How can you set limits that will empower you and provide balance?

- *Know what distracts you.* Be honest with yourself about what draws your attention and drains your time—chatting or texting on your cell phone, watching reality TV, visiting Facebook, managing your Twitter account, and so on.

- *Manage your distractions with boundaries.* Determine when, and for how long, you can perform these activities without jeopardizing your studies. Then schedule them with built-in boundaries: "I will spend 10 minutes on Facebook for every 50 minutes of studying." "I will choose one TV show per day." Stick to your limits—use a cell phone alarm if you need it. You can even use browser plug-ins that you set up to block certain time-wasting sites for specific periods of time. Check out LeechBlock (for Firefox) or StayFocused (for Google Chrome). Setting boundaries is especially important when you are meeting or working online for a hybrid or fully online course.

- *Think before you commit.* Whatever you are asked to do—whether work-related, family-related, in connection with a school organization, or another activity—don't say yes right away. Consider how the commitment will affect your schedule now and in the near future. If you determine the reward isn't worth the risk, say "no" respecfully but firmly.

- *Be realistic about time commitments.* Many students who attempt to combine work and school find they have to trim one or the other to reduce stress and promote success. Overloaded students often fall behind and experience high stress levels that can lead to dropping out. Determine what is reasonable for you; you may find that taking longer to graduate is a viable option if you need to work while in school. You may also decide that you can survive with less income and ease up on work hours in order to spend more time on schoolwork.

The Myth of Multitasking

Over the years, people have come to believe that multitasking is a crucial skill. However, recent research has shown that the human brain is biologically capable of doing only one thinking task at a time—at best, it can only switch rapidly between tasks. When you think you are multitasking, you are really only "switch-tasking."[4]

This means that if you try to do two tasks at once, you can actually work on only one at a time. What you do is interrupt the first activity with the second and then switch back. The time it takes to switch from one thinking activity to another called *switching time*. For example, suppose you're talking to a member of your study group by phone, discussing a homework assignment. If you decide to read through your email while you are on the phone, you will be unable to listen effectively to what's being said on the phone call.

According to two researchers, David Meyer and Dr. John Medina, switching time increases errors and the amount of time it takes to finish the tasks you are working on by an average of 50%. This means the more activities you juggle, the more your brain is interrupted, the more switching you do, the longer it takes to complete your activities, and the more mistakes you make.[5] The cost to the quality of your work may not be worth the juggling.

If you want to be successful at your work, consider the words of Tony Schwarz: "Difficult as it is to focus in the face of the endless distractions we all now face, it's far and away the most effective way to get work done."[6] Focusing on one task at a time will save you time, mistakes, and stress. The minor risks of managing yourself in the present will reward you with learning and accomplishment in the future—and, don't worry, you will still find time to play.

Complete the following on paper or in digital format.

KNOW IT *Think Critically*

After completing your online time-tracking activity, review your log of how you spent your time for a week. Answer the following questions:

- What surprises you about how you spend your time?
- Do you spend the most time on the activities that represent your most important values, or not?
- Where do you waste the most time? What do you think that is costing you?
- On which activities do you think you should spend *more* time? On which should you spend *less* time?

What changes are you willing to make to get closer to how you want to ideally spend your time? Write a short paragraph describing, in detail, two time-management changes you plan to make this term so you focus your time more effectively on your most important goals and values.

WRITE IT *Communicate*

How You Feel About Your Time Management

Think and then write about how your most time-demanding activities make you feel. Paying attention to your feelings can be a key step toward making time management choices that are more in line with your values. What makes you happiest, most fulfilled, and most satisfied? What makes you the most anxious, frustrated, and drained? What do these feelings tell you about your day-to-day choices? Describe how you could adjust your mindset or make different choices to feel better about how you spend your time.

Financial Literacy

MANAGING YOUR MONEY

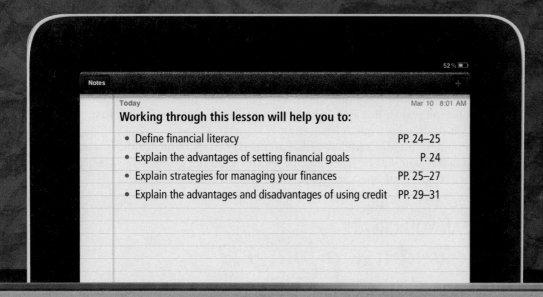

3 LESSON

THIS LESSON WILL HELP YOU EXPLORE WHO YOU ARE AS A MONEY MANAGER. YOU WILL IDENTIFY YOUR SPENDING AND SAVING HABITS AND DEVELOP A CONCEPT OF WHAT YOU WANT VERSUS WHAT YOU NEED. YOU WILL LEARN A STRAIGHTFORWARD BUDGETING STRATEGY AND IDEAS ABOUT HOW TO INCREASE INCOME THROUGH WORK AND FINANCIAL AID.

Today   Mar 10 8:01 AM

Working through this lesson will help you to:

- Define financial literacy   PP. 24–25
- Explain the advantages of setting financial goals   P. 24
- Explain strategies for managing your finances   PP. 25–27
- Explain the advantages and disadvantages of using credit   PP. 29–31

WHAT DOES MONEY
mean in your life?

According to the American Psychological Association, nearly three out of four people in the United States cite money as the number one stressor in their lives.[1] The cost of college tuition continues to rise more quickly than the rate of inflation, and books and other college expenses take a toll on bank accounts. Self-supporting students have to pay for living and family expenses on top of college costs. Students who take longer than expected to complete a degree or certificate often pay more for the additional time in school. Add the recession that the United States is currently experiencing, and it adds up to challenging financial situations for the vast majority of college students.

Thinking analytically, creatively, and practically about money management can help you take calculated risks that reward you with increased control over your finances. First, analyze who you are as a money manager and examine the relationship between money and time.

How You Perceive and Use Money

How you interact with money is unique. Some people spend earnings right away, some save for the future. Some charge everything, some make cash purchases only, others do something in between. Some pay bills online and others mail checks. Some rewards people seek are measured in dollar amounts and others in nonmaterial terms. Your spending and saving behaviors tend to reflect your values and goals.

Improving how you handle money requires that you analyze your attitudes and behaviors. Says money coach Connie Kilmark, "If managing money was just about math and the numbers, everyone would know how to manage their finances some-time around the fifth grade."[2] Begin your analysis by looking at needs versus wants.

Needs versus Wants

People often confuse what they *need* with what they *want*. True needs are absolutely essential for your survival: food, water, air, shelter (rent or mortgage, as well as home maintenance costs and utilities), family and friends, and some mode of transportation. Everything else is technically a want—something you would like to have but could live without. When people spend too much on wants, they may not have enough cash for needs. You might want to buy a $1,000 flat-screen TV, but might regret the purchase if your car broke down and needed a $1,000 repair.

Check your spending for purpose. What do you buy with your money? Are the items you purchase necessary? When you do spend on a want rather than a need, do you plan the expense into your budget with an eye toward a specific reward, or buy on the spur of the moment? With a clear idea of what you want and what you need, you can think through spending decisions more effectively. This is not to say that you should never spend money on wants. Just take calculated risks that satisfy your needs first, and then decide what to do with what is left over.

With more of an idea of what values and perspectives influence the financial decisions you make, you will be more able to choose and take productive risks that move you toward meaningful financial goals. Start with creating a budget.

HOW CAN YOU CREATE
and use a budget?

Everything you will read about money management in this lesson falls under the "umbrella" of one central concept: Live below your means, or in other words, spend less than you earn whenever possible. When money in is more than money out, you will have extra to save or spend.

How can you find out the difference between what you spend and what you earn? Track your spending and earning, and create a budget that balances both. A budget is a place to coordinate resources and expenditures—basically, a set of goals regarding money. Because many expenses are billed monthly, most people use a month as a unit of time when budgeting. Creating a budget involves several steps:

1. Gather information about what you earn (money flowing in).
2. Figure out your expenditures (money flowing out).
3. Analyze the difference between earnings and expenditures.
4. Come up with creative ideas about how you can make changes.
5. Take practical action to adjust spending or earning so you come out even or ahead.

Your biggest expense right now is probably tuition. However, if you have taken out student loans that you don't begin to pay until after you earn your degree, that expense may not hit you fully until after you finish school. (Financial aid options will be explored later in the lesson.) For now, as you consider your budget, include only the part of the cost of your education you are paying for while you are still in school.

Figure Out What You Earn

To determine what is available to you on a monthly basis, start with the money you earn in a month's time at any regular job. Then, if you have savings set aside for your education or any other source of income, determine how much of it you can spend each month and add that amount. For example, if you have a grant for the entire year, divide it by 12 (or by how many months you are in school over the course of a year) to see how much you can use each month.

Figure Out What You Spend

First, note regular monthly expenses like rent, phone, and cable (look at past checks and electronic debits to estimate what the month's bills will be). Some expenses, like automobile and health insurance, may be billed only once or twice a year. In these cases, divide the yearly cost by 12 to see how much you spend every month. Then, over a month's time, keep a spending log in a small notebook to record each day's cash or debit card expenditures. Be sure to count smaller purchases if they are frequent (for example, one or two pricey coffees a day add up over time). By the end of the month, you will have a good idea of where your dollars go.

Use the total of all your monthly expenses as a baseline for other months, realizing that spending will vary depending on events in your life or factors such as seasons. For example, if you pay for heating, that cost will be far greater in cold weather.

A note about technology: One advantage to managing your bank and credit accounts online or using a personal finance software program, such as Quicken, is that you can quickly access information about what you are earning and spending over a period of time. However, you need to be careful to avoid issues like phishing scams. If an email asks you to verify information such as your social security number or PIN number, do not respond to it, and do not click on any link it provides.

Evaluate the Difference

Once you know what you earn and what you spend, calculate the difference: Subtract your monthly expenses from your monthly income. Ideally, you have money left over to save or spend. However, if you are spending more than you take in, examine these areas of your budget.

- *Expenses.* Did you forget to budget for recurring expenses such as the cost for semi-annual dental visits or car insurance? Or was your budget derailed by an emergency expense?
- *Spending patterns and priorities.* Did you spend money wisely during the month, or did you overspend on wants?
- *Income.* Do you bring in enough money? Do you need another income source or a better job?

Adjust Spending or Earning

If you spend more than you are earning, you can spend less, earn more, or better yet, do both. First, consider how to manage spending using strategies such as the following:

- *Set up automatic payments.* If you set up electronic monthly payments for bills and tuition, you will take care of your needs first without thinking about it.
- *Comparison shop.* Think before you buy an expensive item such as a car or a computer. Use websites such as ShopLocal, NexTag, and Woot to compare prices.
- *Show your student ID.* Your student identification card can get you discounts on items such as movies, shows, concerts, food, books and clothing, electronics, and more.

- Share living space.

- Rent movies or borrow them from friends or the library.

- Cook at home more often.

- Use grocery and restaurant coupons from the paper or online.

- Take advantage of sales, buy store brands, and buy in bulk.

- Walk, bike, carpool, or use public transport.

- Bring lunch from home.

- Shop in secondhand or consignment stores or swap clothing with friends.

- Communicate via email or snail mail rather than calling or texting (minutes and texts can add up fast).

- Ask a relative to help with childcare, or create a babysitting co-op.

- Reduce electricity costs by turning off lights when you leave a room, cut back on air conditioning, and switch to compact fluorescent bulbs (CFLs) in your lamps.

Finally, work to save money on a day-to-day basis. The effort of saving small amounts regularly can eventually bring significant reward. Key 3.1 has some suggestions.

Call on your dominant multiple intelligences when planning your budget. For example, logical-mathematical learners may choose a classic detail-oriented budgeting plan, visual learners may want to create a budget chart, and bodily-kinesthetic learners may want to make budgeting more tangible by dumping receipts into a big jar and tallying them at the end of the month. Consider using online tools such as Mint.com or Thrive.com.

Juggle Work and School

If working while in school is a necessity for you, you are not alone. According to a 2007 survey, nearly 50% of college freshmen work to earn money for tuition.[3] If you want or need to work, try to balance it with your academic work and goals. Thinking analytically and creatively, come up with productive risks that bring your desired reward.

Establish your needs

Think about what you need from a job. Ask questions like these:

- How much money do I need to make—weekly, per term, per year?

- What time of day is best for me? Should I consider night or weekend work?

- Can my schedule handle a full-time job, or should I look for part-time work?

- Do I want hands-on experience in a particular field?

- How flexible do I need the job to be?

- If I want a job that isn't as flexible, can I make my coursework more flexible by taking some classes online?

- Can I or should I find work at my school or as part of a work–study program?

Many students are able to fit part-time work into their schedules if they stay local. Look for jobs at nearby businesses, such as restaurants and retailers.

Analyze the impact

Working while in school has both positive and negative effects. Think through these pros and cons when considering or evaluating any job:

- *Pros:* General and career-specific experience; developing contacts; possible enhanced school performance (although full-time work can be problematic, working up to 15 hours a week may actually improve your ability to use time efficiently)
- *Cons:* Time commitment that reduces available study time; reduced opportunity for social and extracurricular activities; having to shift gears mentally from work to classroom; stretching yourself too thin; fatigue

With the information you have gathered and analyzed, look carefully at what is available on and off campus, and apply for the job or jobs that best suit your needs. After you start, continue to evaluate whether the reward of your job is worth the risk. If you make careful choices about work and about how you schedule your life around it, you can earn the rewards you need most and minimize the negative effects on your life.

HOW CAN YOU MAKE THE
most of financial aid?

Financing your education—alone or with the help of your family—involves gathering financial information and making decisions about what you can afford and how much help you need. Never assume you are not eligible for aid. Almost all students are eligible for some kind of need-based or merit-based financial assistance.

Know What Aid Is Available

Aid comes in the form of student loans, grants, and scholarships. The federal government administers the primary loan and grant programs, although many private sources may offer grants and scholarships as well.

- *Student loans.* Student loan recipients are responsible for paying back the amount borrowed, plus interest, according to a payment schedule that may stretch over a number of years.
- *Grants.* Unlike student loans, grants do not require repayment. Grants are awarded to students who show financial need.
- *Scholarships.* Scholarships are awarded to students who show talent or ability in specific areas (academic achievement, sports, the arts, citizenship, or leadership). They do not require repayment.

Information about federal grant and loan programs is available in various federal student aid publications, which you can find at your school's financial aid office, request by phone (800-433-3243), or access online at http://studentaid.ed.gov.

Apply for Aid

The key word for success in this process is *early*. Research early, get forms early, and apply early. The earlier you complete the process, the greater your chances of being considered for financial aid.[4]

- *Seek government aid.* Fill out the Free Application for Federal Student Aid (FAFSA) form electronically. The form can be found through your college's financial aid office, the FAFSA website (www.fafsa.ed.gov), or on the U.S. Department of Education's website (www.ed.gov/finaid.html). You will create a personal portfolio, called MyFSA, on the site. This is where you will enter and store information, including your FAFSA form and any other pertinent forms. The U.S.

Department of Education has an online tool called FAFSA Forecaster to help you estimate how much aid you qualify for. You will need to reapply every year for federal aid. *Note:* This is a free tool. If you hear about services that charge a fee for completing your FAFSA for you, avoid them.

- *Seek private aid.* Thoroughly investigate what you may be eligible for. Search libraries and your school's website, go through books that list scholarships and grants, talk with a financial aid advisor on your campus, and check scholarship search sites such as Scholarships.com and Fastweb.com. Know details that may help you identify sources available to you (you or your family's military status, ethnic background, membership in organizations, religious affiliation, and so on).

If you do receive aid from your college or elsewhere, follow all rules and regulations, especially maintaining good academic standing and meeting yearly application deadlines (in most cases, you have to reapply every year for aid). Finally, take a new look each year at what's available. You may be eligible for different grants or scholarships than when you first applied.

Think Critically about Aid

The decisions you make now about how to finance your education will affect your future. Ask careful questions about the following:

- *Where you get your money.* Scholarships and grants, if you can get them, are best because you don't have to pay them back. Federal loans are the next best option because they tend to have lower interest rates than private loans, which can also have less flexible terms of repayment and tougher consequences for late payments or defaults.
- *How much money you get.* Financial aid experts recommend that you borrow only what you truly need and no more.[5] Look at the Bureau of Labor Statistics online to see what you might expect to earn when you graduate. One rule says that your total debt should be less than twice your expected yearly salary.[6] If your debt looks as though it will be too large, this may mean changing your career goal, finding a less expensive school, or searching for additional sources of aid.
- *The terms of your loan.* Understand your loan—how long you can wait before starting to pay it, how much you will need to pay per month, how long you have to pay it back, what your interest rate is, and any other important details. Make sure you fulfill all obligations set out in the terms.

In response to rising education costs, students are borrowing ever-larger amounts of money. Consequently, the number of students *defaulting* on loans (walking away from them without paying) is on the rise, and even personal bankruptcy won't make student loans go away.[7] The consequences for defaulting on a loan are severe and include credit trouble, inability to apply for further aid, money taken from your salary or social security payment, and more. Borrow only what you need. For helpful information about managing loans, see www.finaid.org.

WHAT WILL HELP YOU USE CREDIT CARDS *and debit cards wisely?*

Student loans are one way of borrowing the money you need to live and study. Another much more expensive form of borrowing is credit. Credit cards are a handy alternative to cash and can reward you with a strong credit history if used with a reasonable level of risk. But they also can plunge you into a hole of debt. Students are acquiring cards in droves. In fact, in 2009, only 2% of undergraduates had no credit history.[8]

Credit cards are a particular danger for students. Credit companies often target students by presenting a positive spin about credit cards, knowing that many students lack knowledge about how credit works. Too much focus on *what* they can purchase with credit cards (rather than *how much* it will really cost them) leads students into trouble because they spend more than they can afford. Recent statistics from a survey of undergraduates illustrate the situation.[9]

- 84% of all students had at least one credit card, and 50% had four or more credit cards.
- Students who hold credit cards carry an average outstanding balance of $3,173, and seniors graduate with an average of $4,100 in credit card debt.
- 82% of students don't pay their cards in full each month, and therefore pay finance charges.
- 90% of students pay for some type of education expense on credit, including 76% who charge textbooks and 30% who use cards to pay tuition.

Many college students charge a wide variety of expenses like car repair, food, and clothes, in addition to school costs. Before they know it, they are deeply in debt. It's hard to notice trouble brewing when you don't see your wallet taking a hit.

How Credit Cards Work

To charge means to create a debt that must be repaid. The credit card issuer, such as Bank of America, Chase, CitiGroup, or Wells Fargo, earns money by charging interest on unpaid balances. The interest is usually 18% or higher. Here's an example: Say you have a $3,000 unpaid balance on your card at an annual interest rate of 18%. If you make the $60 minimum payment every month, it will take *eight years* to pay off your debt, assuming that you make no other purchases. The effect on your wallet is staggering:

Original debt	$3,000
Cost to repay credit card loan at an annual interest rate of 18 percent for 8 years	$5,760
Cost of using credit	$2,760 ($5,760 – $3,000)

By the time you finish, you will repay almost *twice* your original debt.

Keep in mind that credit card companies are in the business to make money off card owners and do *not* have your financial best interests at heart. Focusing on what's best for your finances is *your* job, and the first step is to know as much as you can about credit cards. Start with the important concepts presented in Key 3.2, read the fine print about any card you are considering, and stay focused on productive rewards that are worth the risk of spending on credit.

Watch for Problems

In response to recent economic changes, credit card disclaimers and policies can cause problems unless you stay alert. Here are a few you should note, both when seeking a new card and when looking at existing card statements:[10]

- *New fees.* In addition to annual fees, a card may charge fees for reward programs, paying your bill by phone, or even checking your balance. Find out what the fees are, and switch cards if you feel they are excessive.

WHAT TO KNOW ABOUT ...	... AND HOW TO USE WHAT YOU KNOW
Account balance. A dollar amount that includes any unpaid balance, new purchases and cash advances, finance charges, and fees. Updated monthly.	Charge only what you can afford to pay at the end of the month. Keep track of your balance. Hold on to receipts and call customer service if you have questions.
Annual fee. The yearly cost that some companies charge for owning a card.	Look for cards without an annual fee or, if you've paid your bills on time, ask your current company to waive the fee.
Annual percentage rate (APR). The amount of interest charged yearly on your unpaid balance. This is the cost of credit if you carry a balance in any given month. The higher the APR, the more you pay in finance charges.	Shop around (check Studentcredit.com). Also, watch out for low, but temporary, introductory rates that skyrocket to over 20% after a few months. Always ask what the long-term interest rate is and look for fixed rates (guaranteed not to change).
Available credit. The unused portion of your credit line, updated monthly on your bill.	It is important to have credit available for emergencies, so avoid charging to the limit.
Cash advance. An immediate loan, in the form of cash, from the credit card company. You are charged interest immediately and may also pay a separate transaction fee.	Use a cash advance only in extreme emergencies because the finance charges start as soon as you complete the transaction and interest rates are greater than the regular APR. It is a very expensive way to borrow money.
Credit limit. The debt ceiling the card company places on your account (e.g., $1,500). The total owed, including purchases, cash advances, finance charges, and fees, cannot exceed this limit.	Credit card companies generally set low credit limits for college students. Owning more than one card increases the credit available, but most likely increases problems as well. Try to use only one card.
Delinquent account. An account that is not paid on time or one for which the minimum payment has not been met.	Always pay on time, even if it is only the minimum payment. If you do not pay on time, you will you be charged substantial late fees and will risk losing your good credit rating, which affects your ability to borrow in the future. Delinquent accounts remain part of your credit records for years.
Due date. The date your payment must be received and after which you will be charged a late fee.	Avoid late fees and finance charges by paying at least a week in advance.
Finance charges. The total cost of credit, including interest, service fees, and transaction fees.	The only way to avoid finance charges is to pay your balance in full by the due date. If you keep your balance low, you will be more able to pay it off.
Minimum payment. The smallest amount you can pay by the statement due date. The amount is set by the credit card company.	Making only the minimum payment each month can result in disaster if you charge more than you can afford. When you make a purchase, think in terms of total cost.
Outstanding balance. The total amount you owe on your card.	If you carry a balance over several months, additional purchases are hit with finance charges. Pay cash for new purchases until your balance is under control.
Past due. Your account is considered "past due" when you fail to pay the minimum required payment on schedule.	Look for past due accounts on your credit history by getting a credit report from one of the credit bureaus (Experian, TransUnion, and Equifax) or myFICO or Credit Karma.

- *Shrinking or disappearing grace periods.* In the past, a "grace period" of a few days may have given you a chance to pay late but avoid fees. Now, even just slightly late payments result in a late fee. And in many cases, once you pay late, the credit card company immediately increases your interest rate.

- *Reward program changes.* A reward program such as airline miles or cash back may change, so keep checking your statements. Cards may begin charging for reward programs or may change or remove them if you are late with a payment.

- *"Fee harvesting" cards.* Some cards feature low credit limits and come loaded with extra fees. After the fees are tacked onto the low credit limit, very little is left to spend and consumers often end up going over their limits, resulting in more fees.

The best way to avoid problems is to read the fine print, pay attention to your balances, and pay your bills on time. Even with careful use, credit debt can still add up quickly.

Manage Credit Card Debt

Many older students are familiar with the pros and cons of credit, and may already work hard to focus credit card use on items they or their families can't do without. However, even if you limit your card use to your needs, you can still get into trouble. Debt can escalate quickly and can even lead to personal bankruptcy—a major blot on your credit that can last for years, and one to avoid at all costs. The following strategies require small risks of time and attention for the significant reward of staying in control of credit spending.

To maintain an accurate perspective on where your money goes, keep credit card receipts and include those purchases as you track expenses.

- *Choose your card wisely.* Look for cards with low interest rates, no annual fees, a rewards program, and a grace period.
- *Ask questions before charging.* Would you buy that item if you had to pay cash? Can you pay the balance at the end of the billing cycle?
- *Pay bills regularly and on time, and try to make more than the minimim payment.* Set up a reminder system that activates a week or so before the due date. You can create an email alert through your card account, make a note in your datebook, or set an alarm on your electronic planner.
- *If you get into trouble, call the credit company and ask to set up a payment plan.* You may even be able to make partial payments or get a reduced interest rate. Then, going forward, try to avoid the same mistakes. If you still need help, contact the following organizations such for help: National Foundation for Credit Counseling or American Financial Solutions. *Note:* These organizations do not charge for their services.

Build a Good Credit Score

Your credit score is a measure of how likely you are to pay your bills, calculated from a credit report using a standardized formula. Credit scores are on a scale running from 300 to 850. In general, having a higher score is related to getting better interest rates. For instance, suppose you have a score of 520 and another person has a score of 720, and both of you have $100,000, 30-year mortgages. Because of your lower credit score, you will have a higher APR (annual percentage rate) on your loan, and will ultimately pay $110,325 more in interest charges—the cost of another whole mortgage.[11]

Building, maintaining, and repairing credit is an ongoing challenge. Three primary credit bureaus will send you a report containing your credit score and credit history: Experian, TransUnion, and Equifax (they will provide one free report per year, and charge for any additional reports). For more information, see www.annualcreditreport.com.

HOW CAN YOU PLAN FOR
a solid financial future?

Being able to achieve long-term financial goals—buying a car or a house, taking a vacation, saving money for retirement and for emergencies—requires that you think critically about short-term risks that will bring long-term financial reward. The strategies

get analytical

EXAMINE CREDIT CARD USE

Complete the following on paper or in digital format.

Take a careful look at who you are as a credit consumer. Gather your most recent credit card statements to prepare for this exercise. Answer questions 1 through 5.

1. How many credit cards do you have? For each, list the following:

   ■ Name of card and who issued it (for example, VISA from Home State Bank)
   ■ Current interest rate
   ■ Current balance
   ■ Late fee if you do not pay on time
   ■ Approximate due date for card payment each month

2. Add your balances together. This total is your current credit debt.

3. How much did you pay last month in finance charges? Total your finance charges from the most recent statements of all cards.

4. Do you pay on time, do you tend to pay late, or does it vary?

5. Estimate how many times a year you pay a late fee. Looking at how much your cards charge for late fees, estimate how much money you spent in the last year in late fees.

When you've gathered all your information, analyze how effectively you currently use credit. If you are satisfied with your habits, keep up the good work. If not, identify your bad habits and write specific plans about how to change those habits.

you've examined so far contribute to your long-term goals because they help you spend wisely and maximize your savings.

Save and Invest Your Money

When you live below your means, the money left over can go into savings accounts and investments, which can help you with regular expenses, long-term financial plans, and emergencies (financial advisors recommend a cash "emergency fund" that will cover at least three months worth of expenses). Savings accounts, CDs, and money market accounts can help your money grow.

   ■ *Savings accounts.* Most savings accounts earn *compound interest*. Here's how it works: If you put $1,000 in an account that carries 5% interest, you will earn $50 over the course of the first year. Your account then holds $1,050. From that point on, interest is calculated on that $1,050, not just on the original $1,000. Imagine this: If you invested $1,000 at the age of 22 and put $50 in the account each month, by the time you turned 62 you would have over $100,000.

   ■ *Certificates of deposit (CDs) and money market accounts.* CDs deliver a fixed rate of interest on an amount of money that you put away for a specific period of time (three months, six months, one year). Money market accounts also deliver a fixed rate of interest and allow you to withdraw money, but tend to require a minimum balance and restrict you to a certain number of withdrawals per month. Both types of accounts earn slightly more than a regular savings account.

Begin Saving for Retirement

As more employers reduce or eliminate pension benefits, it is up to workers to save for retirement. Some employers offer full-time workers a 401(k) retirement savings plan, for which you agree to have a certain amount of money automatically withdrawn from your paycheck and deposited in a retirement account. Your employer will often match your contribution.

If no such plan is offered, or if you are self-employed, consider looking into Individual Retirement Accounts (IRAs) offered by financial institutions or banks. When you open an IRA, you can contribute to it monthly or at the end of each year. There are two kinds of IRAs, both of which you can withdraw money from starting at 59-1/2 years of age. The type of IRA you choose will depend on your employment, income, and the money you have available to invest.

If you're feeling a bit overwhelmed about finances at this point in your life, keep in mind the University of Arizona report that "the benefits of financial knowledge extend beyond having money into realms of physical and psychological well-being."[12] Continue to learn about money management, take future risks based on the rewards you need most, and your actions will contribute to success for life.

Complete the following on paper or in digital format.

KNOW IT *Think Critically*

Your Relationship with Money

Getting a handle on money anxiety starts with an honest examination of how you relate to money. First, analyze yourself as a money manager. Look back earlier in the lesson for a description of what influences the way people handle money. Make some notes about your personal specifics in the following areas.

1. What do you most value spending money on?
2. How do you manage money?
3. How does your culture tend to view money?
4. How do your family and friends tend to handle money?

If you had extra money, would you save it, spend it, a little of both? Imagine what you would do if you had an extra $10,000 to spend this year. Describe your plan. Then look for practical ways to make that imagined scenario a reality over time. Describe two specific plans involving changes and sacrifices that will move you toward the goal of having an extra $10,000 to spend at some point in your future.

WRITE IT *Communicate*

Needs and Wants

Make two lists—one of what you consider needs, and the other of what you consider wants. Looking at your lists, describe how you handle your money in relation to what you need and want. Do you prioritize needs and avoid wants until you have cash available? Do you buy wants on credit when you can't afford them? Name one want you would be willing to give up in the next month to see how much money you could save.

Critical, Creative, and Practical Thinking

SOLVING PROBLEMS AND MAKING DECISIONS

THIS LESSON GOES INTO DETAIL ABOUT THE SKILLS INVOLVED IN ANALYTICAL (CRITICAL), CREATIVE, AND PRACTICAL THINKING. IT PROVIDES A PRACTICAL, RESULTS-FOCUSED, STEP-BY-STEP STRATEGY FOR HOW TO USE THESE SKILLS TO DEFINE, THINK THROUGH, AND RESOLVE PROBLEMS AND DECISIONS.

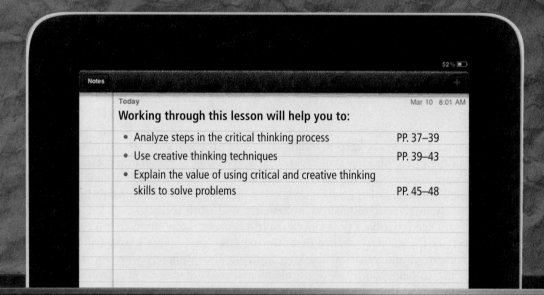

Notes		
Today		Mar 10 8:01 AM
Working through this lesson will help you to:		
• Analyze steps in the critical thinking process		PP. 37–39
• Use creative thinking techniques		PP. 39–43
• Explain the value of using critical and creative thinking skills to solve problems		PP. 45–48

52% 🔋

WHY IS IT IMPORTANT TO
ask and answer questions?

What is thinking? According to experts, it is what happens when you ask questions and move toward the answers.[1] "To think through or rethink anything," says Dr. Richard Paul, director of research at the Center for Critical Thinking and Moral Critique, "one must ask questions that stimulate our thought. Questions define tasks, express problems and delineate issues. . . . only students who have questions are really thinking and learning."[2] It's human to feel as though asking questions makes you look ignorant. However, the risk of questioning is what *combats* ignorance and earns you the reward of learning.

MyStudentSuccessLab (www.mystudentsuccesslab.com) is an online solution designed to help you "Start Strong, Finish Stronger" by building skills for ongoing personal and professional development.

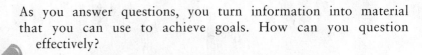

As you answer questions, you turn information into material that you can use to achieve goals. How can you question effectively?

Know why you question. To ask useful questions, you need to know *why* you are questioning. Start by defining your purpose: "What am I trying to accomplish, and why?" For example, if your purpose for questioning your choice of a major was to change majors, that would generate an entirely different set of questions than if your purpose was to find a range of viable jobs that you would qualify for using your current major. As you continue your thought process, you will find more specific purposes that help you generate questions along the way.

Question in different ways. Use questions to:

- Analyze ("How bad is my money situation?")
- Come up with creative ideas ("How can I earn more money?")
- Apply practical solutions ("Who do I talk to about getting a job on campus?")

Want to question. Knowing why you are questioning also helps you *want* to think. "Critical-thinking skills are different from critical thinking dispositions, or a willingness to deploy these skills," says cognitive psychologist D. Alan Bensley of Frostburg State University in Maryland. In other words, having the skills isn't enough—you also need the willingness to risk using them.[3] Having a clear understanding of your desired reward can motivate you to work to achieve it.

As you read and work, keep in mind your sense of where your strengths and challenges lie in the three thinking skill areas. If you are using MyStudentSuccessLab, you may also want to complete the My Thinking Styles inventory to get a view of your thinking skills in terms of the seven styles this inventory evaluates (insightful, open-minded, timely, analytical, inquisitive, systematic, and truth seeking).

When you need to solve a problem or make a decision, combining all three thinking skills gives you the greatest chance of achieving your goal.[4] This lesson will explore analytical, creative, and practical thinking individually, ultimately showing how they work together to help you to solve problems and make decisions effectively. Asking questions opens the door to each thinking skill, and in each section you will find examples of the kinds of questions that drive that skill. Begin by exploring analytical thinking skills.

HOW CAN YOU IMPROVE YOUR
analytical thinking skills?

Analytical thinking is the process of gathering information, breaking it into parts, examining and evaluating those parts, and making connections for the purposes of gaining understanding, solving a problem, or making a decision.

Through the analytical process, you look for how pieces of information relate to one another, setting aside any pieces that are unclear, unrelated, unimportant, or biased. You may also form new questions that change your direction. Be open to them and to where they may lead you.

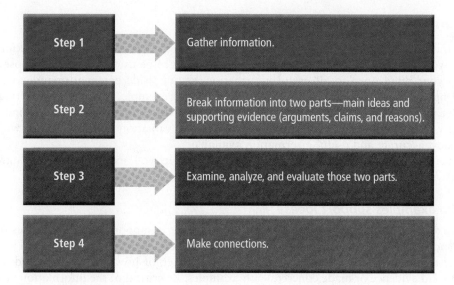

Step 1 → Gather information.

Step 2 → Break information into two parts—main ideas and supporting evidence (arguments, claims, and reasons).

Step 3 → Examine, analyze, and evaluate those two parts.

Step 4 → Make connections.

Gather Information

Information is the raw material for thinking, so to start the thinking process you must first gather your raw materials. This requires analyzing how much information you need, how much time you should spend gathering it, and whether it is relevant. Say, for instance, that you have to write a paper on one aspect of the media (TV, radio, Internet) and its influence on a particular group. Here's how analyzing can help you gather information for that paper:

- Reviewing the assignment terms, you note two important items: The paper should be approximately 10 pages, and it should describe at least three significant points of influence.
- At the library and online, you find thousands of articles in this topic area. Analyzing your reaction to them and how many articles focus on certain aspects of the topic, you decide to focus your paper on how the Internet influences young teens (ages 13–15).
- Examining the summaries of six comprehensive articles leads you to three in-depth sources.

In this way, you achieve a subgoal—a selection of useful materials—on the way to your larger goal of writing a well-crafted paper.

Break Information into Parts

The next step is to search for the two most relevant parts of the information: The main idea or ideas (perhaps in the form of an *argument*—a set of connected ideas, supported by examples, made by a writer to prove or disprove a point) and the evidence that supports them (also called *reasons* or *supporting details*).

Separate the Ideas. Identify each of the ideas conveyed in what you are reading. You can use lists or a mind map to visually separate ideas from one another. For instance, if you are reading about how teens aged 13 to 15 use the Internet, you could identify the goal of each method of access they use (websites, blogs, messaging through social networking).

Identify the Evidence. For each main idea, identify the evidence that supports it. For example, if an article claims that young teens rely on app-based messaging three times more than on emails, note the facts, studies, or other evidence cited to support the truth of the claim.

Examine and Evaluate

The third step is by far the most significant, and lies at the heart of analytical thinking. Now you examine the information to see if it is going to be useful for your purposes. Keep your mind open to all useful information, setting aside personal prejudices. A student who thinks that the death penalty is wrong, for example, may have a hard time analyzing arguments that defend it, or may focus his research on materials that support his perspective. The extra time you risk with careful evaluation will reward you with the most accurate and useful information available.

Here are four different questions that will help you examine and evaluate effectively.

1. Do examples support ideas?

When you encounter an idea or claim, examine how it is supported with examples or *evidence*—facts, expert opinion, research findings, personal experience, and so on. How useful an idea is to your work may depend on whether, or how well, it is backed up with solid evidence or made concrete with examples. Be critical of the information you gather; don't take it at face value.

For example, a blog written by a 12-year-old may make statements about what kids do on the Internet. The word of one person, who may or may not be telling the truth, is not adequate support. However, a study of youth technology use by the Department of Commerce under the provisions of the Children's Internet Protection Act may be more reliable.

2. Is the information factual and accurate, or is it opinion?

A *statement of fact* is information presented as objectively real and verifiable ("The Internet is a research tool"). In contrast, a *statement of opinion* is a belief, conclusion, or judgment that is inherently difficult, and sometimes impossible, to verify ("The Internet is always the best and most reliable research tool"). When you critically evaluate materials, one test of the evidence is whether it is fact or opinion.

3. Do causes and effects link logically?

Look at the reasons given for why something happened (causes) and the explanation of its consequences (effects, both positive and negative). For example, an article might detail what causes young teens to use the Internet after school, and the effects that this has on their family life. The cause-and-effect chain in the article should make sense to you.

An important caution: Analyze carefully to seek out *key* or *root causes*—the true, most significant causes of a problem or situation. For example, many factors may be involved in why young teens spend large amounts of time on the Internet, including availability of service, previous experience, and education level of parents, but on careful examination, one or two factors seem to be more significant than others.

4. Is the evidence biased?

When evidence has a bias, it reflects a preference or inclination in a particular direction, often one that prevents even-handed judgment. Searching for a bias involves looking for hidden perspectives or assumptions that lie within the material.

Many types of work, such as the construction project these architects are discussing, involve analytical thinking.

A *perspective* is a characteristic way of thinking about people, situations, events, and ideas. It can be broad (such as a generally optimistic or pessimistic view of life) or more focused (such as an attitude about whether students should commute or live on campus). Perspectives are associated with *assumptions*—judgments or generalizations influenced by experience and values. For example, the perspective that people can maintain control over technology leads to assumptions such as "Parents can control children's exposure to the Internet." Having a particular experience with children and the Internet can build or reinforce a perspective. Examining perspectives and assumptions helps you judge whether material is *reliable*. The less bias you can identify, the more reliable the information.

After the questions: What information is most useful to you?

You've examined your information, looking at its evidence, its validity, its perspective, and any underlying assumptions. Now, based on that examination, you evaluate whether an idea or piece of information is important or unimportant, relevant or not, strong or weak, and why. You then set aside what is not useful and use the rest to form an opinion, possible solution, or decision.

In preparing your paper on young teens and the Internet, for example, you've analyzed a selection of information and materials to see how they applied to the goal of your paper. You then selected what you believe will be most useful, in preparation for drafting.

Make Connections

The last part of analytical thinking is where, after you have broken information apart, you find new and logical ways to connect pieces together. This step is crucial for research papers and essays because it is where your original ideas are born—and it is also where your creative skills get involved (more on that in the next section). When you begin to write, you focus on your new ideas, supporting them effectively with information you've learned from your analysis.

Here are some ways to make connections.

Compare and contrast. Look at how ideas are similar to, or different from, each other. You might explore how different young teen subgroups (boys versus girls, for example) have different purposes for setting up pages on sites such as Facebook or creating Twitter handles.

Look for themes, patterns, and categories. Note connections that form as you look at how bits of information relate to one another. For example, you might see patterns of Internet use that link young teens from particular cultures or areas of the country together into categories.

Come to new information ready to hear and read new ideas, think about them, and make informed decisions about what you believe. The process will educate you, sharpen your thinking skills, and give you more information to work with as you encounter life's problems. See Key 4.1 for some questions you can ask to build and use analytical thinking skills.

Pursuing your goals, in school and in the workplace, requires not only analyzing information, but also thinking creatively about how to use what you've learned from your analysis.

HOW CAN YOU IMPROVE YOUR *creative thinking skills?*

Think of the word *creativity*, and of people whom you consider to be creative. What comes to mind? Are you thinking of music, visual arts, design, and dance? Are Adele, Zac Posen, Natalie Portman, or Jay-Z in your thoughts? Because creativity is often equated with visual and performing arts, many people don't grasp

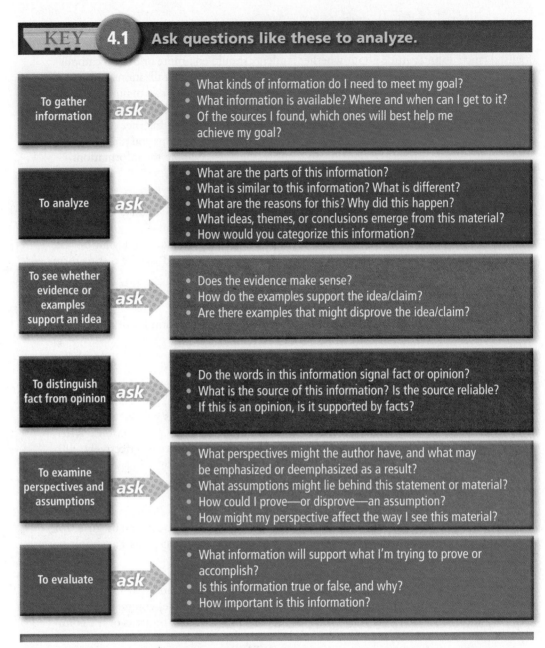

KEY 4.1 Ask questions like these to analyze.

To gather information — *ask*
- What kinds of information do I need to meet my goal?
- What information is available? Where and when can I get to it?
- Of the sources I found, which ones will best help me achieve my goal?

To analyze — *ask*
- What are the parts of this information?
- What is similar to this information? What is different?
- What are the reasons for this? Why did this happen?
- What ideas, themes, or conclusions emerge from this material?
- How would you categorize this information?

To see whether evidence or examples support an idea — *ask*
- Does the evidence make sense?
- How do the examples support the idea/claim?
- Are there examples that might disprove the idea/claim?

To distinguish fact from opinion — *ask*
- Do the words in this information signal fact or opinion?
- What is the source of this information? Is the source reliable?
- If this is an opinion, is it supported by facts?

To examine perspectives and assumptions — *ask*
- What perspectives might the author have, and what may be emphasized or deemphasized as a result?
- What assumptions might lie behind this statement or material?
- How could I prove—or disprove—an assumption?
- How might my perspective affect the way I see this material?

To evaluate — *ask*
- What information will support what I'm trying to prove or accomplish?
- Is this information true or false, and why?
- How important is this information?

Source: Adapted from www-ed.fnal.gov/trc/tutorial/taxonomy.html (Richard Paul, *Critical Thinking: How to Prepare Students for a Rapidly Changing World*, 1993) and from www.kcmetro.edu/longview/ctac/blooms.htm (Barbara Fowler, Longview Community College "Bloom's Taxonomy and Critical Thinking").

what this section of your text will illustrate—the range of human experience that depends on creativity.

There are many ways to define creativity. Here are a few to ponder:

- Combining existing elements in an innovative way to create a new purpose or result (using a weak adhesive to mark pages in a book, a 3M scientist created Post-It notes).
- Generating new ideas from looking at how things are related (noting what ladybugs eat inspired organic farmers to bring them in to consume crop-destroying aphids).[5]
- The ability to make unusual connections—to view information in quirky ways that bring about unique results (after examining how burrs stuck to his dog's fur after a walk in the woods, an inventor imagined how a similar system of hooks and loops could make two pieces of fabric stick to each other).

To think creatively is to generate new ideas that promote useful change, whether the change consists of world-altering communication technology or a tooth brushing technique that more effectively prevents cavities. Prepare to power up your creative thinking ability by gathering the following five ingredients.

The Five Ingredients of Creativity

This recipe produces both the mindset and the inspiration that allow you to think creatively.

1. *Belief that you can be creative.* Creative thinking is a skill that can be developed. Writing about the role of creativity in medicine, Jennifer Gibson, PharmD, notes that "Creativity is not restricted to great artists, but it can be fostered by training, encouragement, and practice. . . . Everyone can be curious, seek change and take risks."[6]

2. *Curiosity and exploration.* Seeking out new information and experiences will broaden your knowledge, giving you more raw materials with which to build creative ideas.[7] Think about what sparks your curiosity, and make a point to know more about it—take a course in it, read a book about it, check out a website or some music.

3. *Time alone.* Despite how American society values speed (so much so that we equate being "quick" with being smart)[8] and working in teams, research indicates that creativity demands time and independent thinking.[9] Think of the stereotypes of the writer alone in a cabin or a painter alone in an attic studio. Steve Wozniak, co-founder of Apple, provides advice that he says "might be hard to take. That advice is: Work alone."[10]

4. *Risk-taking and hard work.* Although most people think of creativity as coming in lightning flashes of inspiration, it demands that you risk time, ideas, and enormous effort in the quest for reward. Creativity expert Michael Michalko notes that "the more times you try to get ideas, the more active your brain becomes and the more creative you become."[11]

5. *Acceptance of mistakes as part of the process.* When you can risk messing up, you open yourself to ideas and promote productivity. Michalko says, "Whenever you try to do something and do not succeed," he says, "you do not fail. You have learned something that does not work."[12]

You have set the stage for creativity with this recipe. Next, explore actions that will help you build your creative thinking skill—braingaming, shifting your perspective, and taking risks.

Go Beyond Brainstorming

You've likely heard of *brainstorming*—letting your mind free to generate ideas or answers to a question, and evaluating their quality later. However, new research suggests that constructive criticism and dissent produce *more* ideas and promote rethinking and refining that leads to an idea's most productive form.[13] "All these errant discussions . . . may even be the most essential part of the creative process," says Lehrer. "It is the human friction that makes the sparks."[14]

Teamwork is crucial in today's workplace, and the most productive teamwork will incorporate constructive dissent and questioning. Instead of brainstorming, think of it as *braingaming*—a term that incorporates the challenges and back-and-forth that can take groups to new heights of creativity.[15] Remember that you don't have to sacrifice civility. At Pixar, groups use a technique called "plussing," which refers to positive, productive criticism that includes ways of improving on the idea being discussed.[16] Keep the "plus" in mind as you contribute and evaluate.

Use these strategies to get the most out of your braingaming.

When you think through something with others in a group, the variety of ideas gives you a better chance of finding a workable solution to a problem.

Avoid looking for one right answer. Questions may have many right answers with degrees of usefulness. The more possibilities you generate, the better your chance of finding the best one. Thomas Edison is said to have tried over 2,000 filaments before he found the right one for the tungsten electric bulb.

Mix collaboration with private time. Group members can become inspired by, and make creative use of, one another's ideas.[17] However, creativity also requires time alone, and working in groups can have drawbacks, including team members letting others do all the work or mimicking others' ideas out of peer pressure.[18] Consider having members generate ideas on their own before bringing them to the group. Sharing ideas electronically is often a productive strategy.

Keep recording tools at the ready. Get in the habit of recording ideas as you think of them. Keep a pen and paper by your bed, your smartphone in your pocket, a notepad in your car, or a recorder in your backpack so that you can grab creative thoughts before they fade.

Shift Your Perspective

If no one ever questioned established opinion, people would still think the sun revolved around the Earth. Here are some ways to change how you look at a situation or problem.

Challenge assumptions. Taking the risk of going against what people assume to be true can lead you down innovative paths. In the late 1960s, for example, most people assumed that schools provided education and television provided entertainment. Jim Henson, a pioneer in children's television, asked, "Why can't we use TV to educate young children?" From that question, the characters of *Sesame Street,* and many other educational programs, were born.

Try on another point of view. Ask others for their perspectives, read about new ways to approach situations, or risk going with the opposite of your first instinct.[19] Then use what you learn to inspire creativity. For a political science course, for example, you might craft a position paper for a senatorial candidate that goes against your position on that particular issue.

Ask "what if" questions. Set up imaginary environments in which new ideas can grow, such as "What if I had unlimited money or time?" For example, the founders of Seeds of Peace, faced with long-term conflict in the Middle East, took the risk to ask: What if Israeli and Palestinian teens met at a summer camp in Maine to build mutual understanding and respect? Based on the ideas that came up, they created an organization that provides enormous reward to teenagers from the Middle East, helping them to develop leadership and communication skills.

Take Risks

Creative breakthroughs can come from targeted risk-taking.

Go against established ideas. The founders of Etsy.com went against the idea that the American consumer prefers cheap, conventional, mass-produced items. In 2005, they took the risk of creating an online company that allows artisans to offer one-of-a-kind, handmade products to the consumer, and were rewarded with a thriving site that has also created a community of artists and connects each artist personally to his or her customers.

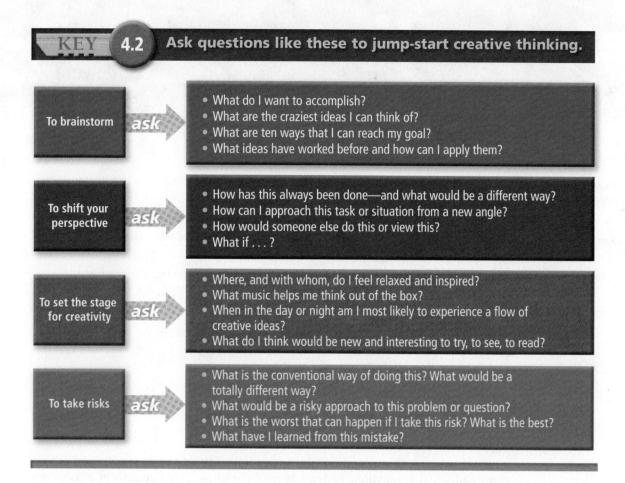

KEY 4.2 Ask questions like these to jump-start creative thinking.

To brainstorm	ask	• What do I want to accomplish? • What are the craziest ideas I can think of? • What are ten ways that I can reach my goal? • What ideas have worked before and how can I apply them?
To shift your perspective	ask	• How has this always been done—and what would be a different way? • How can I approach this task or situation from a new angle? • How would someone else do this or view this? • What if . . . ?
To set the stage for creativity	ask	• Where, and with whom, do I feel relaxed and inspired? • What music helps me think out of the box? • When in the day or night am I most likely to experience a flow of creative ideas? • What do I think would be new and interesting to try, to see, to read?
To take risks	ask	• What is the conventional way of doing this? What would be a totally different way? • What would be a risky approach to this problem or question? • What is the worst that can happen if I take this risk? What is the best? • What have I learned from this mistake?

Risk leaving your comfort zone. Rewards can come when you seek out new experiences and environments. Go somewhere you've never been. Play music you've never heard of. Seek out people who interest you but whom you would not normally connect with. Check out an international or independent film or documentary that is completely outside of your experience. Even small risks like these can create ideas that generate big changes.

As with analytical thinking, asking questions powers creative thinking. See Key 4.2 for examples of the kinds of questions you can ask to get your creative juices flowing.

Creativity connects analytical and practical thinking. When you generate ideas, solutions, or choices, you need to think analytically to evaluate their quality. Then, you need to think practically about how to make the best solution or choice happen.

HOW CAN YOU IMPROVE YOUR
practical thinking skills?

Practical thinking refers to how you adapt to your environment (both people and circumstances), or how you shape or change your environment to adapt to you, to pursue important goals. An example: Your goal is to pass freshman composition. You learn most successfully through visual presentations. To achieve your goal, you can use the instructor's PowerPoints or other visual media to enhance your learning (adapt to your environment) or enroll in a heavily visual online version of the course (change your environment to adapt to you)—or both.

get creative

ACTIVATE YOUR CREATIVE POWERS

Complete the following on paper or in digital format.

Think about your creativity over the past month.

1. First, describe three creative acts you performed—one in the process of studying course material, one in your personal life, and one at work or in the classroom.
2. Now think of a problem or situation that is on your mind. Generate one new idea for how to deal with it.
3. Write down a second idea, but focus on the risk-taking aspect of creativity. What would be a risky way to handle the situation? How do you hope it would pay off?
4. Finally, sit with the question. Write down one more idea *only* after you have been away from this exercise for at least 24 hours.

Keep these ideas in mind. You may want to use one soon!

Real-world problems and decisions require you to add understanding of experiences and social interactions to your analytical abilities. Your success in a sociology class, for example, may depend almost as much on getting along with your instructor as on your academic work. Similarly, the way you solve a personal money problem may have more impact on your life than how you work through a problem in an accounting course.

Put Emotional Intelligence to Work

You gain much of your ability to think practically from personal experience, rather than from formal training.[20] What you learn from experience answers "how" questions—how to talk, how to behave, how to proceed.[21] For example, after completing several papers for a course, you may learn what your instructor expects—or, after a few arguments with a friend or partner, you may learn how to manage "hot button" topics more effectively.

Emotional intelligence gives you steps you can take to promote success. For example, if you are fuming about a low grade on an assignment, engage emotional intelligence to make the best of the situation:

- *Perceive your emotion:* You sense anger, frustration.
- *Think about the emotion:* Note what perception arose from those feelings (at first, "I'm not good enough") and how it affected your mindset (at first, it made you feel badly about yourself).
- *Understand the emotion:* Determining that the emotions did not reflect your value, you consider how to adjust that mindset to increase determination.
- *Manage the emotion:* Decide to meet with your instructor to hear her reasoning behind the grade and ask about what you can do to improve it.

If you know that social interactions are difficult for you, enlist someone to give you some informal coaching. As Dr. Norman Rosenthal reports in "10 Ways to Enhance

KEY 4.3 Ask questions like these to activate practical thinking.

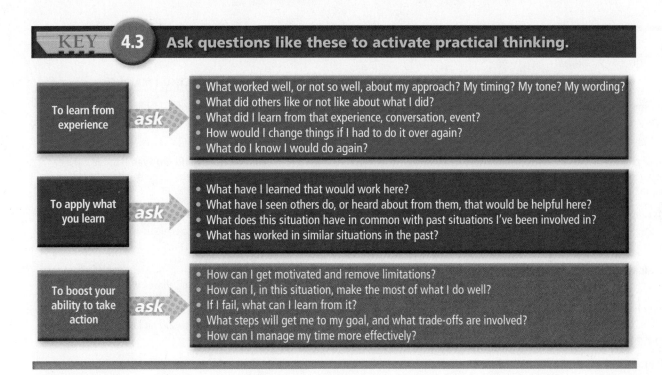

To learn from experience ask
- What worked well, or not so well, about my approach? My timing? My tone? My wording?
- What did others like or not like about what I did?
- What did I learn from that experience, conversation, event?
- How would I change things if I had to do it over again?
- What do I know I would do again?

To apply what you learn ask
- What have I learned that would work here?
- What have I seen others do, or heard about from them, that would be helpful here?
- What does this situation have in common with past situations I've been involved in?
- What has worked in similar situations in the past?

To boost your ability to take action ask
- How can I get motivated and remove limitations?
- How can I, in this situation, make the most of what I do well?
- If I fail, what can I learn from it?
- What steps will get me to my goal, and what trade-offs are involved?
- How can I manage my time more effectively?

Your Emotional Intelligence," you may not realize how much others can tell what you are feeling. "Ask someone who knows you (and whom you trust) how you are coming across," he recommends.[22]

Practical Thinking Means Action

Action is the logical result of practical thinking. Basic student success strategies that promote action—staying motivated, making the most of your strengths, managing time, seeking help from instructors and advisors, and believing in yourself—will keep you moving toward your goals.[23] Learning from mistakes and failure is an especially important part of practical thinking. As psychologist Barry Schwartz points out, "Wisdom comes from experience, and not just any experience. You need permission to be allowed to improvise, to try new things, occasionally to fail, and to learn from your failures."[24] When people resist making mistakes, they deny themselves a chance to learn and develop their powers of reasoning.

See Key 4.3 for some questions you can ask in order to apply practical thinking to your problems and decisions.

HOW CAN YOU SOLVE PROBLEMS
and make decisions effectively?

Problem solving and decision making follow similar paths, both requiring you to identify and analyze a situation, generate possibilities, choose one, follow through on it, and evaluate its success. Key 4.4 gives an overview of the paths, indicating how you think at each step. You can use this path, and a visual organizer, to map out problems and decisions effectively. Remember, too, that whereas all problem solving involves decision making, only some decision making requires you to solve a problem.

LESSON 4

PROBLEM SOLVING	THINKING SKILL	DECISION MAKING
Define the problem—recognize that something needs to change, identify what's happening, look for true causes.	**STEP 1** DEFINE	**Define the decision**—identify your goal (your need) and then construct a decision that will help you get it.
Analyze the problem—gather information, break it down into pieces, verify facts, look at perspectives and assumptions, evaluate information.	**STEP 2** ANALYZE	**Examine needs and motives**—consider the layers of needs carefully, and be honest about what you really want.
Generate possible solutions—use creative strategies to think of ways you could address the causes of this problem.	**STEP 3** CREATE	**Name and/or generate different options**—use creative questions to come up with choices that would fulfill your needs.
Evaluate solutions—look carefully at potential pros and cons of each, and choose what seems best.	**STEP 4** ANALYZE (EVALUATE)	**Evaluate options**—look carefully at potential pros and cons of each, and choose what seems best.
Put the solution to work—persevere, focus on results, and believe in yourself as you go for your goal.	**STEP 5** TAKE PRACTICAL ACTION	**Act on your decision**—go down the path and use practical strategies to stay on target.
Evaluate how well the solution worked—look at the effects of what you did.	**STEP 6** ANALYZE (REEVALUATE)	**Evaluate the success of your decision**—look at whether it accomplished what you had hoped.
In the future, apply what you've learned—use this solution, or a better one, when a similar situation comes up again.	**STEP 7** TAKE PRACTICAL ACTION	**In the future, apply what you've learned**—make this choice, or a better one, when a similar decision comes up again.

Solve a Problem

Use these strategies as you move through the problem-solving process.

Use probing questions to define problems. Ask: What is the problem? And what is *causing* the problem? Engage your emotional intelligence. If you determine that you are not motivated to do your work for a class, for example, you could ask questions like these:

- Do my feelings stem from how I interact with my instructor or classmates?
- Is the subject matter difficult? Uninteresting? Is the volume of work too much?

Chances are that how you answer one or more of these questions may help you define the problem—and ultimately solve it.

Analyze carefully. Gather information that will help you examine the problem. Consider how the problem is similar to, or different from, other problems. Clarify facts. Note your own perspective, and look for others. Make sure your assumptions are not getting in the way.

Generate possible solutions based on causes, not effects. Addressing a cause provides a lasting solution, whereas "putting a Band-Aid on" an effect cannot. Say, for example, that your shoulder hurts when you type. Getting a massage is a helpful but temporary solution, because the pain returns whenever you go back to work. Changing your keyboard height is a better idea and a lasting solution to the problem, because it eliminates the cause of your pain.

Consider how possible solutions affect you and others. Which risk rewards you most? Which takes other people's needs into consideration? Is it possible to maximize reward for all involved?

Evaluate your solution and act on it in the future. Once you choose a solution and put it into action, ask yourself: What worked that you would do again? What didn't work that you would avoid or change in the future?

What happens if you don't work through a problem comprehensively? Take, for example, a student having an issue with an instructor. He may get into an argument with the instructor, stop showing up to class, or take a quick-and-dirty approach to assignments. All of these choices have negative consequences. Now look at how the student might work through this problem using analytical, creative, and practical thinking skills. Key 4.5 shows how his effort can pay off.

Make a Decision

As you use the steps to make a decision, remember these strategies.

Look at the given options—then try to think of more. Some decisions have a given set of options. For example, your school may allow you to major, double major, or major and minor. However, with an advisor's help, you may come up with more options such as an interdisciplinary major. Consider similar situations you've been in or heard about, what decisions were made, and what resulted from those decisions.

Think about how your decision affects others. What you choose might have an impact on friends, family, and others around you.

Gather perspectives. Talk with others who made similar decisions. If you listen carefully, you may hear ideas you never thought about. Consider choices with different levels of risk.

Look at the long-term effects. As with problem solving, it's key to examine what happened after you put the decision into action. For important decisions, do a short-term evaluation and another evaluation after a period of time. Consider whether your decision sent you in the right direction or whether you should rethink your choice.

What happens when you make important decisions too quickly? Consider a student trying to decide whether to transfer schools. If she makes her decision based on a reason that ultimately is not the most important one for her (for example, a boyfriend or close friends go to the other school), she may regret her choice later.

"Successfully intelligent people," says Sternberg, "defy negative expectations, even when these expectations arise from low scores on IQ or similar tests. They do not let other people's assessments stop them from achieving their goals. They find their path and then pursue it, realizing that there will be obstacles along the way and that surmounting these obstacles is part of the challenge."[25] Let the obstacles come, as they will for everyone, in all aspects of life. You can take the risk to face them, and earn the reward of overcoming them, with the power of your successfully intelligent thinking.

KEY 4.5 Work through a problem relating to an instructor.

DEFINE PROBLEM HERE:

I don't like my Sociology instructor

ANALYZE THE PROBLEM

We have different styles and personality types—I am not comfortable working in groups and being vocal.

I'm not interested in being there, and my grades are suffering from my lack of motivation.

Use boxes below to list possible solutions:

POTENTIAL POSITIVE EFFECTS	SOLUTION #1	POTENTIAL NEGATIVE EFFECTS
List for each solution: Don't have to deal with that instructor Less stress	Drop the course	*List for each solution:* Grade gets entered on my transcript I'll have to take the course eventually; it's required for my major
Getting credit for the course Feeling like I've honored a commitment	**SOLUTION #2** Put up with it until the end of the semester	Stress every time I'm there Lowered motivation Probably not such a good final grade
A chance to express myself Could get good advice An opportunity to ask direct questions of the instructor	**SOLUTION #3** Schedule meetings with advisor and instructor	Have to face instructor one-on-one Might just make things worse

Now choose the solution you think is best—circle it and make it happen.

ACTUAL POSITIVE EFFECTS	PRACTICAL ACTION	ACTUAL NEGATIVE EFFECTS
List for chosen solution: Got some helpful advice from advisor Talking in person with the instructor actually promoted a fairly honest discussion I won't have to take the course again	I scheduled and attended meetings with both advisor and instructor and opted to stick with the course.	*List for chosen solution:* Still have to put up with some group work I still don't know how much learning I'll retain from this course

FINAL EVALUATION: Was it a good or bad solution?

The solution has improved things. I'll finish the course, and I got the chance to fulfill some class responsibilities on my own or with one partner. I feel more understood and more willing to put my time into the course.

Complete the following on paper or in digital format.

KNOW IT *Think Critically*

Think of a school-related problem you have—this could be a fear, a challenge, a sticky situation, or a roadblock. Use the empty problem-solving flow chart (Key 4.6) to fill in your work.

Analyze: *Define and examine the problem.* Look at the negative effects and state your problem specifically. Write down the causes and examine them to see what's happening. Verify facts, go beyond assumptions.

Create: *Generate possible solutions.* From the most likely causes of the problem, derive possible solutions. List all the ideas that you come up with, and record your three best ideas in the chart.

Analyze: *Evaluate each solution.* As you think through each solution, (a) weigh the positive and negative effects, (b) consider similar problems, and (c) describe how the solution affects the causes of the problem. Will your solution work?

Get practical: *Choose a solution.* Which solution is the best? You may have a tie or may want to combine two different solutions. Try to find the solution that works best for you. Then, come up with a plan for how you would put your solution to work.

WRITE IT *Communicate*

Emotional intelligence journal: *Examine a problem.* Describe a problem that you are currently experiencing in school—it could be difficulty with a course, a scheduling nightmare, a conflict with a classmate. Create an imaginary letter—to an advisor, instructor, friend, medical professional, or anyone else who may help—that asks for help with your problem. Be specific about what you want and how the person to whom you are writing can help you.

KEY 4.6 Work through a decision or problem using this flowchart.

DEFINE PROBLEM/DECISION: **ANALYZE PROBLEM/DECISION**

Use center boxes to list possible options:

POTENTIAL POSITIVE EFFECTS	OPTION #1	POTENTIAL NEGATIVE EFFECTS
List for each:		*List for each:*

OPTION #2

OPTION #3

Now choose the one you think is best—circle it and make it happen.

ACTUAL POSITIVE EFFECTS	PRACTICAL ACTION	ACTUAL NEGATIVE EFFECTS
List for chosen option:		*List for chosen option:*

FINAL EVALUATION: Did your action, overall, have a positive or negative result?

Source: Based on heuristic created by Frank T. Lyman Jr. and George Eley, 1985.

Learning How You Learn

MAKING THE MOST OF YOUR ABILITIES

LESSON 5

THIS LESSON PROVIDES AN OPPORTUNITY TO INVESTIGATE YOUR LEARNING PREFERENCES IN TWO AREAS—HOW YOU TAKE IN AND PROCESS INFORMATION, AND HOW YOU RELATE TO OTHERS AROUND YOU. YOU WILL LEARN HOW TO TAILOR STUDY STRATEGIES TO YOUR PREFERENCES, TO ADJUST TO TEACHING STYLES, AND TO BUILD YOUR LESSER-DEVELOPED PREFERENCES.

Notes   52% 🔋

Today   Mar 10 8:01 AM

Working through this lesson will help you to:

- Describe different learning preferences   PP. 51–52
- Determine your learning preferences   PP. 55–56
- Recognize classroom and study tactics for different
  learning preferences   PP. 59–62

WHY EXPLORE WHO
you are as a learner?

Have you thought about how you learn? College is an ideal time to think about how you learn, think, and function in the world. "Thinking about thinking" is known as *metacognition*. Building metacognition and self-knowledge can help you choose the risks that will most effectively lead you to rewards you value. The more you know about yourself, the more effectively you can analyze courses and study environments, evaluate partners, and decide what, how, and where to study.

Use Assessments to Learn about Yourself

Each person in the world is born with particular levels of ability and potential in different areas. As you grow, you develop learning preferences based on your ability and potential. A *learning preference* is a way in which a person receives and processes information

MyStudentSuccessLab (www.mystudentsuccesslab.com) is an online solution designed to help you "Start Strong, Finish Stronger" by building skills for ongoing personal and professional development.

51

effectively. Learning preferences combine with effort and environment to create a "recipe" for what you can achieve. Part of this recipe is the way you perceive yourself, a perception that may come from many different sources. Maybe your mother thinks you are "the funny one" or "the quiet one." A grade school teacher may have called you a "thinker" or "slacker," a "go-getter" or "shy." These labels—from yourself and others—influence your ability to set and achieve goals, and can prevent you from taking productive risks if you use them to define yourself too rigidly.

Accepting a label as truth can put you in a fixed mindset and limit your potential. Instead, realize that you are not simply stuck with a label. Brain studies show that humans of any age can build new neuropathways and thereby learn new ideas and skills. This means that intelligence can grow when you risk the work to keep learning.

Picture a bag of rubber bands of different sizes. Some are thick and some thin; some are long and some short—*but all of them can stretch*. A small rubber band, stretched out, can reach the length of a larger one that lies unstretched. In other words, with effort and focus, you can develop whatever raw material you start with, perhaps beyond the natural gifts of someone who makes no effort.

Ask yourself: Who am I right now? Where would I like to be in five years? Assessments focused on how you prefer to learn and interact with others can help you answer some of these big questions. Whereas a test attempts to identify a level of performance, an *assessment*, according to professor and psychologist Howard Gardner, is "the obtaining of information about a person's skills and potentials . . . providing useful feedback to the person."[1] Think of an assessment as an honest exploration that will produce interesting and helpful information.

The assessment in this lesson provides questions to get you thinking about your strengths and challenges. As you search for answers, you are gathering important information about yourself. With this information, you will be able to define your rubber band and get ready to stretch it to its limit.

Use Assessments to Make Choices and to Grow

There may be much about yourself, your surroundings, and your experiences that you cannot control. However, with self-knowledge, you do have control over how you respond to circumstances. For example, even though you cannot control the courses you are required to take or how your instructors teach, you can manage how you respond to those courses and instructors.

The assessment in this lesson—Multiple Pathways to Learning—will give you greater insight into your strengths and weaknesses. The material following the assessment shows you how to maximize what you do well and compensate for challenging areas by making specific choices about what you do in class, during study time, and in the workplace.

Understanding yourself and others as learners also helps you choose how to respond to people in a group situation. In a study group, in-person or online class environment, or workplace, each person takes in material in a unique way. You can use what you know about others' learning preferences to improve communication and teamwork.

Remember: There are no "right" answers, no "best" scores. Completing a self-assessment is like wearing glasses to correct blurred vision. The glasses don't create new paths and possibilities, but they help you to see more clearly the ones in front of you at this moment. As you gain experience, build skills, and learn, your learning preferences are apt to change over time. If you take the assessment again in the future, your results may shift. Finally, to enjoy the reward of useful results, take the risk of answering questions honestly, reflecting who you *are* as opposed to who you *wish* you were.

WHAT TOOLS CAN HELP YOU
assess how you learn and interact with others?

A variety of tools exist to help you become more aware of different aspects of yourself. Some tools focus on learning preferences, some on areas of potential, and others on personality type. This lesson examines one assessment in particular. Multiple Pathways to Learning is a learning preferences assessment focusing on eight areas of potential, referred to as *intelligences*. It is based on Howard Gardner's Multiple Intelligences (MI) theory.

As defined by Gardner, an intelligence is an ability to solve problems or create products that are of value in a culture. Following the assessment is information about the typical traits of each type of intelligence. As you will see from your scores, you have abilities in all areas, though some are more developed than others.

Assess Your Multiple Intelligences with Pathways to Learning

In 1983, Howard Gardner changed the way people perceive intelligence and learning with his theory of Multiple Intelligences. Like Robert Sternberg, Gardner believed that the traditional view of intelligence, based on mathematical, logical, and verbal measurements that made up an "intelligence quotient" (IQ), did not reflect the true spectrum of human ability. Sternberg focused on the spectrum of actions that help people achieve important goals, but Gardner chose to examine the idea that humans possess a number of different areas of natural ability and potential that he called "multiple intelligences."

The theory of Multiple Intelligences

Gardner's research identified eight unique types of intelligence or areas of ability. These included two areas traditionally associated with the term *intelligence*—verbal and logic skills—but expanded beyond them, to encompass a wide range of potentials of the human brain.[2] These intelligences almost never function in isolation. You will almost always use several at the same time for any significant role or task.[3]

As you look at Key 5.1, study the description of each intelligence and then examine the examples of people who have unusually high levels of ability in that area. Although few people have the verbal-linguistic intelligence of William Shakespeare or the interpersonal intelligence of Oprah Winfrey, everyone has some level of ability in every intelligence. Your goal is to identify what your levels are and to work your strongest intelligences to your advantage.

The way Gardner defines intelligence heightens the value of different abilities in different arenas. In Tibet, for example, mountain dwellers prize the bodily-kinesthetic ability of a Himalayan mountain guide. In Detroit, automakers appreciate the visual-spatial talents of a master car designer. Send the car designer up Mount Everest, or have the Sherpa design a car for Chrysler, and suddenly a person who is exceptionally intelligent in one area may falter in another.

Students drawn to the sciences may find that they have strengths in logical-mathematical or naturalistic thinking.

INTELLIGENCE	DESCRIPTION AND SKILLS	HIGH-ACHIEVING EXAMPLE
Verbal-Linguistic	Ability to communicate through language; listening, reading, writing, speaking	• Author J.K. Rowling • Orator and President Barack Obama
Logical-Mathematical	Ability to understand logical reasoning and problem solving; math, science, patterns, sequences	• Physicist Stephen Hawking • Mathematician Svetlana Jitomirskaya
Bodily-Kinesthetic	Ability to use the physical body skillfully and to take in knowledge through bodily sensation; coordination, working with hands	• Gymnast Nastia Liukin • Survivalist Bear Gryllis
Visual-Spatial	Ability to understand spatial relationships and to perceive and create images; visual art, graphic design, charts and maps	• Artist Walt Disney • Designer Stella McCartney
Interpersonal	Ability to relate to others, noticing their moods, motivations, and feelings; social activity, cooperative learning, teamwork	• Media personality Ellen Degeneres • Former Secretary of State Colin Powell
Intrapersonal	Ability to understand one's own behavior and feelings; self-awareness, independence, time spent alone	• Animal researcher Jane Goodall • Philosopher Friedrich Nietzsche
Musical	Ability to comprehend and create meaningful sound; sensitivity to music and musical patterns	• Singer and musician Alicia Keys • Composer Andrew Lloyd Webber
Naturalist	Ability to identify, distinguish, categorize, and classify species or items, often incorporating high interest in elements of the natural environment	• Social activist Wangari Maathai • Bird cataloger John James Audubon

Your own eight intelligences

Gardner believes that all people possess all eight intelligences, but each person has developed some intelligences more fully than others. When you find a task or subject easy, you are probably using a more fully developed intelligence. When you have trouble, you may be using a less developed intelligence.[4]

Gardner also believes your levels of development in the eight intelligences can grow or recede throughout your life, depending on effort and experience. For example, although you will not become a world-class pianist if you have limited musical ability, you can develop what you have with focus and work. Conversely, even a highly talented musician will lose ability without practice. This reflects how the brain grows with learning and becomes sluggish without it.

MULTIPLE PATHWAYS TO LEARNING

Each intelligence has a set of numbered statements. Consider each statement on its own. Then, on a scale from 1 (lowest) to 4 (highest), rate how closely it matches who you are right now and write that number on the line next to the statement. Finally, total each set of six questions. Enter your scores in the grid on page 56.

1. rarely   2. sometimes   3. usually   4. always

1. _____ I enjoy physical activities.
2. _____ I am uncomfortable sitting still.
3. _____ I prefer to learn through doing.
4. _____ When sitting I move my legs or hands.
5. _____ I enjoy working with my hands.
6. _____ I like to pace when I'm thinking or studying.

_____ **TOTAL for BODILY-KINESTHETIC**

1. _____ I enjoy telling stories.
2. _____ I like to write.
3. _____ I like to read.
4. _____ I express myself clearly.
5. _____ I am good at negotiating.
6. _____ I like to discuss topics that interest me.

_____ **TOTAL for VERBAL-LINGUISTIC**

1. _____ I use maps easily.
2. _____ I draw pictures/diagrams when explaining ideas.
3. _____ I can assemble items easily from diagrams.
4. _____ I enjoy drawing or photography.
5. _____ I do not like to read long paragraphs.
6. _____ I prefer a drawn map over written directions.

_____ **TOTAL for VISUAL-SPATIAL**

1. _____ I like math in school.
2. _____ I like science.
3. _____ I problem-solve well.
4. _____ I question how things work.
5. _____ I enjoy planning or designing something new.
6. _____ I am able to fix things.

_____ **TOTAL for LOGICAL–MATHEMATICAL**

1. _____ I listen to music.
2. _____ I move my fingers or feet when I hear music.
3. _____ I have good rhythm.
4. _____ I like to sing along with music.
5. _____ People have said I have musical talent.
6. _____ I like to express my ideas through music.

_____ **TOTAL for MUSICAL**

1. _____ I need quiet time to think.
2. _____ I think about issues before I want to talk.
3. _____ I am interested in self-improvement.
4. _____ I understand my thoughts and feelings.
5. _____ I know what I want out of life.
6. _____ I prefer to work on projects alone.

_____ **TOTAL for INTRAPERSONAL**

1. _____ I like doing a project with other people.
2. _____ People come to me to help settle conflicts.
3. _____ I like to spend time with friends.
4. _____ I am good at understanding people.
5. _____ I am good at making people feel comfortable.
6. _____ I enjoy helping others.

_____ **TOTAL for INTERPERSONAL**

1. _____ I like to think about how things, ideas, or people fit into categories.
2. _____ I enjoy studying plants, animals, or oceans.
3. _____ I tend to see how things relate to, or are distinct from, one another.
4. _____ I think about having a career in the natural sciences.
5. _____ As a child I often played with bugs and leaves.
6. _____ I like to investigate the natural world around me.

_____ **TOTAL for NATURALISTIC**

Source: Developed by Joyce Bishop, PhD, Golden West College, Huntington Beach, CA. Based on Gardner, Howard. *Frames of Mind: The Theory of Multiple Intelligences.* New York: HarperCollins, 1993.

Learning How You Learn

SCORING GRID FOR MULTIPLE PATHWAYS TO LEARNING

For each intelligence, shade the box in the row that corresponds with the range where your score falls. For example, if you scored 17 in bodily-kinesthetic intelligence, you would shade the middle box in that row; if you scored a 13 in visual-spatial, you would shade the last box in that row. When you have shaded one box for each row, you will see a "map" of your range of development at a glance.

A score of 20–24 indicates a high level of development in that particular type of intelligence, 14–19 a moderate level, and below 14 an underdeveloped intelligence.

	20–24 (HIGHLY DEVELOPED)	14–19 (MODERATELY DEVELOPED)	BELOW 14 (UNDERDEVELOPED)
Bodily-Kinesthetic			
Visual-Spatial			
Verbal-Linguistic			
Logical-Mathematical			
Musical			
Interpersonal			
Intrapersonal			
Naturalistic			

Note: A related self-assessment is the VAK or VARK questionnaire. VAK/VARK assesses learning preferences in three (or four) areas: Visual, Auditory, Read/Write (in VARK), and Kinesthetic. This lesson focuses on the Multiple Intelligences (MI) assessment because it incorporates elements of VAK/VARK and expands upon them, giving you a comprehensive picture of your abilities. Keep in mind that auditory learning is part of two MI dimensions:

- Many auditory learners have strong verbal intelligence but prefer to hear words (in a lecture or discussion or on a recording) instead of reading them.
- Many auditory learners have strong musical intelligence and remember and retain information based on sounds and rhythms.

If you tend to absorb information better through listening, try study suggestions for these two intelligences. Some instructors convert their lectures into podcasts, which can be very helpful. For further information about VAK/VARK, go to www.vark-learn .com or search online using the keywords "VAK assessment."

Complete the Multiple Pathways to Learning assessment and scoring grid to determine where you are right now in the eight intelligence areas. Then look at Key 5.2, immediately following the assessment, to identify specific skills associated with each area.

HOW CAN YOU USE
your self-knowledge?

As you analyze learning preferences through completing this assessment as well as any others associated with your course, you develop a clearer picture of who you are and how you interact with others. Then, and most importantly, you figure out what to do with this heightened self-knowledge. Use your thinking skills to choose effective strategies for interacting in the classroom, managing study time, dealing with your workplace, and working with technology. These more targeted and personal efforts can help you earn the reward of deeper and more lasting learning.

Verbal-Linguistic		• Remembering terms easily • Mastering a foreign language • Using writing or speech to convince someone to do or believe something
Musical-Rhythmic		• Sensing tonal qualities • Being sensitive to sounds and rhythms in music and in spoken language • Using an understanding of musical patterns to hear music
Logical-Mathematical		• Recognizing abstract patterns • Using facts to support an idea, and generating ideas based on evidence • Reasoning scientifically (formulating and testing a hypothesis)
Visual-Spatial		• Recognizing relationships between objects • Representing something graphically • Manipulating images
Bodily-Kinesthetic		• Strong mind–body connection • Controlling and coordinating body movement • Using the body to create products or express emotion
Intrapersonal		• Accessing your internal emotions • Understanding your own feelings and using them to guide your behavior • Understanding yourself in relation to others
Interpersonal		• Seeing things from others' perspectives • Noticing moods, intentions, and temperaments of others • Gauging the most effective way to work with individual group members
Naturalistic		• Ability to categorize something as a member of a group or species • Understanding of relationships among natural organisms • Deep comfort with, and respect for, the natural world

Learning How You Learn

Classroom Choices

Most students have to complete a set of "core curriculum" courses, as well as whatever courses their majors or certificates require. As you sign up for the sections that fit into your schedule, you may be asking, "How is it possible to make choices based on my learning preferences?"

The opportunity for choice lies in how you interact with your instructor and function in the classroom. It is impossible for instructors to tailor classroom presentations to 15, 40, or 300 unique learners. As a result, you may find yourself in sync with one teacher and mismatched with another. Sometimes, the way the class is structured can affect your success more than the subject matter; for example, a strong interpersonal

Broaden your experience of your courses, and your education, by interacting with instructors outside of class time.

learner who generally struggles in the sciences might do well in a lab section that depends on group work.

Just as you have learning preferences, instructors have ways they are most comfortable teaching. After several class meetings, you should be able to assess each instructor's dominant teaching styles (see Key 5.3) and determine how those fit with your learning preferences. As with learning preferences, most instructors will demonstrate a combination of teaching styles.

Although styles vary and instructors may combine styles, the word-focused lecture is still most common. For this reason, the traditional college classroom generally works best for the verbal or logical learner. Online coursework may provide more material suited to visual learners. What can you do when your learning preferences don't match up with how your instructor teaches? Here are three suggestions:

- *Play to your strengths.* For example, if you're a kinesthetic learner, you might rewrite or type your lecture notes, make flash cards, or take walks while saying important terms and concepts out loud. Likewise, if you are an interpersonal learner with an instructor who delivers straight lectures, consider setting up a study group to go over details and fill in factual gaps.

- *Work to strengthen weaker areas.* As a visual learner reviews notes from a structured lecture, he could use logical-mathematical strategies such as outlining notes or thinking about cause-and-effect relationships within the material. A logical-mathematical learner, studying for a test from notes delivered

KEY 5.3 Instructors often prefer one or more teaching styles.

TEACHING STYLE	WHAT TO EXPECT IN CLASS
Lecture, verbal focus	Instructor speaks to the class for the entire period, with little class interaction. Lesson is taught primarily through words, either spoken or written on the board, on PowerPoints in class or online, with handouts or text, or possibly through podcasts.
Lecture with group discussion	Instructor presents material but encourages class discussion.
Small groups	Instructor presents material and then breaks class into small groups for discussion or project work.
Visual focus	Instructor uses visual elements such as PowerPoint slides, diagrams, photographs, drawings, transparencies, in-class or "YouTube for Schools" videos, or movies.
Logical presentation	Instructor organizes material in a logical sequence, such as by steps, time, or importance.
Random presentation	Instructor tackles topics in no particular order, and may jump around a lot or digress.
Conceptual presentation	Instructor spends the majority of time on the big picture, focusing on abstract concepts and umbrella ideas.
Detailed presentation	Instructor spends the majority of time, after introducing ideas, on the details and facts that underlie them.
Hands-on presentation	Instructor uses demonstrations, experiments, props, and class activities to show key points.

get analytical

IMPROVE A CLASSROOM EXPERIENCE

Complete the following on paper or in digital format.

Considering what you know about yourself as a learner and about your instructors' teaching styles this term, decide which classroom situation is the most challenging for you. Use this exercise to analyze the situation.

1. Name the course and describe the instructor's style.

2. Analyze how your learning preference interacts with your instructor's teaching style, describing what about this interaction makes the class challenging.

3. Based on your analysis, identify a change you can make to improve the situation. Describe the change, noting specifically what you plan to do and when.

by an instructor with a random presentation, could organize her material using tables and timelines.

■ *Ask your instructor for help.* Connect through email or during office hours. Communicating your struggle can feel like a risk, but building a relationship with an instructor or teaching assistant can be extremely rewarding. This is especially true in large lectures where you are anonymous unless you speak up. For example, a visual learner might ask the instructor to recommend figures or videos to study that illustrate the lecture.

The adjustments you make for your instructor's teaching style will build flexibility that you need for career and life success. Just as you can't hand pick your instructors, you will rarely, if ever, be able to choose your work colleagues. You will have to adjust to them, and help them adjust to you. Keep in mind, too, that research shows a benefit from learning in a variety of ways—kind of like cross-training for the brain. Knowing this, some instructors may challenge you to learn in ways that aren't comfortable for you.

A final point: Some students try to find out more about an instructor by asking students who have already taken the course or looking up comments online. Be cautious, as you may not be able to trust an anonymous poster. Even if you hear a review from a friend you trust, every student–instructor relationship is unique, and an instructor your friend loved may be a bad match for you. Prioritize the courses you need, and know that you can make the most of what your instructors offer, regardless of their teaching styles.

Study Choices

Start now to use what you learned about yourself to choose the best study techniques. If you tend to learn successfully from a linear, logical presentation, look for order (for example, a timeline of how information organized by event dates) as you review notes. If you are strong in interpersonal intelligence, you could work with study groups whenever possible.

When faced with a task that challenges your weaknesses, use strategies that boost your ability. For example, if you do *not* respond well to linear information, try applying your strengths to the material by using a hands-on approach. Or you could try developing your area of weakness by learning study skills that work well for logical-mathematical learners.

When you study with others, you and the entire group will be more successful if you understand one another's learning preferences, as in the following examples.

- An Interpersonal learner could take the lead in teaching material to others.
- A Visual learner could create a table to illustrate the group schedule.
- A Naturalistic learner might organize facts into categories that solidify concepts.

Look at Key 5.4 for study strategies that suit each intelligence. Because you have some level of ability in each area and because you will sometimes need to boost your

KEY 5.4 Choose study techniques to maximize each intelligence.

Verbal-Linguistic		• Read text; highlight selectively • Use a computer to retype and summarize notes • Outline chapters • Recite information or write scripts/debates
Musical-Rhythmic		• Create rhythms out of words • Beat out rhythms with hand or stick while reciting concepts • Write songs/raps that help you learn concepts • Write out study material to fit into a wordless tune you have on a CD or MP3 player; chant or sing the material along with the tune as you listen
Logical-Mathematical		• Organize material logically; if it suits the topic, use a spreadsheet program • Explain material sequentially to someone • Develop systems and find patterns • Analyze and evaluate information
Visual-Spatial		• Develop graphic organizers for new material • Draw "think-links" (mind maps) • Use a computer to develop charts and tables • Use color in your notes for organization
Bodily-Kinesthetic		• Move while you learn; pace and recite • Rewrite or retype notes to engage "muscle memory" • Design and play games to learn material • Act out scripts of material
Intrapersonal		• Reflect on personal meaning of information • Keep a journal • Study in quiet areas • Imagine essays or experiments before beginning
Interpersonal		• Study in a group • As you study, discuss information over the phone or send instant messages • Teach someone else the material • Make time to discuss assignments and tests with your instructor
Naturalistic		• Break down information into categories • Look for ways in which items fit or don't fit together • Look for relationships among ideas, events, facts • Study in a natural setting if it helps you focus

ability in a weaker area, you may find useful suggestions under any of the headings. Try different techniques. Pay attention to what works best for you. You may be surprised at what is useful.

Technology Choices

Technology is everywhere. People communicate using email, text messaging, and social networking sites; they read blogs, listen to podcasts, and use apps on their cell phones. Technology also plays a significant role in academic settings, where you may encounter:

- Hybrid or fully online courses
- Instructors who communicate primarily via email
- Course websites where you can access the syllabus and connect with resources and classmates
- Textbooks with their own websites where you complete and email assignments
- Online research that takes you from website to website as you follow links
- Projects where students create media such as a YouTube video or social media campaign

Technology has profoundly affected how we get information and share it with others. According to the Pew Research Center, it "is producing a fundamentally new kind of learner, one that is self-directed, better equipped to capture information, more reliant on feedback from peers, [and] more inclined to collaborate."[6] These "new learners" are more likely to research online, share content through social media sites, and create media content.

For some students, forms of technology such as search engines and Google Docs come easily, but others may struggle. Knowing your learning preferences can help you fit technology tools to your assignment and use online resources effectively. Are you strong in intrapersonal intelligence? Working with an online tutorial may be a good choice. Are you an interpersonal learner? Find a tech-savvy classmate to help you get the hang of it. A visual learner may try out the features of a text or course website according to what looks interesting, whereas a logical-mathematical learner may click through features in their listed order.

If you're having trouble with a particular type of technology, find a teaching assistant, instructor, or skilled classmate to help you understand how to use it. Finally, remember that technology cannot make you learn—it can simply make information accessible to you. To achieve the reward of learning, evaluate different technologies carefully and use them in ways that are most productive for you.

Workplace Choices

Knowing how you learn and interact with others will help you work more effectively and take more targeted and productive career planning risks. How can an employee or job candidate benefit from self-awareness?

Better performance and teamwork

When you understand your strengths, you can find ways to use them on the job more readily, as well as determine how to compensate for tasks that take you out of your areas of strength. In addition, you will be better able to work with others. For example, a team leader might offer an intrapersonal team member the chance to take material home to think about before attending a meeting; a bodily-kinesthetic learner might find hands-on ways to spearhead new projects, while delegating the detailed research to a naturalistic learner on the team.

Better career planning

Exploring ways to use your strengths in school will help you make better choices about what internships, jobs, or careers will suit you. For most college students, majors and *internships*—temporary work programs that offer supervised, practical experience in a job and career area—are more immediate steps on the road to a career. Internships can be extremely rewarding risks, giving you a chance to "try out" your major in a workplace setting. You might even discover you don't have an interest in a career in that area and you need to switch majors.

With self-awareness comes the opportunity to make the best of both favorable and challenging situations, because it gives you the power to choose how to handle those situations. Remember that you always have options for how to respond, even when you can't change your course, your instructor, your school, or your required core curriculum. Use those options with a positive outlook and you will continue to learn and grow in any situation.

Complete the following on paper or in digital format.

KNOW IT *Think Critically*

Link How You Learn to Coursework and Major

Apply what you know about yourself to some future academic planning.

1. Summarize in a paragraph or two what you know about yourself as a learner. Focus on what you learned from the assessment you have taken in connection with this lesson.

2. Schedule a meeting with your academic advisor. Note the following:

   - Name of advisor
   - Office location/contact information
   - Time/date of meeting

   At the meeting, give the advisor an overview of your learning strengths and challenges based on the summary you wrote. Ask for advice about courses that might interest you and majors that might suit you. Take notes. As a result of your discussion, name two courses to consider in the next year.

3. Think about the courses you listed and other courses related to them. Toward what majors might each of them lead you? Based on those courses, name two majors to investigate. Then, create a separate to-do list of how you plan to explore one course offering and one major. Set a deadline for each task. If you are having trouble choosing a major because you are unsure of a career direction, see an advisor in the career center for guidance.

WRITE IT *Communicate*

With your assessment results in mind, think about how you generally relate to people. Describe the type(s) of people with whom you tend to get along. How do you feel when you are around these people? Then, describe the types that tend to irk you. How do those people make you feel? Use your emotional intelligence to discuss what those feelings tell you. Consider how you can adjust your mindset or take action to create the best possible outcome when interacting with people with whom you don't naturally get along well.

Learning How You Learn

6 Listening and Note Taking

TAKING IN AND RECORDING INFORMATION

THIS LESSON GIVES YOU A SET OF PRACTICAL STRATEGIES FOR RECORDING EFFECTIVE NOTES IN CLASS AND REVIEWING THEM TO STRENGTHEN RECALL AND LEARNING. YOU'LL LEARN WHICH NOTE-TAKING FORMAT FEELS MOST COMFORTABLE FOR YOU, UNDERSTANDING THAT YOUR CHOICE OF FORMAT MAY CHANGE DEPENDING ON SITUATION AND COURSE TOPIC OR OVER TIME.

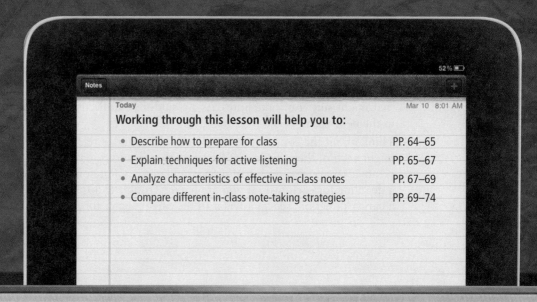

52% 🔋

Notes ➕

Today   Mar 10 8:01 AM

Working through this lesson will help you to:

- Describe how to prepare for class   PP. 64–65
- Explain techniques for active listening   PP. 65–67
- Analyze characteristics of effective in-class notes   PP. 67–69
- Compare different in-class note-taking strategies   PP. 69–74

HOW CAN YOU BECOME
a better listener?

The act of hearing is not the same as the act of listening. *Hearing* refers to sensing spoken messages from their source, while *listening* is a process that involves sensing, interpreting, evaluating, and reacting to spoken messages. You can hear all kinds of things and not understand or remember any of them. Listening starts with hearing, but then continues with focused thinking about what you hear. Listening is a learnable skill that engages your analytical, creative, and practical thinking abilities. It extends far beyond the classroom and rewards you with increased ability to relate to work and school colleagues, friends, and family.

Manage Listening Challenges

Sitting in your classes, you may notice students engaged in activities that interfere with listening: texting or surfing the Internet, talking, sleeping, and daydreaming. These students are probably not absorbing much (or any) information from the instructor, and may be distracting you as well. Read on to learn how to address this challenge and others on your path to better listening. Even if you are taking an online class, you can apply the following to improve your concentration when working on class materials online or listening to recorded or streaming lectures or discussions.

Issue #1: Distractions that divide your attention

Common distractions that interfere with listening include *internal distractions* (worry, anticipation, hunger, feeling too hot or too cold) or *external distractions* (chatting, texting, computer use, any kind of movement or noise). These distractions prevent you from paying full attention to what is said. As a result, you can easily miss or misunderstand things.

Fix #1: Focus, focus, focus

First of all, remind yourself you're risking the effort of college for the reward of education, which at the moment means learning the material for this course. You may even want to remind yourself how much it costs to participate in one class meeting. Find practical ways to minimize distractions.

- Sit near the front of the room.
- Move away from talkative classmates.
- Turn off your cell phone or put it in silent mode, and don't text during class time.
- Consider writing your notes by hand, rather than using a laptop.
- If you use a computer to take notes, stay on task—no gaming, Facebook, Twitter, or surfing during class.
- If you take a class online, find a time and location that encourage you to focus.
- Get enough sleep to stay alert.
- Eat enough so you're not hungry, or bring small snacks if allowed.

It's important to try to put stray thoughts and worries aside while in class. "Switch-tasking"—switching back and forth between tasks—reduces focus and increases the chance of making mistakes. In a study at Stanford, people switching between fewer tasks ("low" multitaskers) actually outperformed people switching between more tasks ("high" multitaskers) on all tasks.[1] Even when it is hard, risk keeping your focus on one thing at a time.

Issue #2: Listening lapses

Even the most fantastic instructor cannot *make* you listen. Only you can do that. If you decide that a subject is too difficult or uninteresting, you may tune out and miss what comes next. Or, you may also focus on only certain points and shut out everything else. Either way, you may miss valuable information and not gain much reward for your time spent.

Fix #2: An I-can-do-it attitude

- *Start with a productive mindset.* If the class is hard, you have more incentive to pay attention. Instructors are generally more sympathetic to, and eager to help, students who've obviously been trying even when the subject matter is difficult.
- *Concentrate.* Work to take in the whole message so you can later review with your textbook notes, and think critically about what is important. Making connections between ideas can reduce both the difficulty of the material in some cases, and boredom if you're familiar with the concepts.
- *Refocus.* If you experience a listening lapse, try to get back into the lecture quickly instead of worrying about what you missed. After class, look at a classmate's notes to fill in the gaps.

Listening to other students can be as important as listening to instructors. These students may learn something useful from their fellow students' perspectives.

- *Be aware.* Pay attention to *verbal signposts.* These are words or phrases that call attention to what comes next, help organize information, connect ideas, and indicate what is important and what is not. See Key 6.1 for examples.

Issue #3: Rushing to judgment

It's common to stop listening when you hear something you don't like, don't agree with, or don't understand. Unfortunately, that type of emotional reaction may cause you to miss important information, which can hurt you at test time. Judgments also involve reactions to speakers themselves. If you do not like your instructors or have preconceived notions about their race, ethnicity, gender, physical characteristics, or disability, you may dismiss their message and miss out on your opportunity to learn.

Fix #3: Recognize and correct your patterns

Emotions are very powerful. They can warp what you hear or prevent you from hearing completely. College is about broadening your horizons and looking for what different people can teach you, even though their beliefs may differ from yours. So, what do you do if you react emotionally to a speaker or a message?

- *Recognize your pattern so you can change it.* When you feel yourself reacting to something, stop and take a deep breath. Count to 10. Take one more breath and see how you feel.
- *Know that you cannot hear or learn from others if you are filled with preconceived notions about them and their ideas.* Put yourself in their shoes; would you want them to stop listening to you if they disagreed with you, or would you want to be heard completely?
- *Stop it.* It's as simple as that. Risk listening with an open mind. Even when you disagree or have a negative reaction about an instructor, keep listening. Being open to the new and different, even when it makes you a bit uncomfortable, can bring the reward of learning that changes you for the better.

Issue #4: Partial hearing loss and learning disabilities

If you have a hearing loss or a learning disability, listening effectively in class may prove challenging. Learning disabilities come in a variety of forms affecting different parts of cognition.

Fix #4: Get help

If you have a hearing loss, find out about available equipment. For example, listening to a taped lecture at a higher-than-normal volume can help you hear things you missed in class. Ask instructors if digitalized recordings are available for download to a computer or iPod. Meet with your instructor outside of class to clarify your notes or sit near the front of the room.

If you have, or think you have, a learning disability, learn what services are available. Seek connections with people who can reward you with productive help. Talk to your advisor and instructor about your problem, seek out a tutor, visit academic centers that can help (such as the writing center if you have a writing issue), scan the college website, and connect with the office of students with disabilities.

Issue #5: Comprehension difficulties for non-native English speakers

If English is not your first language, it may be challenging to listen and understand material in the classroom. Specialized vocabulary,

KEY 6.1 Pay attention to verbal signposts.

SIGNALS THAT POINT TO KEY CONCEPTS	SIGNALS THAT SUPPORT
A key point to remember . . .	A perfect example . . .
Point 1, point 2, etc. . . .	Specifically, . . .
The impact of this was . . .	For instance, . . .
The critical stages in the process are . . .	Similarly, . . .

SIGNALS THAT POINT TO DIFFERENCES	SIGNALS THAT SUMMARIZE
On the contrary, . . .	From this you have learned . . .
On the other hand, . . .	In conclusion, . . .
In contrast, . . .	As a result, . . .
However, . . .	Finally, . . .

informal language, and the rate of speech can add to the challenge. Succeeding in the classroom will require concentration, dedication, and patience.

Fix #5: Take a proactive approach to understanding

Talk to your instructor as soon as possible about your situation. Discussing your needs with your instructor early in the course keeps the instructor informed and shows your dedication. In some cases, your instructor will give you a list of key terms to review before class. During class, keep a list of unfamiliar words and phrases to look up later, but try not to let the terms prevent you from understanding the main ideas. Focus on the main points of the lecture and meet with classmates after class to fill in the gaps in your understanding.

If, after several weeks, you're still having difficulties, consider enrolling in an English refresher course, getting a tutor, or visiting the campus advising center for more assistance. Be proactive about your education.

Listening isn't always easy and it isn't always comfortable. Keeping an open, engaged mind takes practice and sometimes exposes you to information that you disagree with or that even upsets you. However, only by taking the risk to listen well can you be rewarded with the ability to focus on and remember the most important information.

Effective listening skills are the basis for effective note taking—an essential and powerful study tool.

HOW CAN YOU IMPROVE
your note-taking skills?

Taking notes makes you an active class participant, even when you don't say a word. Notes also provide you with study materials. Note taking is key to your academic success.

Class notes serve two primary purposes: (1) They record what happened in class, and (2) they provide study materials. Because it is virtually impossible to write or type every word you hear, note taking encourages you to use your analytical intelligence to critically evaluate what is worth remembering. Exploring the strategies outlined next helps you prepare for class, take notes in class, and review notes after class.

Prepare

Showing up for class on time is just the start. Here's more about preparing to take notes:

- *Preview your reading material.* Reading assigned materials before class will give you the background to take effective notes, and is one of the most rewarding possible study strategies. Check your class syllabi daily for assignment due dates, and plan your reading time with these deadlines in mind.
- *Review what you know.* Taking 15 minutes before class to review previous notes and reading will help you to follow the lecture from the start.
- *Set up your environment.* Find a comfortable seat, away from friends if you are in a classroom and sitting with them distracts you. Set up your notebook or, if you use a laptop, open the file containing your class notes. Be ready to write (or type) as soon as the instructor begins speaking.
- *Gather support.* In each class, set up a support format with one or two students so you can meet to discuss questions you have or look at their notes after an absence. Find students whose work you respect.

Record Information Effectively during Class

The following practical suggestions will help you record information to review later:

- Write down all key terms and definitions.
- For difficult concepts, note relevant examples, applications, and links to other material.
- Ask questions. If questions are welcome during class, ask them. If you prefer to ask questions after class, jot down questions as you think of them through the class period.
- Write down every question your instructor raises, since these questions may be on a test.
- Be organized, but not fussy. Remember that you can always improve your notes later.
- Draw pictures and diagrams to illustrate ideas.
- Be consistent. Use the same system to show importance—such as indenting, spacing, or underlining—on each page.
- If you have trouble with a concept, leave space for an explanation and flag it with a question mark. After class, consult your text or ask a classmate or instructor for help.
- Go beyond the PowerPoint. When instructors use electronic resources, expand on the main points listed there with details from the lecture.
- Use personal shorthand. When words appear frequently in your notes, abbreviate or replace them in ways that make them quicker to write.

Finally, don't stop taking notes when your class engages in a discussion. Even though it isn't part of the instructor's planned presentation, it often includes important information.

Good listening powers note taking. When taking notes in class, stop to listen to the information before deciding what to write down.

Review and Revise

The process of note taking is not complete when you put your pen down or close your computer at the end of the class period. Notes are only useful to you if you review and revise them, and within as short a time period as you can manage. The longer you wait to review those notes, the less likely you will understand them.

Class notes often have sections that are incomplete, confusing, or illegible. Review and revise your notes as soon as possible after class to fill in gaps while the material is still fresh, clarify sloppy handwriting, and raise questions. Rewriting or retyping notes is a great way to reinforce what you heard in class, review new ideas, and create easy-to-read study aids. It also prepares you to combine class and textbook notes, a rewarding test preparation strategy you may choose to try.

WHAT NOTE-TAKING
formats can you use?

Now that you have gathered some useful strategies for what goes into your notes and how to study that material, take a look at different note-taking formats. As you read, keep some questions in mind:

- For what class or type of instruction is this format best suited? Why?
- How could I make use of this format?
- Which format seems most comfortable to me?
- What format might be most compatible with my learning preferences? Why?

This section discusses different note-taking formats. To select a format that works best in each class, take the following into account:

- *The instructor's style* (which will be clear after a few classes). In the same term, you may have an instructor who is organized, another who jumps around and talks rapidly, and a third who goes off topic in response to questions. Be flexible as you adapt.
- *The course material.* You may decide that an informal outline works best for a highly structured lecture and that a mind map (discussed later in the lesson) is right for a looser presentation. Try one note-taking format for several classes, then adjust if necessary.
- *Your learning preferences.* For the greatest reward in exchange for your effort, choose strategies that make the most of your strengths and compensate for weaknesses.

Now look at examples of various note-taking formats and how they work.

Outlines

Outlines use a standard structure to show how ideas interrelate. *Formal outlines* indicate idea dominance and subordination with Roman numerals, uppercase and lowercase letters, and numbers. In contrast, *informal outlines* show the same associations but replace the formality with a format of consistent indenting and dashes. When a lecture seems well organized, an informal outline can show how ideas and supporting details relate and indicate levels of importance. Key 6.2 shows how the structure of an informal outline could help a student take notes on the topic of tropical rain forests.

From time to time, an instructor may give you a guide, usually in outline form, to help you take notes in class. This outline, known as *guided notes*, may be on the board, on an overhead projector, or on a handout that you receive at the beginning of class. Guided notes do *not* replace your own notes. Designed to be sketchy and limited, they require you to fill in the details during class, which helps you to pay attention. In addition, the act of writing helps anchor your memory of information.

Tropical Rain Forests

—What are tropical rain forests?
    —Areas in South America and Africa, along the equator
    —Average temperatures between 25° and 30° C (77°–86° F)
    —Average annual rainfalls range between 250 to 400 centimeters
      (100–160 inches)

—Rainforests are the Earth's richest, most biodiverse ecosystem.
    —A biodiverse ecosystem has a great number of organisms co-existing within
      a defined area.
    —Examples of rainforest biodiversity
      —2½ acres in the Amazon rainforest has 283 species of trees
      —a 3-square-mile section of a Peruvian rain forest has more than
        1,300 butterfly species and 600 bird species.
    —Compare this biodiversity to what is found in the entire U.S.
      —only 400 butterfly species and 700 bird species

—How are humans changing the rainforest?
    —Humans destroy an estimated 50,000 square miles of rainforest a year
      (10 times the area of Connecticut).
      —Cutting down trees for lumber
      —Clearing the land for ranching or agriculture
    —Rain forest removal is also linked to the increase in atmospheric carbon dioxide,
      which worsens the greenhouse effect (where gases such as carbon dioxide trap
      the sun's energy in the Earth's atmosphere as heat resulting in global warning).

Source: Audesirk, Teresa, Gerald Audesirk, and Bruce E. Byers. *Biology: Life on Earth, 9/E.* Upper Saddle River, NJ: Prentice Hall, 2011, pp. 559–561.

When an instructor's presentation is disorganized, it may be difficult to use an outline. Focus instead on taking down whatever information you can as you try to connect key topics. The following note-taking methods can be beneficial in such situations.

Cornell T-Note Format

The Cornell note-taking format, also known as the *T-note format,* consists of three sections on ordinary notepaper.[2]

- *Notes,* the largest section, is on the right. Record your notes here in whatever form you choose. Skip lines between topics so you can clearly see where a section begins and ends.
- The *cues* column goes on the left side of your notes. Leave it blank while you read or listen, and then fill it in later while you review. You might insert key words or comments that highlight ideas, clarify meaning, add examples, link ideas, or draw diagrams. Many students use this column to raise questions, which they answer when they study.
- The *summary* goes at the bottom of the page. Here you reduce your notes to critical points, a process that helps you learn the material. Use this section to provide an overview of what the notes say.

Create this note-taking structure *before* class begins by following these directions:

- Start with a sheet of 8½-by-11-inch lined paper. Label it with the date and lecture title.
- To create the cue column, draw a vertical line about 2½ inches from the left side of the paper. End the line about 2 inches from the bottom of the sheet.
- To create the summary area, start at the point where the vertical line ends (about 2 inches from the bottom of the page) and draw a horizontal line that spans the entire paper.

    Key 6.3 shows how the Cornell format was used to take notes in a business course.

Mind Map

A *mind map,* also known as a think-link or word web, is a visual form of note taking that encourages flexible thinking and making connections. When you draw a mind map, you use shapes and lines to connect ideas with supporting details and examples. The visual design makes the connections easy to see, and shapes and pictures extend the material beyond words.

To create a mind map, start by circling or boxing your topic in the middle of the paper. Next, draw a line from the topic and write the name of one major idea at the end of the line. Circle that idea. Then, jot down specific facts related to the idea, linking them to the idea with more lines. Continue the process, identifying thoughts with words and circles, and connecting them to one another with lines. Key 6.4 shows a mind map illustrating the sociological concept called stratification.

A mind map does not have to include circles and lines; it can take on a number of different forms such as a "jellyfish" (main idea at the top with examples dangling down below) or a series of stairs with examples building to the idea at the top. Engage your creativity to develop a shape that works for you. If a mind map is difficult to construct during class time, consider transforming your notes into a mind map format later when you review.

Label a sheet of paper with the date and title of the lecture.

Create the **cue column** by drawing a vertical line about 2-½ inches from the left side of the paper. End the line about 2 inches from the bottom of the sheet.

Create the **summary area** by starting where the vertical line ends (about 2 inches from the bottom of the page) and drawing a horizontal line across the paper.

October 3, 2010, p. 1

Understanding Employee Motivation

Why do some workers have a better attitude toward their work than others?	Purpose of motivational theories — To explain role of human relations in motivating employee performance — Theories translate into how managers actually treat workers
Some managers view workers as lazy; others view them as motivated and productive.	2 specific theories — Human resources model, developed by Douglas McGregor, shows that managers have radically different beliefs about motivation. — Theory X holds that people are naturally irresponsible and uncooperative — Theory Y holds that people are naturally responsible and self-motivated

Why do some workers have a better attitude toward their work than others?

Some managers view workers as lazy; others view them as motivated and productive.

Maslow's Hierarchy

self-actualization needs (challenging job)
esteem needs (job title)
social needs (friends at work)
security needs (health plan)
physiological needs (pay)

Purpose of motivational theories
— To explain role of human relations in motivating employee performance
— Theories translate into how managers actually treat workers

2 specific theories
— Human resources model, developed by Douglas McGregor, shows that managers have radically different beliefs about motivation.
 — Theory X holds that people are naturally irresponsible and uncooperative
 — Theory Y holds that people are naturally responsible and self-motivated
— Maslow's Hierarchy of Needs says that people have needs in 5 different areas, which they attempt to satisfy in their work.
 — Physiological need: need for survival, including food and shelter
 — Security need: need for stability and protection
 — Social need: need for friendship and companionship
 — Esteem need: need for status and recognition
 — Self-actualization need: need for self-fulfillment
Needs at lower levels must be met before a person tries to satisfy needs at higher levels.
— Developed by psychologist Abraham Maslow

Two motivational theories try to explain worker motivation. The human resources model includes Theory X and Theory Y. Maslow's Hierarchy of Needs suggests that people have needs in 5 different areas: physiological, security, social, esteem, and self-actualization.

Charting Method

Sometimes instructors deliver information in such quantities and at such speeds that taking detailed notes becomes nearly impossible. When a lot of material comes at you quickly, the charting method might be useful. It is also excellent for information presented chronologically or sequentially.

To create charting notes, look ahead in your syllabus to determine the day's lecture topic, or contact your instructor. Then separate your paper into columns such as definitions, important phrases, and key themes. As you listen to the lecture, fill in the columns. For example, here is a section of charting notes for a history class:

TIME PERIOD	IMPORTANT PEOPLE	EVENTS	IMPORTANCE
1969–1974	Richard Nixon	Watergate, Vietnam War	Ended Vietnam War, opened relations with China, first president to resign

Electronic Strategies

If you take notes using an electronic device, saving them safely is essential. You can save notes on your device or on a remote server (known as "the cloud") connected to the Internet. Evernote is a software package that lets you take notes using any computer or Android phone. These notes include text, webpage URLs and content, photographs, or voice memos—all of which can have attachments. You can save your notes on your own computer or on a special Evernote server.

GoogleDocs is another example of a documentation and note-taking tool that lets you save text to the cloud. With GoogleDocs, you need only connect to the Internet, open GoogleDocs, and start typing. When you're done, you save your work to a collection (folder) of your choice, hosted on a Google server. You can also download the

KEY 6.4 Use a mind map to connect ideas visually.

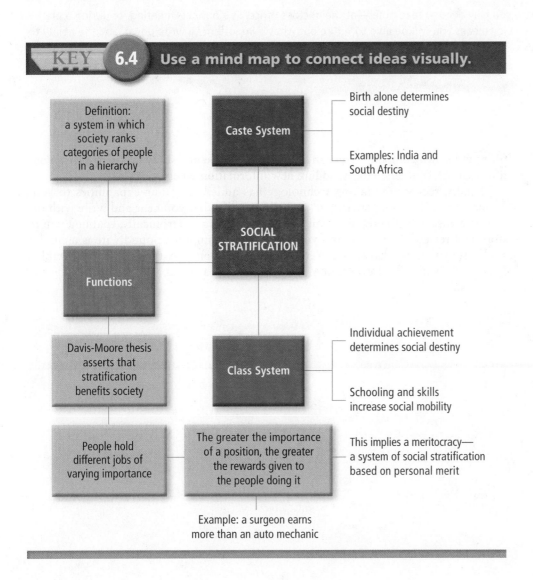

get practical

FACE A NOTE-TAKING CHALLENGE

Complete the following on paper or in digital format.

Get set to take in and record information in your most difficult class.

1. What is the name of the course that is most challenging for you right now?

2. Consult your syllabus for this course. What do you have to read (text sections and/or other materials) before your next class?

3. Where will you sit in class to focus your attention and minimize distractions?

4. Which note-taking format is best suited for the class and why?

5. Who are two classmates whose notes you can borrow if you miss a class or are confused about material? Include phone numbers and/or email addresses.

In life, you never know where you may need to take notes—at the doctor's office, in a business meeting, or during a presentation. The ability to listen well means you will be able to figure out what is important to write down, and the ability to take effective notes rewards you with the ability to recall and use that information in the future.

file to your own computer. You can allow other people in a study group to access your file in GoogleDocs and edit it, adding new information where necessary.

Finally, recent note-taking technology has added recording capabilities to your arsenal. The Livescribe "smartpen" records exactly what you hear and write with the pen on a specialized notebook which saves everything electronically, enabling you to store and review the lecture and your notes on a computer. SoundNote is a similar application that works with tablet computers. When you type notes on a tablet, SoundNote will record everything you type as well as what you are hearing during the class.[3]

Complete the following on paper or in digital format.

KNOW IT *Think Critically*

Your Best Listening and Note-Taking Conditions

Think of a recent class where you were able to listen and take notes effectively.

1. Describe the environment (course title, classroom setting, and so on):
2. Describe the instructor's style (lecture, group discussion, question and answer):
3. Describe your level of preparation and attitude toward the class:
4. Describe the note-taking style you typically use in the class and note how effective it is:
5. Describe any barriers to effective listening in the class:

Now think of a recent class in which you found it hard to listen and take notes.

1. Describe the environment (course title, classroom setting, and so on):
2. Describe the instructor's style (lecture, group discussion, question and answer):
3. Describe your level of preparation and attitude toward the class:
4. Describe the note-taking style you typically use in the class, and note how effective it is:
5. Describe any barriers to effective listening in the class:

Examining the two situations you identified, identify three conditions that seem to be crucial for you to effectively listen and take notes.

WRITE IT *Communicate*

Determining the best method for you. Over the next week, commit to trying at least two types of note-taking formats in your classes. If possible, choose a different format for each subject. Before entering the class, prepare by readying your notebook with the correct formatting for the particular note-taking format. Take your class notes using the new format. When the week is over, reflect in writing about how each style worked for you and which would be the most beneficial going forward.

Active Reading

MAKING MEANING FROM YOUR MATERIALS

THIS LESSON TEACHES THE STEPS OF THE SQ3R READING TECHNIQUE, A PROVEN STRAT-
EGY THAT HELPS YOU CHOOSE WHAT IS IMPORTANT TO REMEMBER AND RETAIN IT MORE
EFFECTIVELY. YOU'LL ALSO LEARN HOW TO PUT YOUR NOTES AND READING MATERIALS
TO WORK AS YOU STUDY USING ANNOTATIONS, SUMMARIES, AND THE CREATION OF A
MASTER NOTE SET.

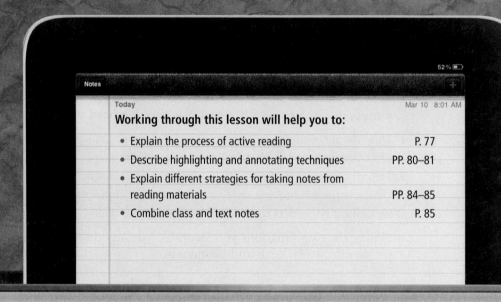

52% 🔋

Notes   ✛

| Today | Mar 10 8:01 AM |

Working through this lesson will help you to:

• Explain the process of active reading	P. 77
• Describe highlighting and annotating techniques	PP. 80–81
• Explain different strategies for taking notes from reading materials	PP. 84–85
• Combine class and text notes	P. 85

WHAT SETS YOU UP
for reading comprehension?

Reading comprehension is the gateway to success in school and beyond. Why?
Because if you can read and *understand* something, you can learn it and *use* it.
In exchange for your risk of effort and commitment, you can earn the following
rewards:

- A broad and deep range of knowledge
- A solid foundation of learning that will help you perform in advanced courses
- The ability to digest and use information on the job and to stay up-to-date on changes

College reading assignments are often challenging, requiring more focus and new
strategies on your part. During any given week, you may have a variety of assignments
such as:

- A text chapter on the history of South African apartheid (world history)
- An original research study on the relationship between sleep deprivation and memory problems (psychology)
- The first three chapters in John Steinbeck's classic novel *The Grapes of Wrath* (American literature)
- A technical manual on the design of computer anti-virus programs (software design)

To face reading challenges like these, use specific techniques. Here's how to prepare for making the most of your reading, even before you open a book or log onto a computer.

Take an Active and Positive Approach

Instructors expect you to complete most reading assignments on your own. How can you approach difficult reading material actively and positively?

- *Define your purpose.* Know *why* you are reading the material. To comprehend concepts and details? To evaluate critically? To learn how to do something? With a clear purpose or reward in mind, you can decide how much time and effort to risk. Key 7.1 provides more details about reading purposes.
- *Have an open mind.* Be careful not to pre-judge assignments as impossible or boring or a waste of time before you even begin.
- *Plan for multiple readings.* Don't expect to master challenging material on the first pass. Get an overview of key concepts and basic organization during your first reading. Use later readings to build understanding, relate information to what you already know, and apply information.
- *Get help.* If material is tough to understand, consult resources including instructors, study-group partners, tutors, related texts, and websites. Build a library of texts in your major and minor areas of study and refer to them whenever necessary.

Organize Your Study Area for Maximum Focus

Where, when, and with whom you study has a significant effect on your success.

Use locations that work. Choose settings that distract you least: at home, at a library, outdoors, in an empty classroom, whatever works. Your schedule may limit your choices. For example, if you can only study when libraries are closed, you will probably have to work at home; if you commute, mass transit may be a good study spot. Evaluate how effectively you focus. If you spent too much time being distracted at a particular location, try somewhere different.

KEY 7.1 **Establish why you are reading a given piece of material.**

WHAT'S MY PURPOSE?	EXPLANATION
1. To Understand	Read to comprehend concepts and details, and to explain them in your own words. Concepts provide a framework for details and details help explain or support general concepts.
2. To Evaluate Analytically	Read with an open mind as you examine causes and effects, evaluate ideas, and ask questions that test arguments and assumptions. Analysis develops a level of understanding beyond basic information recall.
3. For Practical Application	Read to find information to help reach a specific goal. For instance, when you read a lab manual for chemistry, your goal is to successfully perform the lab experiment.
4. For Pleasure	Read for entertainment, such as reading *Sports Illustrated* magazine or a science fiction, mystery, or romance novel.

Choose times that work. Pay attention to your natural rhythms, and try to read when you tend to be most alert and focused. For example, night owls tend to be productive when everyone else is sleeping, but morning people may have a hard time reading late at night.

Concentrate. When you pay attention to one thing and one thing only, you are concentrating. The following tips can help you improve your focus and your understanding:

1. *Deal with internal distractions.* If you are hungry, get a snack; if you lose focus, an exercise break may energize you and help you concentrate. When worries come up, such as to-do list items for other projects, write them down and deal with them later.
2. *Take control of technology.* Web surfing, emailing, texting, or instant messaging can distract, especially if you are reading online material. Plus, forcing your brain to switch back and forth between tasks can increase work time and errors. Instead, save technology for breaks or after you finish your work.
3. *Structure your work session.* Set realistic goals and a specific plan for dividing your time. Tell yourself: "I'm going to read 30 pages and then go online for 30 minutes."
4. *Manage family obligations.* Set up activities or childcare if you have kids. Tell them what your education means to them and to you. Help them understand the importance of uninterrupted study time.
5. *Have a break planned.* Think of something you would look forward to. You deserve it!

The strongest motivation to concentrate comes from within. When you see the connection between what you study and your short- and long-term goals, you will be better able to focus, to remember, to learn, and to apply what you have learned.

You may be more able to concentrate in some locations than in others. Try many, at different times of day, and see what works best for you. This student enjoys reading in her room in the daytime.

Expand Your Course Vocabulary

Every subject has its own specialized vocabulary. Mastering the new terms will improve your reading speed and comprehension, so it's worth the time to learn them. Try making flash cards, reviewing the end-of-text glossary, or simply using the words in your own sentences. The more you work with new ideas, the more embedded they will become. Don't discount the value of a standard dictionary.

HOW CAN SQ3R *improve your reading?*

Reading is an interactive form of communication. The author communicates ideas to you and invites your response. How can you respond? One answer is provided by the SQ3R reading strategy, which stands for Survey, Question, Read, Recite, and Review.[1] This technique requires that you interact with reading material by asking questions, marking ideas, discovering connections, and more. In return, it rewards you with greater ability to take in, understand, and remember what you read.

As you move through the stages of SQ3R, you will first skim and scan your text. *Skimming* refers to rapidly reading chapter elements such as section introductions and conclusions, boldfaced or italicized terms, pictures and charts, and summaries. The goal of skimming is to quickly identify the main ideas. In contrast, *scanning* involves a careful search for specific information. You might use scanning during the SQ3R review phase to locate particular facts.

Just like many strategies presented to you throughout your college career, SQ3R works best if you adapt it to your own needs. Explore the techniques, evaluate what works, and then make the system your own. Use it for both hard copy and online text materials. As you become familiar with SQ3R, keep in mind that it works best with textbook-based courses like science, math, social sciences, and humanities. SQ3R is *not* recommended for literature courses.

Step 1: Survey

Surveying, the first stage in SQ3R, is the process of previewing or pre-reading a book before you study it. Compare surveying to looking at a map before a road trip; determining the route in advance will save time and trouble while you travel. Survey tools include the following:

Front matter. Skim the table of contents for the chapter titles, main topics in each chapter and the order in which they will be covered, as well as special features. Then skim the preface, which is a personal note from the author telling you what the book will cover and its point of view.

Chapter elements. Text chapters generally use different devices to structure their information and highlight content.

- Chapter titles establish the topic and often the author's perspective.
- Chapter introductions or outlines generally list objectives or key topics.
- Level headings (first, second, third), including those in question form, break down material into bite-size chunks.
- Margin materials can include definitions, quotes, questions, and exercises.
- Tables, charts, photographs, and captions illustrate important concepts visually.
- Sidebars or boxed features are connected to text themes and introduce extra tidbits of information that supplement the text.
- Different styles or arrangements of type (**boldface**, *italics*, underlining, larger fonts, • bullet points, and boxed text) can flag vocabulary or important ideas.
- End-of-chapter summaries review chapter content and main ideas.
- Review questions and exercises help you understand and apply content in creative and practical ways.

Back matter. Some texts include a glossary that defines text terms, an index to help you locate topics, and a bibliography that lists additional readings.

Step 2: Question

The next step in SQ3R is to ask questions about your assignment. Questioning leads you to discover knowledge, rewarding you with a greater investment in the material and improved ability to remember it. Here's the process.

Ask yourself what you know. Before you begin reading, think about, and summarize in writing if you can, what you already know about the topic. This prepares you to apply what you already know to new material. Building on current knowledge helps you learn faster. It is especially important in your major, where the concepts you learn in introductory courses prepare you for higher-level courses.

Write questions linked to chapter headings. Next, examine the chapter headings and, on a separate page or document or in the text margins, write questions about them. When you encounter an assignment without headings, divide the material into logical sections and develop questions based on what you think is the main idea of each section. There are no "correct" questions. Given the same headings, two students could create two different sets of questions. The goal of questioning is to guide your reading so you learn more from it.

Key 7.2 shows how questioning works. The column on the left contains primary and secondary headings from a section of *Out of Many*, a U.S. history text. The column on the right rephrases these headings in question form.

Step 3: Read

Your text survey and questions give you a starting point for reading, the first R in SQ3R. Remembering what you read requires an active approach.

Focus on the key points of your survey. Pay special attention to information in the headings, in boldface type, in chapter objectives, in the summary, and in other emphasized text.

Focus on your Q-stage questions. Read the material with the purpose of answering each question. Write down or highlight ideas and examples that relate to your questions.

Create text tabs. Place plastic index tabs or adhesive notes at the start of different chapters so you can flip back and forth with ease. If you are reading online, use any tabbing tools the electronic file provides.

Annotate your text

You are now ready to dig into the text, ask more questions, and identify what's important. Here are two ways to identify important information. If you are reading an ebook, use the "insert comments" feature or other available marking tools to implement the following suggestions on electronic materials.

Mark up your text. If the book is yours, write notes in the margins or on separate paper, circle main ideas, or underline supporting details. These cues will boost memory

KEY 7.2 Create questions from headings.

HEADINGS	QUESTIONS
The Meaning of Freedom	What did freedom mean for both slaves and citizens in the United States?
Moving About	Where did African Americans go after they were freed from slavery?
The African American Family	How did freedom change the structure of the African American family?
African American Churches and Schools	What effect did freedom have on the formation of African American churches and schools?
Land and Labor after Slavery	How was land farmed and maintained after slaves were freed?
The Origins of African American Politics	How did the end of slavery bring about the beginning of African American political life?

and help you study for exams. Here are some tips for *annotating*—taking notes in the margins of textbook pages:

- Use pencil so you can erase comments or questions that are answered later.
- Write your Q-questions in the margins next to text headings.
- Mark critical sections with marginal notations such as: *Def.* for definition, *E.g.* for helpful example, *Concept* for an important concept, and so forth.
- Write notes at the bottom of the page connecting the text to what you learned in class or in research. You can also attach adhesive notes with your comments.
- Circle the topic sentence in a paragraph to focus on the most important information.

Highlight your text. The goal of highlighting is to call out important concepts and information so that they get your attention. Use these tips to make highlighting work for you:

- *Develop a system and stick to it.* Decide whether you will use different colors to highlight different elements, bracket long passages, or underline. When working with e-books, use the highlighting function to color over important text.
- *Consider using a regular pencil or pen instead of a highlighter pen.* The copy will be cleaner and look less like a coloring book than a textbook.
- *Mark text carefully if you are using a rented book or a book to be re-sold.* Use pencil and erase your marks at the end of the course. Write on sticky notes. Make copies of important chapters or sections and mark up the pages. If renting, check with the rental service to see what they permit.
- *Read an entire paragraph before you begin to highlight, and don't start until you have a sense of what is important.* Only then put pencil or highlighter to paper as you pick out the main idea, key terms, and crucial supporting details and examples.
- *Avoid overmarking.* Underlining or highlighting everything makes it impossible to tell what's important. If you decide that a whole passage is important to call out, try marking it with brackets.
- *Know that highlighting is just the beginning of learning the material.* To learn the information you've highlighted, interact with it through surveying, questioning, reciting, and review.

Yes, annotating your textbook carries the risk that you will not be able to sell it back. However, the student who interacts with material stands to gain much greater depth of learning than the student who doesn't touch a page. If you aim to learn, the reward of annotating your text is likely worth the financial risk.

Use specific techniques for different disciplines

Just as not all instructors are the same, neither are all course materials. Math textbooks often move sequentially—in other words, your understanding of later material depends on how well you have learned concepts in earlier chapters—and are problem-and-solution based, so you may want to work through problem steps as you read. Science textbooks are packed with vocabulary and formulas, so you may want to use memory tricks to remember information. For social sciences, humanities, and literature, look for themes and think through problems and solutions.

Know how to read online materials

Screen readers tend to notice heads and subheads, bullet points, and visuals, scanning material for the important points instead of staying focused through long paragraphs or articles.[2] They may also develop what web researcher Jakob Nielsen calls *F-pattern reading*—reading across the line at the beginning of a document, then reading less and less of the full width of the line as you move down the page, and only seeing the left-hand text by the time you reach the bottom of the document.[3]

Nielsen suggests making the most of screen reading using a step-by-step process:

1. *Skim through the article.* See whether it contains important ideas.
2. *Before reading in depth, save the article on your computer or device.* This gives you the ability to print the article if you prefer to highlight and add notes on hard copy.
3. *Survey the article.* Read the title, subtitle, headings, figures, charts, and tables.
4. *Come up with questions to guide your reading.* Ask yourself what general and specific information you want to learn from the article.
5. *Read the article in depth.* You have already judged that the material is important, so take it much slower than you would normally.
6. *Highlight and take notes.* Use the program's highlighter and comment functions.
7. *Print out articles you would rather study on hard copy.* Make sure printouts include any electronic highlighting and comments you've created.
8. *Review your notes.* Combine them with your class and text notes (details later in this lesson).

Step 4: Recite

Once you finish reading a topic, stop and answer the questions you raised in the Q stage of SQ3R. Even if you already did this during the reading phase, deliberately reciting the answers helps you commit the material to memory. This is the second R in SQ3R.

You can say each answer aloud, silently speak the answers to yourself, "teach" the answers to another person, or write your ideas and answers in note form. The motion of speaking or writing helps to anchor the material in your brain. Whatever method you choose, make sure you know how the ideas connect to one another and to the general concept being discussed.

Writing is often the most effective way to learn new material. Write responses to your Q-stage questions and use your own words to explain new concepts. Save your writing as a study tool for review. Writing gives you immediate feedback. When your writing agrees with the material you are studying, you know the information. When it doesn't, you still need work.

When do you stop to recite? Waiting until the end of a chapter is too late, but stopping at the end of one paragraph is too soon. The best plan is to recite at the end of each text section, right before a new heading. Repeat the question-read-recite cycle until you complete the chapter. If you fumble for thoughts, reread the section until you are on solid ground.

Step 5: Review

Reviewing is the third R in SQ3R. When you review early and often in the days and weeks after you read, you will better memorize, understand, and learn material. If you close the book after reading it once, chances are you will forget almost everything, which is why reading material for the first time right before a test usually doesn't work. Reviewing is your key to learning.

Reviewing the same material over several short sessions will also help you identify knowledge gaps. It's natural to forget material between study sessions, especially if it's complex. When you come back after a break, you can focus on where you need the most help.

get creative

USE SQ3R TO MAKE A CONNECTION

Complete the following on paper or in digital format.

For this exercise, partner with someone in your class. Before you meet, each of you will write a mini-autobiography, approximately three paragraphs in length, answering the following questions:

- Where are you from?
- How would you describe your family?
- How has your family influenced the student you are today?
- What are three things you would like someone to know about you?

When you finish, read over what you've written for spelling, punctuation, and clarity. Title the biography. Switch papers with your partner and read his or her biography using SQ3R:

1. *Survey:* Scan your partner's paper for any words that stand out or phrases that seem important. Circle or highlight anything you notice right away.

2. *Question:* Thinking about what you learned from your survey, write questions in the margins. Your questions should reflect what you expect to learn.

3. *Read:* Read through the biography. Make notes in the margins when you find answers to your Q-stage questions. Use your pen to circle or underline main ideas.

4. *Recite:* Discuss what you learned from the paper with your partner. How accurate was your comprehension of the biography? Were there any areas that were not clear or that you misunderstood? If so, what might help in those cases?

5. *Review:* Write a summary of the biography of your partner. If there is time, recite the summary aloud in front of the class. Introduce your partner to the class as if he or she had just joined, focusing on the most interesting and unique information.

Finally, discuss the impact of using SQ3R with your partner. How did it impact your comprehension of their biography? What might you try differently next time?

Active Reading

Examine the following reviewing techniques. Try them all, and use the ones that work best for you. Try using more than one strategy when you study. Switching among several different strategies tends to strengthen learning and memory.

- Reread your notes, then summarize them from memory.
- Review and summarize in writing the text sections you highlighted or bracketed.
- Rewrite key points and main concepts in your own words. Create written examples that will help solidify the content in your mind.
- Answer the end-of-chapter review, discussion, and application questions.
- Reread the preface, headings, tables, and summary.
- Recite important concepts to yourself (although you may risk looking silly, this technique's high effectiveness may be a worthwhile reward).
- Record information and play it back.
- Listen to MP3 audio recordings of your text and other reading materials on your iPod.

- Make hard-copy or electronic flash cards with a word or concept on one side and a definition, examples, or other related information on the other. Test yourself daily.
- Quiz yourself, using the questions you raised in the Q-stage.
- Discuss the concepts with a classmate or in a study group. Answer one another's Q-stage questions.
- Ask your instructor for help with difficult material.

Refreshing your knowledge is easier and faster than learning it the first time. Make a weekly review schedule and stick to it. A combination of short daily reviews in the morning, between classes, or in the evening is more effective than an all-night cramming session before a test.

HOW CAN YOU TAKE NOTES *from reading materials?*

Using what you know about note taking and reading, you can maximize what you learn from anything you read. Especially in the later stages of review, strategies that help you combine and condense materials provide significant reward for the extra time they require. They help you connect information in new ways and boost analytical and creative thinking, which are especially important for essay exams.

Taking Notes from a Text

Note taking can also help you decide and reinforce what is most important to remember when you read textbooks, articles, or any other materials assigned for class or used for research. You may decide to take separate notes on reading material if the book is a library copy or borrowed from a classmate. Or, you might do so when you don't have enough room to take notes in the margin. Some students simply prefer to take separate notes on reading material as a study strategy.

Start the process by identifying what you want to get from the notes. Basic topics? An in-depth understanding of a particular concept? Once you've established the goal, identify the best format. For instance, mind maps work well to understand broad connections, overall relationships, or how your text works in relation to your instructor's lecture. On the other hand, formal outlines make sense of complicated information in a structured way that can provide clarity. After choosing a format, read and take notes on the material using the Survey, Question, and Read stages of SQ3R.

- Survey to get an overview of what the material can offer you.
- Question to focus your attention on what is important enough to record in your notes.
- Read and record your notes on paper or in an electronic file.

Finally, remember that many of the in-class note-taking strategies you just explored will help you take effective notes on reading materials. For example, you can note key terms and definitions, recreate important diagrams, use consistent formatting, and flag areas of confusion with a question mark.

If you are reading an online version of a textbook, you may be able to annotate it electronically using tools embedded in the e-book software.

Create a Summary of Reading Material

When you summarize main ideas in your own words, you engage analytical thinking, considering what is important to include as well as how to organize and link it together. To construct a summary, focus on the main ideas and examples that support them. Don't include your own ideas or evaluations at this point. Your summary should simply condense the material, making it easier to focus on concepts and interrelationships when you review.

Here are suggestions for creating effective summaries:

- Choose material to summarize—a textbook chapter, for example, or an article.
- Identify the main ideas and key supporting details by highlighting or annotating the material.
- Wherever possible, use your own words.
- Make your writing simple, clear, and brief. Eliminate less important details.
- Consider creating an outline of the portion of the text to see how ideas relate.
- Include information from tables, charts, photographs, and captions in your summary; these visual presentations may contain important information not written in the text.
- Combine word-based and visual note-taking forms that effectively condense the information, such as a concept map, timeline, chart, or outline.

Combine Class and Reading Notes into a Master Set

The process of combining class and text notes enables you to see patterns and relationships among ideas. It strengthens memory and offers a cohesive and comprehensive study tool, especially useful at midterm or finals time. Follow these steps to create and use a *master note set* (a complete, integrated note set containing both class and text notes).

Step 1: Condense down to what's important. Combine and reduce your notes so they contain only main ideas and key supporting details, such as terms, dates, formulas, and examples. Tightening and summarizing forces you to critically evaluate which ideas are most important.

Step 2: Recite what you know. As you approach exam time, recite what you know about a topic. Make the process more active by reciting out loud during study sessions, writing your responses on paper, making flash cards, or working with a partner.

Step 3: Use critical thinking. Reflect on ideas as you review your combined notes by generating examples from other sources that illustrate central ideas, evaluating differences between class notes and reading notes, and applying concepts to problems posed in class.

Step 4: Create study sheets. A study sheet is a one-page synthesis of all key points on one theme, topic, or process. Use critical thinking skills to organize information into themes or topics that you will need to know on an exam.

Step 5: Review and review again. To ensure learning and prepare for exams, review your condensed notes, study sheets, and critical thinking questions until you know every topic cold.

Your future demands that you be able to read, understand, and critically evaluate information on a daily basis in school, on the job, and in life (your 401[k] retirement plan, local and world news, the fine print in a cell phone contract). Develop the ability to read with focus, purpose, and follow-through, and you will never stop enjoying the benefits.

RISK ACTION

FOR COLLEGE, CAREER, AND LIFE REWARDS

Complete the following on paper or in digital format.

KNOW IT *Think Critically*

Study a Text Page

The facing page is from the chapter "Groups and Organizations" in the sixth edition of John J. Macionis's *Sociology*. Skim the excerpt. Identify the headings on the page and the relationships among them. Mark primary-level headings with a numeral 1, secondary headings with a 2, and tertiary (third-level) headings with a 3.

   Analyze the headings and text by answering the following questions.

1. Which heading serves as an umbrella for the rest?
2. What do the headings tell you about the content of the page?
3. Name two concepts that seem important to remember.
4. Based on the concepts you pulled out, write two study questions that you can review with an instructor, a teaching assistant, or a fellow student.
5. After reading this page thoroughly, write a short summary paragraph.

WRITE IT *Communicate*

Emotional intelligence journal: *Reading challenges.* Which current course presents your most difficult reading challenge? Describe what makes the reading tough: the type of material, the length of the assignments, the level of difficulty, or something else. What feelings come up for you when you read, and what effect do they have on your reading? Describe techniques you learned in this lesson that can help you get into a growth mindset and read productively.

in a lecture hall do engage one another and share some common identity as college classmates; thus, such a crowd might be called a loosely formed group. By contrast, riders hurtling along on a subway train or bathers enjoying a summer day at the beach pay little attention to one another and amount to an anonymous aggregate of people. In general, then, crowds are too transitory and impersonal to qualify as social groups.

The right circumstances, however, could turn a crowd into a group. People riding in a subway train that crashes under the city streets generally become keenly aware of their common plight and begin to help one another. Sometimes such extraordinary experiences become the basis for lasting relationships.

SOCIAL GROUPS

Virtually everyone moves through life with a sense of belonging; this is the experience of group life. A social group refers to *two or more people who identify and interact with one another.* Human beings continually come together to form couples, families, circles of friends, neighborhoods, churches, businesses, clubs, and numerous large organizations. Whatever the form, groups encompass people with shared experiences, loyalties, and interests. In short, while maintaining their individuality, the members of social groups also think of themselves as a special "we."

Groups, Categories, and Crowds

People often use the term "group" imprecisely. We now distinguish the group from the similar concepts of category and crowd.

Category

A *category* refers to people who have some status in common. Women, single fathers, military recruits, homeowners, and Roman Catholics are all examples of categories.

Why are categories not considered groups? Simply because, while the individuals involved are aware that they are not the only ones to hold that particular status, the vast majority are strangers to one another.

Crowd

A *crowd* refers to a temporary cluster of individuals who may or may not interact at all. Students sitting

Primary and Secondary Groups

Acquaintances commonly greet one another with a smile and the simple phrase, "Hi! How are you?" The response is usually a well scripted, "Just fine, thanks, how about you?" This answer, of course, is often more formal than truthful. In most cases, providing a detailed account of how you are *really* doing would prompt the other person to beat a hasty and awkward exit.

Sociologists classify social groups by measuring them against two ideal types based on members' genuine level of personal concern. This variation is the key to distinguishing primary from secondary groups.

According to Charles Horton Cooley (1864–1929), a **primary group** is a *small social group whose members share personal and enduring relationships.* Bound together by primary relationships, individuals in primary groups typically spend a great deal of time together, engage in a wide range of common activities, and feel that they know one another well. Although not without periodic conflict, members of primary groups display sincere concern for each other's welfare. The family is every society's most important primary group.

Cooley characterized these personal and tightly integrated groups as *primary* because they are among the first groups we experience in life. In addition, the family and early play groups also hold primary importance in the socialization process, shaping attitudes, behavior, and social identity.

8 Memory and Test Taking

STUDYING TO RETAIN AND SHOW WHAT YOU LEARN

IN THIS LESSON YOU WILL LEARN HOW MEMORY WORKS AND HOW TO MAXIMIZE IT, THROUGH MNEMONIC DEVICES AND OTHER STRATEGIES, AS YOU PREPARE FOR TESTS. YOU WILL LEARN STRATEGIES TO MANAGE TEST ANXIETY AND BUILD SKILLS IN ANSWERING DIFFERENT TYPES OF TEST QUESTIONS.

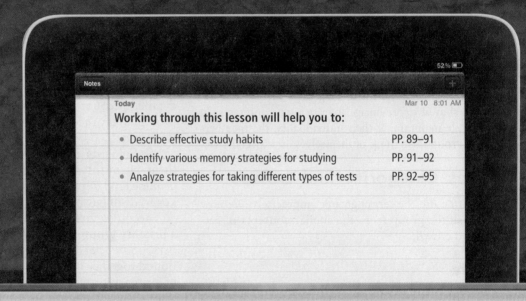

52% 🔋

Notes   ＋

Today   Mar 10 8:01 AM

Working through this lesson will help you to:

- Describe effective study habits   PP. 89–91
- Identify various memory strategies for studying   PP. 91–92
- Analyze strategies for taking different types of tests PP. 92–95

HOW CAN YOU REMEMBER
what you study?

All learning and performance depend on memory, because the information you remember—concepts, facts, processes, formulas, and more—is the raw material with which you think, write, create, build, and perform your day-to-day actions in school and out. *Memory* refers to the way the brain stores and recalls information or experiences acquired through the five senses. Through the effort of studying and a positive attitude, you earn the reward of a memory that can help you move toward your goals.

Why do people forget information? Health issues and poor nutrition can cause memory problems. Stress is also a factor—research shows that even short-term stress can interfere with cell communication in the learning and memory regions of the brain.[1] However, the most common reason that information fails to stay in long-term memory is ineffective studying—not risking the effort necessary to earn the reward of retention. To achieve the goal of remembering important information so that you can use it, you need to find the best strategies for you. One way to do this is to use *journalists' questions*—questions journalists ask as writing aids:

1. *When, Where, and Who:* Determine the times, places, and company (or none) that suit you.
2. *What and Why:* Choose what is important to study, and set the rest aside.
3. *How:* Find the specific tips and techniques that work best for you.

When, Where, and Who: Choosing Your Best Setting

Figuring out the when, where, and who of studying is all about self-management. You analyze what works best for you, create ideas about how to put that self-knowledge to work, and use practical thinking to implement those ideas as you study.

When

The first part of *when* is *how much*. Having the right amount of time for the job is crucial. One formula for success is this: For every hour you spend in an in-person or online classroom each week, spend at least two to three hours preparing for the class. For example, if you are carrying a course load of 15 credit hours, you should spend 30 hours a week studying outside of class.

The second part of *when* is *what time*. First, determine what time is available to you in between classes, work, and other commitments. Then, thinking about when you function best, choose your study times carefully. You may not always have the luxury of being free during your peak energy times, but do the best you can.

The third part of *when* is *how close to original learning*. Because most forgetting happens right after learning, reviewing notes the same day you took them, if possible, will help you retain information most effectively.

The final part of *when* is *when to stop*. Take a break, or go to sleep, when your body is no longer responding. Forcing yourself to study when you're not focused won't reward you with increased retention, and may in fact have detrimental effects.

Where

Where you study matters. As with time, consider your restrictions first—there may be only so many places that are available to you, close by, and open when you have study time free. Also, analyze the effectiveness of the locations of previous study sessions. If you spent too much time blocking out distractions at a particular location, try someplace different.

Many students like to study in a library, where you may find spaces such as quiet rooms that don't allow talking, social areas where study groups can discuss materials, rooms where computer terminals are available for research, and so on. Also, many discipline-specific buildings have their own smaller libraries. Consider outdoor locations or empty classrooms. If you study where you live, find times when distractions are at a minimum.

Who

Some students prefer to study alone, and some in pairs or groups. Many mix it up, doing some kinds of studying (such as first reading) alone, and others (such as problem sets) with one or more people. Some find that they prefer to study certain subjects alone and others with a group. Some groups meet in person, and others in a chat room online or via a conference call.

The study location that works for you depends on individual needs and preferences. These students have found that they can concentrate effectively at individual desks in the library.

Even students who prefer to study alone might consider the risk of working with others from time to time. Besides the reward of greater communication and teamwork skills, group study enhances your ability to remember information because it gets you to say things out loud, exposes you to other ideas, motivates you to study in preparation for a meeting, and subjects you to questions that make you clarify your thinking.[2]

One final part of *who* is dealing with *who might be distracting*. If friends want you to go out, tell them why studying is important to you. If children demand your attention, tell them (if they are old enough to understand) what your education will mean to you and to them.

What and Why: Evaluating Study Materials

It is impossible and unnecessary to study every word and bit of information. Before you study, decide *what* is important to study by examining *why* you need to know it. Here's how:

Choose materials to study. Set aside materials or notes you know you do not need to review. Looking at the notes, textbooks, and other materials left, determine what chapters or sections are important to know for your immediate goal (for example, studying for a test) and why. Thinking about the "why" can increase your focus.

Prioritize materials. Determine what you need the most work on and put it first, then save easier materials for later. Almost every student has more steam at the beginning of a study session than at the end; plus, fatigue or an interruption may prevent you from covering everything.

Set specific goals. Look at what you need to cover and the time you have available, and decide what you will accomplish—for example, you will read pages of a certain textbook chapter, review three sets of class notes, and create a study sheet from both the book and your notes.

How: Using Study Strategies

Now focus on the *how*—the strategies that will anchor the information you need in your brain. You may already use several of them. Try as many as you can, and keep what works.

Put your notes to work. Regularly reread your notes in batches (for example, every one or two weeks) to build your recall of information. As you reread, fill in gaps, highlight main ideas and supporting points, and add test questions in the margins.

Study during short, frequent sessions. You can improve your chances of remembering material if you learn it more than once. A pattern of short sessions, say three 20-minute study sessions followed by brief periods of rest, is more effective than continual studying with little or no rest.

Take care of yourself. Sleep improves your ability to remember what you studied before you went to bed. So does having a good breakfast. Exercise is another key component. The latest research shows that regular exercise followed by food and rest can significantly improve the functioning of the parts of the brain most involved in memory—the cortex and hippocampus.[3]

Use analytical thinking skills. Analytical, or critical, thinking encourages you to associate new information with what you already know. Imagine you have to remember information about the signing of the Treaty of Versailles, which ended World War I. How can critical thinking help?

- Recall everything that you know about the topic.
- Think about how this event is similar to other events in history.

- Consider what is different and unique about this treaty in comparison to other treaties.
- Explore the causes that led up to this event, and look at the event's effects.
- Evaluate how successful you think the treaty was.

This critical exploration makes it easier to remember the material you are studying.

Organize the items you are processing. One way to do this is to use the *chunking* strategy—putting information into smaller units that are easier to remember. For example, while it is hard to remember these ten digits—4808371557—it is easier to remember them in three chunks—480 837 1557. In general, try to limit groups to 10 items or fewer. You can also use an outline or think-link to record material and note logical connections.

Recite, rehearse, and write. The more you can repeat, and the more ways you can repeat, the more likely you are to remember. When you *recite* material, you repeat key concepts aloud, in your own words, to aid memorization. *Rehearsing* is similar to reciting but is done silently. *Writing* is reciting on paper.

Use flash cards. Flash cards provide immediate feedback. Use the front of a 3-by-5-inch index card to write a word, idea, or phrase you want to remember, or find an online site on which you can create electronic flashcards. Use the back for a definition, explanation, example, and other key facts. Use the cards as a self-test, carrying them with you and reviewing them frequently in various orders.

Use audio strategies. Try creating "audio flash cards": Record short-answer study questions by leaving 10 to 15 seconds between questions blank, so you can answer out loud, and then record the correct answer after the pause to give yourself immediate feedback, or get podcasts from your instructors if they provide them.

Mnemonic Devices

Memory techniques known as *mnemonic devices* (pronounced neh-MAHN-ick) make information unforgettable through unusual mental associations and visual pictures, giving you a "hook" on which to hang these facts and retrieve them later. Keep in mind that no matter how clever they are and how easy they are to remember, mnemonics have nothing to do with understanding. Their sole objective is to help you memorize. Use them only when necessary—for instance, to remember a long list of items or events. Here are some common types to try.

Visual images and associations. Turning information into mental pictures helps improve memory, especially for visual learners. To remember that the Spanish artist Picasso painted *The Three Women,* you might imagine the women in a circle dancing to a Spanish song with a pig and a donkey (pig-asso). The best images involve bright colors, three dimensions, action scenes, inanimate objects with human traits, and humor.

Acronyms. An acronym is a word formed from the first letters of a series of words. In a word acronym, the first letters of the items you want to remember spell a word. The word (or words) spelled don't have to be real words. The name Roy G. Biv is an acronym that will help you remember the colors of the spectrum (Red, Orange, Yellow, Green, Blue, Indigo, Violet). Other acronyms take the form of an entire sentence, in which the first letter of each word in each sentence stands for the first letter of the memorized term. This is called a *list order acronym.* Astronomy students memorizing the planets in order of their distance from the sun (Mercury, Venus, Earth, Mars, Jupiter, Saturn, Uranus, and Neptune) might learn this sentence: My very elegant mother just served us nectarines.

Songs and rhymes. Some of the classic mnemonic devices are rhyming poems that stick in your mind. One you may have heard is the rule about the order of "i" and "e" in spelling:

get practical

ANSWER YOUR JOURNALISTS' QUESTIONS

Complete the following on paper or in digital format.

Think about a study session you've had in the past that you believe did not prepare you well for a test, and recall what strategies you used—if any. Now, plan a study session that will take place within the next seven days—one that will help you learn something important to know for one of your current courses. Answer the questions below to create your session:

1. *When* will you study, and for how long?
2. *Where* will you study?
3. *Who* will you study with, if anyone?
4. *What* will you study?
5. *Why* is this material important to know?
6. *How* will you study—what strategy (or strategies) do you plan to use?
7. How do you think the journalists' questions, and this structure, would have helped you get more out of your previous study session?
8. Final step—put this plan to work. Name the date you will use it.

I before E, except after C, or when sounded like "A" as in "neighbor" and "weigh." Four exceptions if you please: either, neither, seizure, seize.

Music can be an exceptional memory tool. Make up your own poems or songs, linking familiar tunes or rhymes with information you want to remember.

HOW CAN PREPARATION
improve test performance?

The goal of a test is to see what you have learned—and learning prepares you for tests. As you attend class, stay on top of assignments, complete readings and projects, participate in class discussions, and do the day-to-day work of learning, you become ever more ready to succeed on tests. The following strategies help you handle the challenge.

Gather Information

Before you begin studying, find out as much as you can about the test.

What type of test? Investigate the types of questions (objective, essay, or a combination), the logistics (time, date, and location and whether it is an in-class or take-home test), permissible tools (whether books, notes, or calculators are allowed), how it will be administered (in person or online), and how the test is graded (what value different questions have).

What are you expected to know? Read your syllabus and talk to your instructor to get a clear idea of the topics that will be covered and assigned material you will be tested on. Other strategies for predicting what will be on a test include reviewing textbook features, going to review sessions, looking at old tests if your instructor makes them available, and meeting with your instructor.

What materials should you study? Go through notes, texts, handouts, and related primary sources, choosing the items that you need to study and setting the rest aside. Then prioritize materials so you focus the bulk of your time on the information you most need to understand.

Schedule Study Time and Set a Goal

Time management is essential to test success, because the most effective studying takes place in consistent segments over time. Use time management skills to lay out an effective study schedule.

When you study with a classmate, you can help each other understand difficult concepts, as well as fill in the holes in each other's notes.

- *Consider relevant factors.* Note the number of days until the test, when in your days you have time available, and how much material you have to cover.
- *Schedule a series of study sessions.* Define what materials you will focus on for each session. Enter sessions in your planner just as you would for any other commitment.

Next, use goal-setting skills to set a SMART goal. Make it:

- *Specific.* Get clear on what you will be tested on and what you need to study.
- *Measurable.* Acknowledge when you accomplish each study session.
- *Achievable.* Stay up-to-date with your coursework so that you feel confident on test day.
- *Realistic.* Give yourself enough time and resources to get the job done.
- *Time frame.* Anchor each step toward the test in your schedule.

A comprehensive study plan will help you work SMART. Try using a plan like the one in Key 8.1. Consider making several copies and filling one out for each major test this term.

Review Using Study Strategies

Now that you have a plan and schedule in place, put it to work. Use what you know about learning, thinking, reading, memory, and studying to remember material:

- *Think analytically.* Ask analytical thinking questions and look for connections with other material.
- *Use SQ3R.* This reading method provides an excellent structure for reviewing your reading materials.
- *Consider your learning preferences.* Use study strategies that engage your strengths. When necessary, incorporate strategies that boost your areas of challenge.
- *Remember your best settings.* From the *when*, *where*, and *who* of your journalists' questions, use the locations, times, and company that suit you best.
- *Employ specific study strategies.* Consider your favorites from the *how* of your journalists' questions.
- *Create mnemonic devices.* These work exceptionally well for remembering lists or groups of items. Use mnemonics that make what you review stick.
- *Actively review your combined class and text notes.* Summaries and master sets of combined text and class notes provide comprehensive study tools.

Complete the following checklist for each exam to define your study goals, get organized, and stay on track:

Course: _____ Instructor: _____

Date, time, and place of test: _____

Type of test (Is it a midterm or a minor quiz?): _____

What instructor said about the test, including types of test questions, test length, and how much the test counts toward your final grade:

_____

_____

Topics to be covered on the test, in order of importance (information should also come from your instructor):

1. _____

2. _____

3. _____

4. _____

5. _____

Study schedule, including materials you plan to study (texts, class notes, homework problems, and so forth) and dates you plan to complete each:

Material	**Completion Date**
1. _____	_____
2. _____	_____
3. _____	_____
4. _____	_____
5. _____	_____

Materials you are expected to bring to the test (textbook, sourcebook, calculator, etc.):

_____

_____

_____

Special study arrangements (such as planning study group meeting, asking the instructor for special help, getting outside tutoring):

_____

_____

_____

Life-management issues (such as rearranging work hours):

_____

_____

_____

Source: Adapted from Fry, Ron. *"Ace" Any Test*, 3rd ed. Franklin Lakes, NJ: Career Press, 1996, pp. 123–124.

- *Prepare physically.* Get as much sleep as you can and eat a light, well-balanced meal before the exam.
- *Make the most of cramming.* If learning is your goal, *cramming*—studying intensively and around the clock right before an exam—will not help you reach it. However, most students cram for tests at some point in their college careers. If you must cram, try to focus on crucial concepts. Create a last-minute study sheet to review right before the test.

Work through Test Anxiety

A moderate amount of stress can have a positive effect, making you alert, ready to act, and geared up to do your best. Some students, however, experience incapacitating stress before and during exams, especially midterms and finals. *Test anxiety* can cause sweating, nausea, dizziness, headaches, and fatigue, reducing concentration and causing you to forget everything you learned. Sufferers may get lower grades because their performance does not reflect what they know or because their fear has affected their ability to prepare effectively.

Test anxiety has two different sources—lack of preparation, and dislike of testing situations.[4] For anxiety that stems from being unprepared, the answer is straightforward—get prepared. For students who dread the event no matter how prepared they are, the fact of having a test—any test—causes anxiety. Because tests are unavoidable, this anxiety is more challenging to manage. Such students need to shift their mindset and build a positive attitude that says, "I know this material and I'm ready to show it."

When it's test time, how can you be calm and focused? These strategies may help.

- *Manage your environment.* Sit away from people or things that might distract you. If it helps, listen to relaxing music on an MP3 player while waiting for class to begin.
- *Reassure yourself with positive self-talk.* Tell yourself that you can do well and that it is normal to feel anxious, particularly before an important exam.
- *Write down your feelings.* Research shows that if students take a few minutes before an exam to put their feelings in writing, they post higher grades and have less anxiety.[5]
- *Practice relaxation.* Close your eyes, breathe deeply and slowly, tense and relax your muscles, and visualize positive mental images like finishing the test with confidence.
- *Bring a special object.* If an object has meaning for you—a photograph, a stone or crystal, a wristband, a piece of jewelry, a hat—it may provide comfort at test time.

WHAT GENERAL STRATEGIES CAN
help you succeed on tests?

Even though every test is different, there are general strategies that will help you handle almost all tests, including short-answer and essay exams.

Test Day Strategies

Choose the right seat. Find a seat that will put you in the right frame of mind and minimize distractions. Choose a place near a window, next to a wall, or in the front row so you can look into the distance. Know yourself: For many students, it's smart to avoid sitting near friends. If you are home or in the computer lab taking the test, be just as selective with your location.

Write down key facts. Before you even look at the test, write down key information, including formulas, rules, and definitions, that you don't want to forget. (Use the back of the question sheet so your instructor knows that you made these notes after the test began.)

Directions count, so read them. Reading test directions carefully can save you trouble. For example, you may be required to answer only one of three essay questions; you may also be told that you will be penalized for incorrect responses to short-answer questions.

Mark up the questions. Note key words. Circle *qualifiers* that can alter the meaning of a test question, such as *always, never, all, none, sometimes,* and *every*; verbs that communicate specific instructions; and concepts that are tricky or need special attention.

Work from easy to hard. Begin with the easiest questions and answer them quickly. This will boost your confidence and leave more time for harder questions.

Watch the clock. If you finish early, check over your work. If you are falling behind, be flexibile about the best use of the remaining time.

Maintain academic integrity. Valid concerns can put students under pressure to succeed. However, cheating generally means not learning, and retention of knowledge is necessary both to complete future coursework and to thrive in jobs that require you to use it. Furthermore, if you cheat, you run the risk of being caught and disciplined (with consequences that can affect your college career as well as your ability to get a job). The choice is yours, and the consequences—positive or negative—will be yours as well.

Objective Questions

Objective questions generally have you choose or write a short answer. They can include multiple-choice, fill-in-the-blank, matching, and true-or-false questions.

Multiple-choice questions. These are the most popular type of question on standardized tests. Read the directions carefully and try to think of the answer before looking at the choices. Then read the choices and make your selection. Focus especially on qualifying words such as *always, never, tend to, most, often,* and *frequently*. Look also for negatives in a question ("Which of the following is *not* . . . ?").

---

1. Although you know that alcohol is a central nervous system depressant, your friend says it is actually a stimulant because he does things that he wouldn't otherwise do after having a couple of drinks. He also feels less inhibited, more spontaneous, and more entertaining. The reason your friend experiences alcohol as a stimulant is that

   a. Alcohol has the same effect on the nervous system as amphetamines.
   b. Alcohol has a strong placebo effect.
   c. The effects of alcohol depend almost entirely on the expectations of the user.
   d. Alcohol depresses areas in the brain responsible for critical judgment and impulsiveness.

   (answer: d)

2. John drinks five or six cups of strong coffee each day. Which of the following symptoms is he most likely to report?

   a. nausea, loss of appetite, cold hands, and chills
   b. feelings of euphoria and well-being
   c. anxiety, headaches, insomnia, and diarrhea
   d. time distortion and reduced emotional sensitivity

   (answer: c)

Source: Charles G. Morris and Albert A. Maisto, *Understanding Psychology*, 10th ed., p. 145. © 2013 Pearson Education, Inc. Reprinted by permission of Pearson Education, Inc., Upper Saddle River, NJ.

True-or-false questions. Read true-or-false questions carefully to evaluate what they are asking. Look for absolute qualifiers (such as *all, only,* and *always* that often make an otherwise true statement false) and conservative qualifiers (*generally, often, usually,* and *sometimes* that often make an otherwise false statement true). Be sure to read *every* word of a true-or-false question to avoid jumping to an incorrect conclusion.

Indicate whether the following statements are true (T) or false (F):

1. Alcohol is implicated in more than two-thirds of all automobile accidents.   *(true)*

2. Caffeine is not addictive.   *(false)*

3. Recurring hallucinations are common among users of hallucinogens.   *(true)*

4. Marijuana interferes with short-term memory.   *(true)*

Source: Charles G. Morris and Albert A. Maisto, *Understanding Psychology*, 10th ed., p. 145. © 2013 Pearson Education, Inc. Reprinted by permission of Pearson Education, Inc., Upper Saddle River, NJ.

Fill-in-the-blank questions. These questions, also known as sentence completion questions, ask you to supply one or more words or phrases to completes the sentence. Be logical—make sure your answer is factually and grammatically correct and matches the number of blanks.

The following examples show fill-in-the-blank questions you might encounter in an introductory psychology course (correct answers follow questions):

1. Our awareness of the mental processes of our everyday life is called _____. *(consciousness)*

2. The major characteristic of waking consciousness is _____. *(selective attention)*

3. In humans, sleeping and waking follow a _____ cycle. *(circadian)*

4. Most vivid dreaming takes place during the _____ stage of sleep. *(REM)*

Source: Charles G. Morris and Albert A. Maisto, *Understanding Psychology*, 10th ed., p. 130. © 2013 Pearson Education, Inc. Reprinted by permission of Pearson Education, Inc., Upper Saddle River, NJ.

Subjective Questions

Also known as essay questions, these questions demand information recall but also require you to plan, organize, draft, and refine a response in a less structured way than short-answer questions. The following steps—basically a shortened version of the writing process—will help you respond effectively.

The following examples show essay questions you might encounter in an introductory psychology course:

1. Experts disagree about how many different kinds of memory there are. Recently, some psychologists have suggested that the classification of memories into different types is artificial and merely confuses matters. They suggest that we should consider memory a unitary thing. What arguments can you come up with to support the practice of making distinctions among different kinds of memory?

2. Primary drives are, by definition, unlearned. But learning clearly affects how these drives are expressed: We learn how and what to eat and drink. Given that information, how might you design a research study to determine what aspects of a given drive, say hunger, are learned and which are not?

3. Obviously, war is not the only cause of extreme stress and trauma. Do you think an individual's response to a personal attack, such as a rape, is similar to or different from that caused by serving in combat?

Source: Charles G. Morris and Albert A. Maisto, *Understanding Psychology*, 10th ed., pp. 196, 260, 385. © 2013 Pearson Education, Inc. Reprinted by permission of Pearson Education, Inc., Upper Saddle River, NJ.

1. *Read every question.* Decide which to tackle (if there's a choice). Read carefully, and use critical thinking to identify exactly what the question is asking.

2. *Map out your time.* Schedule how long to allot for each answer, and then break your time down into smaller segments for each part of the process. For example, if you have 20 minutes to answer a question, use 5 to plan, 10 to draft, and 5 to review and finalize. Be flexible and ready to adjust how you use your time if things don't go as planned.

3. *Focus on action verbs.* Action verbs—such as *compare, describe, evaluate, prove, summarize,* and many more—tell you what to do to answer the question. Underline these words and use them to guide your writing.

4. *Plan.* Thinking about what the question is asking and what you know, define your goal—what you intend to say in your answer. On scrap paper, outline or map your ideas and supporting evidence. Then develop a thesis statement that outlines the goal you've set.

5. *Draft.* Note the test directions before drafting your answer. Your essay may need to be of a certain length, for example, or may need to take a certain format. Then, use the following guidelines as you work:

   - State your thesis, and then get right to the evidence that backs it up.
   - Structure your essay so that each paragraph presents an idea that supports the thesis.
   - Use clear language and tight logic to link ideas to your thesis and create transitions.
   - Look back at your planning notes periodically to make sure you cover everything.
   - Wrap it up with a short, to-the-point conclusion.

6. *Revise.* Although you may not have the time to rewrite your entire answer, you can improve it with minor changes. Check word choice, paragraph structure, and style. If you notice anything missing, use editing marks to insert it (neatly so it remains legible) into the text. When you're done, make sure it's the best possible representation of your ideas.

7. *Edit.* Check for mistakes in grammar, spelling, punctuation, and usage. Correct language and neat, legible handwriting leave a positive impression and help your grade.

Finally, remember that no one aces every test. The purpose of a test is to see how much you know, not merely to get a grade. If you can embrace this attitude, you will be able to learn from your mistakes. Making mistakes on tests and learning from them is part of your academic experience. You can benefit by looking realistically at what you could have done better and making specific changes in the way you study for, or take, your next exam.

Improving your memory and test-taking skills requires energy, time, and work. By using the specific techniques described in this lesson, you will be able to learn more in less time, remember what you learn long after exams are over, and build memory skills that will serve you well in the workplace.

Complete the following on paper or in digital format.

KNOW IT *Think Critically*

Prepare Effectively for Tests

Take a careful look at your performance on and preparation for a test you took recently.

1. First, think about how you did. Were you pleased or disappointed with your performance and grade? Explain your answer.

2. List any of the problems below that you feel you experienced in this exam. If you experienced one or more problems not listed here, include them in your document. For each problem you identified, think about why you made mistakes.

- Incomplete preparation
- Trouble remembering information
- Fatigue
- Feeling rushed during the test
- Shaky understanding of concepts

- Poor guessing techniques
- Feeling confused about directions
- Test anxiety
- Poor essay organization or writing

3. Next, generate ideal test-preparation strategies that would address your problem(s). If you had all the time and materials you needed, how would you have prepared for this test? Describe briefly what your plan would be.

4. Now think back to your actual test preparation. Describe the difference between the ideal study plan you just described and what you actually did.

5. Finally, improve your chances for success on the next exam by coming up with specific changes in your preparation. Describe two things: actions you took this time but do *not* intend to take next time, and actions you did not take this time, but *do* intend to take next time.

WRITE IT *Communicate*

Emotional intelligence journal: How feelings connect to study success. Think about how you were feeling at times when you were most able to recall and use information in a high-stress situation—a test, a workplace challenge, a group presentation. What thought, action, or situation put you in this productive mindset that helped you succeed? Did you go for a run, talk to your best friend, take 30 minutes for yourself? Create a list of thoughts or actions you can call on when you will be faced with a challenge to your memory and want the best possible outcome.

Memory and Test Taking

Diversity and Communication

MAKING RELATIONSHIPS WORK

THIS LESSON TEACHES STRATEGIES FOR EFFECTIVE COMMUNICATION BOTH IN PERSON AND ONLINE. IN THE COVERAGE OF TEAMWORK, YOU WILL LEARN IDEAS FOR HOW TO HANDLE CONFLICT, CRITICISM, AND ANGER ON YOUR WAY TO SUCCESSFUL, COOPERATIVE WORK.

52% 🔋

Notes   +

Today   Mar 10 8:01 AM

Working through this lesson will help you to:

- Explain how to adjust your communication to suit
  your audience   PP. 104–106

- Recommend best practices for forming and
  participating in teams   PP. 108–109

- Explain ways to manage conflict in one-on-one and
  team settings   PP. 109–110

HOW CAN YOU
develop cultural competence?

On an interpersonal level, *diversity* refers to the differences among people and among groups of which people are a part. Differences in gender, skin color, ethnicity and national origin, age, and physical characteristics are most obvious. Differences in cultural and religious beliefs and practices, education, sexual orientation, socioeconomic status, family background, and marital and parental status are less visible, but no less significant.

Another layer of diversity lies within each unique individual. Among the factors defining this layer are personality traits, learning preferences, strengths and weaknesses, and natural talents and interests. Even if friends or family members share your racial and ethnic background, they may differ in how they learn, the way they communicate, or their sexual orientation.

Interacting effectively with all kinds of people is crucial to your school and life success and is the goal of *cultural competence*—the ability to understand and appreciate

MyStudentSuccessLab
(www.mystudentsuccesslab.com) is an online solution designed to help you "Start Strong, Finish Stronger" by building skills for ongoing personal and professional development.

differences among people and adjust your behavior in ways that enhance, rather than detract from, relationships and communication. Risking becoming culturally competent carries significant rewards promoting both school and life success. According to the National Center for Cultural Competence, developing cultural competence involves these five actions:[1]

1. Value diversity.
2. Identify and evaluate personal perceptions and attitudes.
3. Be aware of what happens when different cultures interact.
4. Build knowledge about other cultures.
5. Use what you learn to adapt to diverse cultures as you encounter them.

In developing cultural competence, you develop practical skills that help you connect to others, bridging the gap between who you are and who they are.[2]

Action #1: Value Diversity

Valuing diversity means having a basic respect for the differences among people and an understanding of what is positive about those differences. You may not like everyone you meet, but if you value diversity, you will tolerate and respect people whether you like them or not, avoid assumptions, and grant them the right to think, feel, and believe without being judged.

Valuing diversity is about more than just passive *tolerance* of the world around you (not causing conflict but not seeking harmony either). The reward of productive teamwork and deep friendship demands a more significant risk than that. Valuing diversity is about moving toward *acceptance* by actively celebrating differences as an enriching part of life.

As you get to know people you collaborate with, you will discover both visible and invisible characteristics and qualities.

Action #2: Identify and Evaluate Personal Perceptions and Attitudes

Many who value the *concept* of diversity experience negative feelings about the *reality* of diversity in their own lives. This disconnect reveals prejudices and stereotypes.

Prejudice

Almost everyone has some level of *prejudice*—a preconceived judgment or opinion formed without just grounds or sufficient knowledge—that leads to prejudging others, usually on the basis of gender, race, sexual orientation, disability, or religion. People judge others without knowing anything about them because of factors like the following:

- *Influence of family and culture.* Children learn attitudes—including intolerance, superiority, and hate—from their parents, peers, and community.
- *Fear of differences.* It is human to fear and make assumptions about the unfamiliar.
- *Experience.* One bad experience with a person of a particular race or religion may lead someone to condemn all people with the same background.

Stereotypes

Prejudice is usually based on *stereotypes*—oversimplified opinions or judgments made without proof or critical thinking—about the characteristics of a person or group of people, based on factors such as the following:

- *Desire for patterns and logic.* People often try to make sense of the world by using the labels, categories, and generalizations that stereotypes provide.
- *Media influences.* The more people see stereotypical images—the beautiful blonde airhead, the jolly fat man—the easier it is to believe that stereotypes are universal.
- *Laziness.* People often find it easier to group members according to a characteristic they seem to have in common than to question who each individual really is. It takes conscious thinking to overcome the stereotypes that quickly come to mind.

Stereotypes derail personal connections and block effective communication because pasting a label on a person makes it hard for you to see the real person underneath. Even stereotypes that seem "positive," such as "women are nurturing," may not always be true and can get in the way of perceiving uniqueness.

Risk identifying your stereotypical or prejudicial thinking on the way to the reward of cultural competence. Ask analytical questions about your own ideas and beliefs:

- How do I react to differences?
- What prejudices or stereotypes come to mind when I see people, in real life or in the media, who are a different color than I am? From a different culture? Making different choices?
- Where did my prejudices and stereotypes come from?
- Are these prejudices fair? Are these stereotypes accurate?
- How does having prejudices and believing stereotypes harm me?

With the knowledge you gain as you answer these questions, move on to the next stage: looking carefully at what happens when people from different cultures interact.

Action #3: Be Aware of What Happens When Cultures Interact

Interaction among people from different cultures can promote learning, build mutual respect, and broaden perspectives. However, as history has shown, such interaction can also produce problems caused by lack of understanding, prejudice, and stereotypic thinking. At their mildest, these problems create roadblocks that obstruct relationships and communication. At their worst, they set the stage for acts of discrimination and hate crimes.

Discrimination

Federal law says you cannot be denied basic opportunities and rights because of your race, creed, color, age, gender, national or ethnic origin, religion, marital status, potential or actual pregnancy, or potential or actual illness or disability (unless the illness or disability prevents you from performing required tasks, and unless accommodations are not possible). Despite these legal protections, *discrimination*—actions that deny people equal employment, education, and housing opportunities, or that treat people as second-class citizens—is common and often appears on college campuses. For example, members of campus clubs may reject prospective members because of religious differences, or instructors and students may judge one another according to weight, accent, or body piercings.

When prejudice turns violent, it often manifests itself in *hate crimes*— crimes motivated by a hatred of a specific characteristic thought to be possessed by the victim, usually based on their race, ethnicity, or religious or sexual orientation. Because hate crime statistics include only reported incidents, they tell just a part of the story. Many more crimes likely go unreported by victims fearful of what might happen if they contact authorities.

Action #4: Build Cultural Knowledge

The successfully intelligent response to discrimination and hate is to gather knowledge. Taking the risk to learn about people who are different from you, especially those you are likely to meet on campus or on the job, sets you up for productive relationships. How can you begin?

- Read newspapers, books, magazines, and websites that expose you to different perspectives.
- Ask questions of all kinds of people, about themselves and their traditions.
- Observe how people behave, what they eat and wear, how they interact with others.
- Travel internationally to unfamiliar places where you can experience different ways of life.
- Travel locally to equally unfamiliar, but close-by, places where you will encounter a variety of people.
- Build friendships with fellow students or coworkers you would not ordinarily approach.

Some colleges have international exchange programs that can help you appreciate the world's cultural diversity. Engaging with students from other countries, whether they have come to your college or you have chosen to study abroad, can provide a two-way learning experience, helping each of you learn about each other's culture.

Building knowledge also means exploring yourself. Talk with family, read, and seek experiences that educate you about your own cultural heritage; then share what you know with others.

Action #5: Adapt to Diverse Cultures

Now put what you've learned to work with practical actions. Taking the risk to open your mind can bring the reward of extraordinary relationships and new understanding. Let the following suggestions inspire more ideas about what you can do to improve how you relate to others.

- *Look past external characteristics.* If you meet a woman with a disability, get to know her. She may be an accounting major, a guitar player, and a mother. She may love baseball and politics. These characteristics, not just her physical person, describe who she is.
- *Move beyond your feelings.* Engage your emotional intelligence to note what different people make you feel, and then examine the potential effect of those feelings. By working to move beyond feelings that could lead to harmful assumptions and negative outcomes, you will improve your chances for successful communication.
- *Risk putting yourself in other people's shoes.* Ask questions about what other people feel, especially if there's a conflict. Offer friendship to someone new to your class. Seek the reward of mutual understanding.

- *Adjust to cultural differences.* When you understand someone's way of being and put it into practice, you show respect and encourage communication. For example, if a study group member takes offense at a particular kind of language, avoid it when you meet.
- *Climb over language barriers.* When speaking with someone who is struggling with your language, choose words the person is likely to know, avoid slang expressions, be patient, and use body language to fill in what words cannot say. Invite questions, and ask them yourself.
- *Help others.* There are countless ways to make a difference, from providing food or money to a neighbor in need, to sending relief funds to nations devastated by natural disasters. Every act, no matter how small, makes the world that much better.
- *Stand up against prejudice, discrimination, and hate.* When you hear a prejudiced remark, notice discrimination taking place, or suspect a hate crime, make a comment or get help from an authority such as an instructor or dean. Support organizations that encourage tolerance. The reward of keeping someone safe is worth the risk.
- *Recognize that people everywhere have the same basic needs.* Everyone loves, thinks, hurts, hopes, fears, and plans. When you are trying to find common ground with diverse people, remember that you are united through your essential humanity.

Just as there is diversity in skin color and ethnicity, there is also diversity in the way people communicate. Effective communication helps people of all cultures make connections.

HOW CAN YOU *communicate effectively?*

Clearly spoken communication promotes success at school, at work, and in personal relationships. However, communicating is a skill that takes effort and focus. If you can be strategic, learn to give and receive criticism, and manage communication technology, you will increase your effectiveness as a communicator.

Be Strategic

Every time you communicate, you do so with intent: To clearly convey an idea to someone, often with a goal of encouraging him or her to take action. When you communicate to an instructor that you might miss a paper deadline, perhaps you hope that the instructor will grant you an extension. When you communicate with a friend about your weekend schedule, you may anticipate that the friend will respond with an idea of when you can get together. Here are three strategies that help you get your point across as effectively as possible.

Send "I" messages. "I" messages communicate your needs rather than attacking someone else. Creating these messages involves some simple rephrasing: "You didn't lock the door!" becomes "I was worried when I came home and found the door unlocked." "I" statements soften the conflict by highlighting the effects the other person's actions have on you, rather than focusing on the person or the actions themselves.

Be assertive. Most people tend to express themselves in one of three ways—aggressively, assertively, or passively. *Aggressive* communicators focus primarily on their own needs. *Passive* communicators focus primarily on the needs of others. *Assertive* communicators are able to declare and affirm their opinions while respecting the rights of others to do the same. Assertive behavior promotes the most productive communication. What can aggressive and passive communicators do to move toward

AGGRESSIVE	ASSERTIVE	PASSIVE
Blaming, name-calling, and verbal insults: "You created this mess!"	Expressing yourself and letting others do the same: "I have thoughts about this. First, what is your opinion?"	Feeling you have no right to express anger: "No, I'm fine."
Escalating arguments: "You'll do it my way, no matter what it takes."	Using "I" statements to defuse arguments: "I am uncomfortable with that choice and want to discuss it."	Avoiding arguments: "Whatever you want to do is fine."
Being demanding: "Do this."	Asking and giving reasons: "Please consider doing it this way, and here's why. . . . "	Being noncommittal: "I'm not sure what the best way to handle this is."

an assertive style? Aggressive communicators might take time before speaking, use "I" statements, and listen to others. Passive communicators might acknowledge their anger, express opinions, and exercise the right to make requests. Key 9.1 contrasts these three communication styles.

Adjust to communication styles within generations. Generations come with personal and lifestyle characteristics that can affect intergenerational communication. Recognizing and adapting to differences caused by generation gaps can help you communicate successfully.

Although adjusting to communication styles helps you speak and listen more effectively, you also need to understand, and learn how to effectively give and receive, criticism.

Know How to Give and Receive Criticism

Criticism can be either constructive or unconstructive. *Constructive criticism* promotes improvement or development. It is a practical problem-solving strategy involving good-will suggestions for improving a situation. In contrast, unconstructive criticism focuses on what went wrong, doesn't offer alternatives to help solve the problem, and is often delivered negatively, creating bad feelings.

Constructive criticism can help bring about important changes. Consider someone who is continually late for study group sessions. Which comment from the group leader would encourage a change in behavior?

- *Constructive.* The group leader talks privately with the student: "I've noticed you've been late a lot. We count on you to contribute. Is there a problem that is keeping you from being on time? Can we help?"
- *Unconstructive.* The leader watches the student arrive late and says, in front of everyone, "If you can't start getting here on time, there's really no point in your coming."

At school, instructors criticize classwork, papers, and exams. On the job, criticism may come from supervisors, coworkers, or customers. No matter the source, constructive comments can help you grow. Be open to what you hear, and remember that most people want you to succeed.

Offering constructive criticism. Use the following strategies to be effective:

- *Criticize the behavior, not the person.* Avoid personal attacks. "You've been late to five group meetings" is preferable to "You're lazy."

get analytical

GIVE CONSTRUCTIVE CRITICISM

Complete the following on paper or in digital format.

Think of a situation that could be improved if you were able to offer constructive criticism to a friend or family member.

1. Describe the situation and name the improvement you seek.

2. Imagine that you have a chance to speak to this person. First describe the setting—time, place, and atmosphere—where you think you would be most successful.

3. Now develop your "script." Analyze the situation and decide on what you think would be the most constructive approach. Free write what you would say. Keep in mind the goal you want your communication to achieve. Revise what you wrote as necessary.

4. Finally, if you can, make your plan a reality. Will you do it?

5. If you do have the conversation, analyze the result. Was it worth it?

- *Define the specific problem.* Try to focus on the facts, backing them up with specific examples and minimizing emotions.
- *Suggest new approaches and offer help.* Talk about practical ways to handle the situation. Generate creative options. Help the person feel supported.
- *Use a positive approach and hopeful language.* Express your belief that the person can turn the situation around.

Receiving criticism. Being open to criticism is a challenging risk, but the potential rewards of positive change make it worth the discomfort. When receiving criticism:

- *Analyze the comments.* Listen carefully and then evaluate what you heard. What does it mean? What is the intent? Try to let unconstructive comments go without responding.
- *Ask for suggestions on how to change your behavior.* Be open to what others say.
- *Summarize the criticism and your response.* The goal is for all to understand the situation.
- *Use a specific strategy.* Use problem-solving skills to analyze the problem, brainstorm ways to change, choose a strategy, and take practical action to make it happen.

Plug into Communication Technology without Losing Touch

Modern technology has revolutionized the way people communicate. You can call or text on a mobile phone; write a note via email, instant message, or Twitter; communicate through blogs and chat rooms; and use social networking tools such as Facebook, Instagram, and more. As a college student, you may take courses that operate partially or fully online, meaning that part or all of your communication with instructors and fellow students is in the electronic realm.

Although communication technologies allow you to communicate faster, more frequently, and with more people than ever before, it has its drawbacks. Key 9.2 shows some positive and negative aspects of communication technology.

As freeing and convenient as it may be to communicate electronically in a faceless environment, its low-risk feeling matches its limited potential for reward. Real life demands that people effectively interact face-to-face. Avoid prioritizing electronic communication over in-person real-time interaction (think about how you feel when a friend you are with spends half your time together texting). Your goal is to communicate electronically to *enhance* real-time interaction rather than *replace* it. Ultimately, you will develop your own personal communication "recipe," consisting of how, and how much, you want to communicate.

Whether online or in person, you will be working in teams for much of your college career, as well as your working life. Your success as a team member will depend on your ability to communicate successfully.

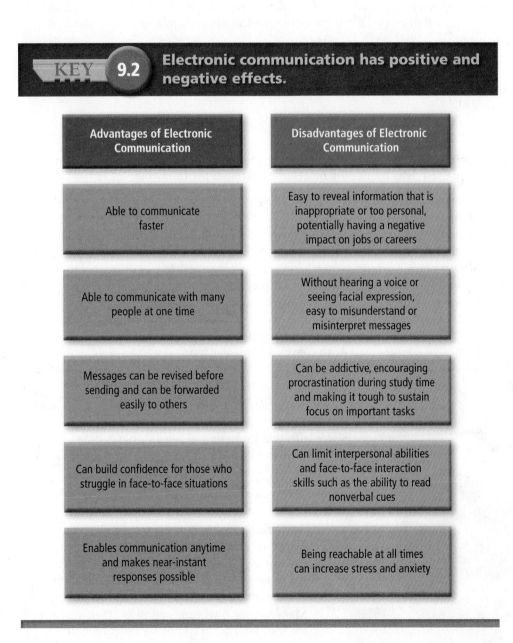

KEY 9.2 Electronic communication has positive and negative effects.

Advantages of Electronic Communication	Disadvantages of Electronic Communication
Able to communicate faster	Easy to reveal information that is inappropriate or too personal, potentially having a negative impact on jobs or careers
Able to communicate with many people at one time	Without hearing a voice or seeing facial expression, easy to misunderstand or misinterpret messages
Messages can be revised before sending and can be forwarded easily to others	Can be addictive, encouraging procrastination during study time and making it tough to sustain focus on important tasks
Can build confidence for those who struggle in face-to-face situations	Can limit interpersonal abilities and face-to-face interaction skills such as the ability to read nonverbal cues
Enables communication anytime and makes near-instant responses possible	Being reachable at all times can increase stress and anxiety

HOW DO YOU WORK
effectively in a team?

A team is a group of people working together toward a common goal.[3] In today's working world, almost everything is accomplished by a team. Large companies often use project teams that span the globe. Nonprofit organizations put teams together to accomplish goals. Instructors teach and develop curriculum in teams, and work in teams with counselors, administrators, and other academic employees. Aware of the importance of working with others, academic institutions have increased the teamwork component of many courses, and students work together both in person and online to create documents, put together presentations, and complete projects.

The prime advantage to working in teams is the ability to combine skills and talents. An academic or work team benefits from a wide array of skills that no single student or employee could possess alone, from analytical skills, to marketing skills, to technical skills, and everything in between. Complex projects at school or in the workplace demand all of these skills, especially when things need to get done in a specific time frame.

Lead and Collaborate Effectively

Being a contributing part of a team means knowing how to collaborate as well as how to lead.

Know how to collaborate

Collaboration means working effectively with others to achieve a common goal. It is built on trust, which can only be achieved through the following:

- *Honesty.* Team members tell one another the truth, not just what each wants to hear, so they can work together to solve problems and overcome obstacles.
- *Openness.* Team members risk saying what is on their minds and share information because they understand the reward of productivity depends on it.
- *Consistency.* Each team member works and interacts in a consistent manner, and team members consistently do what they say they will do.
- *Respect.* Team members see one another as vital parts of the team and speak, listen, and behave respectfully toward one another. Using respectful language is especially important with email communication, where it is tough to convey a particular tone.

Know how to lead

You may be called upon to lead your team as well as participate in it. Being a leader is a risk, but the reward for effective leadership is getting things done. Here are some tips for being an effective leader:

- Communicate clearly so your team understands what you are trying to accomplish and why, and how they fit into your vision.
- Set goals for yourself and your team so everyone knows what to do and when.
- Be clear on the skills and talents you have and those that others have so you know how to best contribute and how to delegate the right tasks to others.
- Manage your own time and help others stay on track so your team completes tasks on time.
- Follow through—finish what you start.

Communication with others is essential to every school and work goal, from team projects to study groups to on-the-job collaborations.

Set and Achieve Goals as a Team

For a team to accomplish a goal, it's a good idea to follow some established guidelines. Here are some that every team should follow.

1. Before anything else, identify the desired goal so the team starts working with the end in mind.

2. Once team members know the goal, define roles and expectations. Who is going to do what and how well does it need to be done? If team members are clear about communicating their skills and talents, the team leader should be able to delegate various tasks.

3. Then it's time for planning and scheduling. Just because the team members know what they are supposed to do, it doesn't mean they know *when* they are supposed to do it. Certain tasks may depend on others, so the team leader needs to figure out a realistic schedule.

4. Throughout the process, the team must monitor its performance to see if deadlines are being met and teammates are performing their tasks to the best of their abilities.

5. Finally, the team needs to evaluate its performance. What went well? What didn't? What might team members change next time, either with this same team or another? Make sure you don't skip this crucial opportunity to learn from the experience and improve on it.

Goal achievement also depends on being efficient and productive during meetings. To ensure you accomplish your goals during a meeting, follow good meeting etiquette:

- *Show up on time.* This is as true for an in-person meeting as it is with a conference call or online chat. If you cannot avoid being late, call, text, or email to let people know. Then apologize briefly when you arrive.

- *Be prepared.* Make sure you have all necessary materials. Do a "tech check" ahead of time to make sure your equipment is working (computer, software, and video projector).

- *Use an agenda and take notes.* Communicate the goal of the meeting, the items that will be covered, and how long it will last. Then stick to that agenda and have someone take notes.

- *Listen and don't interrupt.* Listen to what the person is saying instead of planning your response or interrupting. When it's your turn, you will appreciate not being interrupted.

- *Practice civility.* No matter how angry or frustrated you feel, do not get overly emotional. Also, if you have an issue with someone, talk to him or her privately after the meeting.

- *Avoid distractions.* If you text or take phone calls during a meeting, you will seem rude and may miss important information. Give your full attention to the meeting and your teammates.

- *Meet virtually.* If you encounter scheduling conflicts, keep in mind that you can use virtual meeting technology to communicate when your group cannot gather in person.

Conflict and anger are a natural part of the ebb and flow of team dynamics. Read on for ways to manage both.

Manage Conflict

With different types of personalities on the team, disagreement is bound to occur, but disagreement is what brings new ideas to the floor. So, rather than fear conflict, overreact to it, or escalate it, try the following steps.

1. *Determine what the issue is.* Is it a conflict of interest? A lack of role clarity? A lack of resources? A personality conflict? Once you are clear on the conflict, continue.

2. *Separate emotion from the message.* This means avoiding responding to the emotion in your team member's voice. Instead, listen to the message behind the emotion. What is the concern? Try to listen without judging.

3. *Respond to the group, not the individual.* When someone attacks you or argues with you, take a deep breath and do not respond immediately. Then, once you feel more centered, respond to the entire group. You can still make eye contact with the individual, but make sure to talk to the rest of the group as well. This way, the conflict does not become a personal argument.

4. *Take it offline.* If resolution is not possible during the meeting, ask to take the discussion offline and privately discuss the issue with the individual at another time, outside of the meeting.

One final note about virtual meetings: Although all of the team success skills you just read apply to any team, virtual team interactions demand some particular strategies. When you are on a telephone or videoconference, speak clearly and be sure to take turns (when two people are talking at the same time, often neither can be understood). Because it can be hard to forge a relationship over a WebEx, make an effort to create a personal connection before or after the meeting. Finally, if there is confusion or a misunderstanding, pick up the phone after your meeting is over and clarify the situation with another member of your team. Hearing a voice in a real-time conversation makes things more personal and helps move things toward resolution.

Complete the following on paper or in digital format.

KNOW IT *Think Critically*

Make a Difference

Review the five actions for cultural competence earlier in this section. Then complete the following.

1. Re-read the suggestions for "Action #5: Adapt to Diverse Cultures." Choose three and write them down. Then, for each, give a real-life version (something you've done or know someone else has done). For example, by choosing to wear a blindfold for an entire day as part of a "Blind for a Day" experience, students put themselves in other people's shoes.

2. Make two of these strategies into personal plans. Rewrite them as specific actions you are willing to take in the next six months. For example, "put yourself in other people's shoes" might become "read a memoir written by someone from an unfamiliar culture."

3. Choose one of the plans to put into action in the next 30 days. Choose wisely—recall your knowledge of SMART goals and pick the one that is most attainable and realistic. Name your choice. Describe your goal with this action—how you want to make a difference.

4. Finally, do it. Name the date by which you plan to have taken action.

WRITE IT *Communicate*

Know yourself as a team member. How do you tend to operate in a team? Describe yourself as a team member, including what you tend to do well in a team, what challenges you, how you like and do not like to contribute, what types of people you work well with and not so well with, and so on. Include a team experience from your life as an example.

10 Information Literacy

EVALUATING SOURCES EFFECTIVELY

THIS LESSON EXPLORES THE PROS AND CONS OF BOTH LIBRARY AND ONLINE RESEARCH, EMPHASIZING THE BENEFIT OF USING BOTH. YOU WILL LEARN CRITICAL EVALUATION OF READING MATERIALS, INCLUDING HOW TO USE THE CARS TEST TO EVALUATE THE QUALITY OF INTERNET SOURCES.

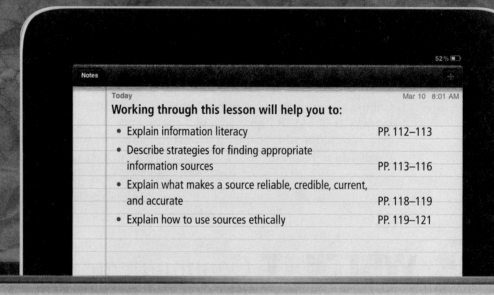

Today   Mar 10   8:01 AM

Working through this lesson will help you to:

- Explain information literacy   PP. 112–113
- Describe strategies for finding appropriate
  information sources   PP. 113–116
- Explain what makes a source reliable, credible, current,
  and accurate   PP. 118–119
- Explain how to use sources ethically   PP. 119–121

HOW CAN YOU BE AN INFORMATION
literate reader and researcher?

Today's students and workers have more information, and more sources of information, available to them than ever before in recorded history. In fact the current time is often referred to as the "information age," and the modern workplace is dominated by *knowledge work*—work that is primarily concerned with information rather than manufacturing or manual labor. For this reason, being an information-literate person is crucial to your success.

What is *information literacy*? The American Library Association defines it as "a set of abilities requiring individuals to 'recognize when information is needed and have the ability to locate, evaluate, and use effectively the needed information.'"[1] This set of abilities includes:[2]

- Determining how much information you need
- Effectively accessing what you need
- Evaluating both the information and its sources using critical thinking
- Using information to accomplish a goal

Many modern students have grown up with technology and are comfortable using electronic devices and computers to research online. However, being technologically savvy does not mean that you are necessarily information literate. For example, when it comes to research, most students' first instinct is to power up the computer and start jumping around on Google. However, there are a myriad of research resources at your fingertips. Materials and electronic databases in a library have been evaluated by librarians and researchers, and for this reason are likely to be credible. By comparison, many of the hundreds or even thousands of Internet sources on a given topic are not monitored or evaluated by any knowledgeable person or organization, and may turn out to be nothing more than conjecture, opinion, and rants.

Risking time and effort to search carefully will reward you with the most useful, accurate, and reliable information. Start to build your information literacy by understanding how to perform an effective information search, both in the library and online.

Map Out the Possibilities

To select the information that is most helpful for your research, you need to first know what is available to you. Sign up for an in-person or online library orientation session.

To gain a key advantage in your search for information, get to know a librarian. This professional can assist you in locating unfamiliar or hard-to-find sources, navigating catalogs and databases, uncovering research shortcuts, and dealing with pesky equipment. Know what you want to accomplish before asking a question. At many schools, you can query a librarian by cell-phone, email, and instant messaging.

Search for Information at the Library

To avoid being overwhelmed by the sheer magnitude of resources available, use a practical, step-by-step search method. Key 10.1 shows how to start wide and then narrow your search for a closer look at specific sources.

When using virtual or online catalogues, you will need to adjust your research methods. Searching library databases requires a *keyword search*—an exploration that uses a topic-related, natural-language word or phrase as a starting point to locate other information. To narrow your search and reduce the number of *hits* (results returned by your search), add more keywords to your search criteria. For example, instead of searching through the broad category "art," focus on "French art" or, more specifically, "nineteenth-century French art." Key 10.2 shows how to use the keyword system to narrow your search with what is called *Boolean logic*.

When your school's library purchases databases and makes them available for student use, those databases have been evaluated by experienced and knowledgeable professionals who determine that they have a high level of integrity and credibility. For you as a researcher, it can help to know that any materials you find in your school's hard copy or electronic holdings are already established as reliable.

Much, although not all, research can be done using online databases. Get to know the databases and other resources your school makes available to students.

KEY 10.1 Use a step-by-step search method.

Start with general reference works	Examples include encyclopedias, almanacs, dictionaries, biographical references.
Move to specialized reference works	Examples include encyclopedias and dictionaries that focus on a narrow field.
Use the electronic catalog to locate materials	Search the library catalog by author, title, or subject to locate specific books, periodicals, and journals. Most library catalogs are virtual and can be accessed by computers throughout the library. Ask a librarian for assistance, if needed.
Browse through relevant books and articles	Using your results from the catalog search, dive in deeper by looking through the books and articles related to your topic.

KEY 10.2 Perform an effective keyword search with Boolean logic.

IF YOU ARE SEARCHING FOR ...	DO THIS	EXAMPLE
A word	Type the word normally.	Aid
A phrase	Type the phrase in its normal word order (use regular word spacing) or surround the phrase with quotation marks ("x"). Quotation marks ensure the search engine finds the words together in the same phrase, rather than the individual words on the same page.	financial aid, "financial aid"
Two or more keywords without regard to order	Type the words in any order, surrounding the words with quotation marks. Use *and* to separate the words.	"financial aid" and "scholarships"
Topic A *and* topic B	Type the words in any order, surrounding the words with quotation marks. Use *and* to separate the words. The search engine will list a result only if it contains BOTH topics A and B.	"financial aid" and "scholarships"
Topic A *or* topic B	Type the words in any order, surrounding the words with quotation marks. Use *or* to separate the words. The search engine will list a result if it contains *either* A or B.	"financial aid" or "scholarships"
Topic A *but not* topic B	Type topic A first within quotation marks, and then topic B within quotation marks. Use *not* to separate the words. The search engine will list a result if it contains only Topic A and does not contain Topic B.	"financial aid" not "scholarships"

Search for Information Online

Unlike your college library collection or databases, Internet resources are not always evaluated by anyone who vouches for their quality. As a result, your research depends on critical thinking to sort out the valid, credible materials from the invalid, not-so-credible ones.

Start with search engines

Among the most popular and effective search engines are Google (www.google.com) and Yahoo! (www.yahoo.com). Search engines aimed at academic audiences include the Librarian's Index to the Internet (www.lii.org) and INFOMINE (www.infomine .com). At these academic directories, someone has screened the sites and listed only those sources that are reputable and regularly updated.

In addition, your school may include access to certain nonpublic academic search engines in the cost of your tuition. Sites like LexusNexus, InfoTrac, GaleGroup, and OneFile are known for their credibility in the academic world as well as their vast amounts of information. Risk going "beyond Google" for the reward of accessing extensive banks of information and resources. Check with your school's library to see how to access these sites.

Use a search strategy

The World Wide Web has been called "the world's greatest library, with all its books on the floor." With no librarian in sight, you need to master a practical Internet search strategy.

1. *Use natural language phrases or keywords to identify what you are looking for.* University of Michigan professor Eliot Soloway recommends first phrasing your search in the form of a question. Then he advises identifying the important words in the question as well as related words. This will give you a collection of terms to use in different combinations as you search (see example below).[3]

> **Initial question:** What vaccines are given to children before age 5?
> **Important words:** vaccines, children, before age 5
> **Related words:** polio, shot, pediatrics
> **Final search criteria (important + related words):** vaccines children "before age 5" "polio shot" pediatrics

   Note: Some of the terms in the final search criteria above are enclosed in quotes and others are not. By putting terms in quotes, you tell the search engine that the words *must* appear next to one another, rather than at different locations on the same web page.

2. *Use a search engine to isolate valuable sites.* Enter your questions, phrases, and keywords in various combinations to generate lists of "hits." Vary word order to see what you can generate. If you get too many hits, try using more specific keywords.

3. *Evaluate the list of results.* The first links in the list of search results are not always the most relevant. Often, the top hits belong to individuals or companies that have paid money to have their sites show up first. Scan through the list of results, reading the short synopsis that accompanies each. You may need to look further down the list of hits, and maybe even go the second or third page of results, to find what you need.

4. *Skim sites to evaluate what seems most useful.* Once you identify a potentially useful link, click it to go to the website. Evaluate the content and provider. Does

get creative

BROADEN YOUR SEARCH

LESSON 10

Complete the following on paper or in digital format.

Identify a topic that you will research online. Ideally, choose a topic that you need to research for one of your courses, so that you will be able to put your work to use. If you have no research assignment currently, select a topic that interests you.

1. Name the topic.

2. Generate 10 keywords closely associated with this topic.

3. Using these keywords, create three different phrases or sets of words that you plan to use when searching.

4. Now go through the steps of the Internet search strategy using each phrase or set of words. For each, make notes about the relevant and useful sites you discover, and how far down the hit list you had to go to find them. Comparing your notes, identify which phrase or set of words helped you find useful information most effectively. Finally, write a short paragraph explaining what you learned from the experience and how you will research in the future.

the site seem relevant and reputable? Is it biased in favor of a particular point of view? What is its purpose? For example, a blog is apt to focus on opinion; a company's site is likely to promote its products; an article in a scholarly journal may focus on research findings.

5. *Save, or bookmark, the sites you want to focus on.* Make sure you can access them again. You may want to copy URLs and paste them into a separate document. Consider printing Internet materials that you know you will need to reference over and over again.

6. *When you think you are done, start over.* Choose another search engine and search again. Different systems may access different sites.

The limitations of Internet-only research make it smart to combine Internet and library research. Search engines cannot find everything for several reasons:

- Not all sources are in digital format.
- The Internet prioritizes current information and may not find older information.
- Some digital sources may not be part of your library's subscription offerings.
- Internet searches require electricity or battery power and an online connection.

Use the Internet as a starting point to get an idea of the various documents you may want to locate in the library and read in print. When you find a blog or website that provides only a short extract of important information and then references the rest, find that original article or book and read the information in its entirety. Often, risking the time and effort that extra searching takes will reward you with more accurate, in-depth, and useful information.

Your need to be an effective researcher doesn't stop at graduation, especially in a workplace dominated by information and media. The skills you develop as you research school projects will serve you well in any kind of job that requires use of the Internet and other resources to find and evaluate information.

HOW CAN YOU RESPOND CRITICALLY
to what you read?

It is crucial to question everything you read—trade books, journal and newspaper articles, Internet documents, primary sources, and even textbooks that are supposed to be as accurate as possible. Critical reading involves questioning, analyzing, and evaluating. Think of the reading process as an archaeological dig. First, you excavate a site and uncover the artifacts. Then you separate out what you've found, make connections among ideas, and evaluate what is important. This process rewards you with the ability to focus on the most important materials.

Reading for different purposes engages different parts of critical reading. When you read to learn and retain information or to master a skill, you focus on important information (analyzing and evaluating how the ideas are structured, how they connect, and what is most crucial to remember). When you read to search for truth, you ask questions to evaluate arguments (analyzing and evaluating the author's point of view as well as the credibility, accuracy, reliability, and relevance of the material).

Focus on Important Information

Before determining how to respond to something you've read, ask yourself what is important and what you need to remember. According to Adam Robinson, co-founder of The Princeton Review, "The only way you can effectively absorb the relevant information is to ignore the irrelevant information."[4] The following questions should help you determine what is relevant (if you answer "yes," it's probably relevant):

- Does it contain headings, charts, tables, captions, key terms and definitions, or an introduction or summary? (For a textbook, check mid-chapter or end-of-chapter exercises.)
- Does it offer definitions, crucial concepts, examples, an explanation of a variety or type, critical relationships, or comparisons?
- Does it spark questions and reactions as you read?
- Does it surprise or confuse you?
- Does it mirror what your instructor emphasizes in class or in assignments?

When trying to figure out what to study and what to skim, ask yourself whether your instructor would expect you to know the material. If you are unsure and the topic is not on your syllabus, email your instructor and ask for clarification.

Ask Questions to Evaluate Arguments

An *argument* refers to a persuasive case—a set of connected ideas supported by examples—that a writer makes to prove or disprove a point. Many scholarly books and articles, in print form or on the Internet, are organized around particular arguments. However, other online articles, websites, and blogs offer *claims* instead—arguments that appear to be factual but don't have adequate evidence to support them. Critical readers evaluate arguments and claims to determine whether they are accurate and logical. When quality evidence combines with sound logic, the argument is solid. Just because you read it online or in print does not mean it's true.

Like an archaeological dig, a productive information search can take time and effort. Resist stopping at your first discovery, and take the time to unearth everything that might serve you.

It's easy to accept or reject an argument according to whether it fits with your point of view. If you risk asking questions, however, you can determine the argument's validity and gain the reward of greater depth of understanding, regardless of your opinion. Evaluating an argument involves several factors:

- The quality of the *evidence* (facts, statistics, and other materials supporting an argument).
- Whether the evidence fits the idea concept.
- The logical connections.

Approach every argument with healthy skepticism. Have an open mind to assess whether you are convinced or still have serious questions.

Evaluate Every Source

It is important to examine the evidence in all reading materials, but especially in those materials on the Internet, since online resources vary widely in reliability. In fact, your Internet research is only as strong as your critical thinking. Robert Harris, professor and Web expert, has developed an easy-to-remember system for evaluating Internet information called the **CARS** test for information quality (Credibility, Accuracy, Reasonableness, Support). Use the information in Key 10.3 to question any source you find as you conduct research. You can also use it to test the reliability of non-Internet sources.

HOW DO YOU WRITE AND RESEARCH
with academic integrity?

Every action you take in college gives you an opportunity to act with integrity. This includes every research and writing assignment that you complete.

Plagiarism and the Role of Electronic Materials

Using another writer's words, content, unique approach, or illustrations without crediting the author is called *plagiarism* and is illegal and unethical. Plagiarism has become more prevalent in recent years because technology has made it quicker and easier than ever before. Thirty years ago, when students had only hard-copy research materials to reference, they had to handwrite or type the information they found. Now, with a few clicks of a mouse, any amount of digitized text can be instantly copied and pasted into a document that a student is creating for an assignment.

The ease of copying and pasting is just part of how technology has made plagiarism more rampant. A *New York Times* article entitled "Plagiarism Lines Blur for Students in Digital Age" contends that the availability of electronic information has changed the concept of who owns an image or selection of text. Director of the ICAI Teresa Fishman states in the article, "Now we have a whole generation of students who've grown up with information that just seems to be hanging out there in cyberspace and doesn't seem to have an author . . . it's possible to believe this information is just out there for anyone to take."[5]

Plagiarism is not always deliberate. In a digital environment it's easy to plagiarize without intending to. You might copy something from a website that doesn't list an author, and then forget to go back and determine the source of the material. You might paste something into a draft with the intention of going back in and putting it into your own words, but in the time crunch before your due date, you forget and hand it in with the copied paragraph still word-for-word from the website.

CREDIBILITY	ACCURACY	REASONABLENESS	SUPPORT
Examine whether a source is believable and trustworthy.	*Examine whether information is correct—i.e., factual, comprehensive, detailed, and up to date (if necessary).*	*Examine whether material is fair, objective, moderate, and consistent.*	*Examine whether a source is adequately supported with citations.*
What are the author's credentials? Look for education and experience, title or position of employment, membership in any known and respected organization, reliable contact information, biographical information, and reputation.	**Is it up to date, and is that important?** If you are searching for a work of literature, such as Shakespeare's play *Macbeth*, there is no "updated" version. However, you may want reviews of its latest productions. For most scientific research, you will need to rely on the most updated information you can find.	**Does the source seem fair?** Look for a balanced argument, accurate claims, and a reasoned tone that does not appeal primarily to your emotions.	**Where does the information come from?** Look at the site, the sources used by the person or group who compiled the information, and the contact information. Make sure that the cited sources seem reliable and that statistics are documented.
Is there quality control? Look for ways in which the source may have been screened. For example, materials on an organization's website have most likely been approved by several members; information coming from an academic journal has to be screened by several people before it is published.	**Is it comprehensive?** Does the material leave out any important facts or information? Does it neglect to consider alternative views or crucial consequences? Although no one source can contain all of the available information on a topic, it should still be as comprehensive as is possible within its scope.	**Does the source seem objective?** While there is a range of objectivity in writing, you want to favor authors and organizations who can control their bias. An author with a strong political or religious agenda or an intent to sell a product may not be a source of the most truthful material.	**Is the information corroborated?** Test information by looking for other sources that confirm the facts in this information—or, if the information is opinion, sources that share that opinion and back it up with their own citations. One good strategy is to find at least three sources that corroborate each other.
Is there any posted summary or evaluation of the source? You may find abstracts of sources (summary) or a recommendation, rating, or review from a person or organization (evaluation). Either of these—or, ideally, both—can give you an idea of credibility before you decide to examine a source in depth.	**For whom is the source written, and for what purpose?** Looking at what the author wants to accomplish will help you assess whether it has a bias. Sometimes biased information will not be useful for your purpose; sometimes your research will require that you note and evaluate bias (such as if you were to compare Civil War diaries from Union soldiers with those from Confederate soldiers).	**Does the source seem moderate?** Do claims seem possible, or does the information seem hard to believe? Does what you read make sense when compared to what you already know? While wild claims may turn out to be truthful, you are safest to check everything out.	**Is the source externally consistent?** Most material is a mix of both current and old information. External consistency refers to whether the old information agrees with what you already know. If a source contradicts something you know to be true, chances are higher that the information new to you may be inconsistent as well.
Signals of a potential lack of credibility: Anonymous materials, negative evaluations, little or no evidence of quality control, bad grammar or misspelled words	*Signals of a potential lack of accuracy:* Lack of date or old date, generalizations, one-sided views that do not acknowledge opposing arguments	*Signals of a potential lack of reasonableness:* Extreme or emotional language, sweeping statements, conflict of interest, inconsistencies or contradictions	*Signals of a potential lack of support:* Statistics without sources, lack of documentation, lack of corroboration using other reliable sources

Source: Harris, Robert. "Evaluating Internet Research Sources." VirtualSalt, November 22, 2010. From http://www.virtualsalt.com/evalu8it.htm

Pitfalls aside, the fact that technology makes plagiarism quick and easy does *not* make it acceptable. To avoid plagiarism, use this one general directive: Do not submit as your own any words you did not write or images you did not create. Resources must be properly cited and either quoted (if used word-for-word) or paraphrased. The risk of the effort and attention required to follow this rule rewards you with true learning.

Note that even as technology facilitates plagiarism, it presents tools to detect it. Sites like Turnitin.com allow instructors to check student work for plagiarism, and WriteCheck helps students do the same with their own work before submitting it. Instructors are far more likely to catch plagiarized material now, with a quick copy and paste to Turnitin.com, than they were in the past when they would have had to pore through books and journals at the library. Make a commitment to hand in your own work and to uphold the highest standards of academic integrity.

Crediting Authors and Sources

The following techniques will help you properly credit sources and avoid plagiarism:

Make source notes as you go. Plagiarism often begins accidentally during research. You may forget to include quotation marks around a quotation, or you may intend to cite or paraphrase a source but never do. To avoid forgetting, write detailed source and content notes as you research.

Learn the difference between a quotation and a paraphrase. A *quotation* repeats a source's exact words and uses quotation marks to set them off from the rest of the text. A *paraphrase,* a restatement of the quotation in your own words, requires that you completely rewrite the idea, not just remove or replace a few words.

Use a citation even for an acceptable paraphrase. Credit every source that you quote, paraphrase, or use as evidence (except when the material is considered common knowledge). To credit a source, write a footnote or endnote that describes it, using the format preferred by your instructor.

Understand that lifting material off the Internet is plagiarism. Words in electronic form belong to the writer just as words in print form do. If you cut and paste sections from a source document onto your draft, you are probably committing plagiarism. Key 10.4 will help you identify what instructors regard as plagiarized work.

Use specific formats and lists. You may be asked to submit different kinds of source lists when you hand in your paper:

- A References list, also called a *List of Works Cited*, includes only the sources you actually cited in your paper.
- A Bibliography includes all the sources you consulted, whether or not they were cited in the paper.
- An Annotated Bibliography includes all the sources you consulted as well as an explanation or critiques of each source.

Your instructor will tell you which documentation style to use. Consult a college-level writers' handbook for an overview of documentation styles. Among the most common are:

- The Modern Language Association (MLA) format is generally used in the humanities, including history, literature, the arts, and philosophy (www.mla.org).
- The American Psychological Association (APA) style is the appropriate format in psychology, sociology, business, economics, nursing, criminology, and social work (www.apa.org).

Plagiarism takes many forms.

Instructors consider the following types of work to be plagiarized:

- Submitting a paper from a website that sells or gives away research papers
- Handing in a paper written by a fellow student or family member
- Copying material in a paper directly from a source without proper quotation marks or source citation
- Paraphrasing material in a paper from a source without proper source citation
- Submitting the same paper in more than one class, even if the classes are in different terms or even different years

No matter where you gather your materials or what your purpose, pursue information with integrity and a critical thinking approach. With this care and attention you will build the information literacy you need to forge ahead in the 21st century.

Complete the following on paper or in digital format.

LESSON 10

KNOW IT *Think Critically*

Information Evaluation for the 21st Century

Information literacy is a requirement for almost every 21st century job. Employers expect you to research independently and master new skills to keep up with change. For example, working in the field of sociology requires you to interpret government regulations and evaluate case reports, court documents, and research materials. Plus, nearly every job requires you to read memos, emails, and reports from an information-literate perspective.

Prepare yourself by honestly assessing your skills *right now*. Write down each ability on the following list. For each, give yourself a rating on a scale of 1 to 10, with 10 being the highest:

- Analyze the credibility of sources.
- Define your research goal and use it to guide your search.
- Find both library and online sources effectively.
- Use only the sources that will move you toward your goal.
- Evaluate the arguments found in research materials.

Identify the two skill areas where you rated yourself lowest and think about how you can improve. For each, describe two actions you can take in the next month to build the skill.

WRITE IT *Communicate*

Emotional intelligence journal: *Plagiarism.* Express your perspective on plagiarism in general and on your school's academic integrity policy. What is your intent with regard to plagiarism? What have you seen or experienced, good or bad, in the realm of academic integrity? In your opinion, what long-term effects do plagiarizers risk? Sum up your view in a statement of advice you would give to a student entering college soon.

Wellness and Stress Management

STAYING HEALTHY IN MIND AND BODY

THIS LESSON PROVIDES AN OVERVIEW OF CAUSES OF STRESS FOR STUDENTS, AS WELL AS WAYS TO MANAGE STRESS EFFECTIVELY THROUGH ATTENTION TO PHYSICAL AND MENTAL HEALTH. YOU WILL LEARN STRATEGIES FOR MANAGING EMOTIONAL DISORDERS AND MAKING EFFECTIVE DECISIONS REGARDING SUBSTANCE USE AND SEXUAL ACTIVITY.

52% 🔋

Notes +

Today   Mar 10   8:01 AM

Working through this lesson will help you to:

HOW CAN FOCUSING ON HEALTH
help you manage stress?

If you're feeling high levels of *stress*—the physical or mental strain that occurs when your body reacts to pressure—you're not alone. Stress levels tend to be high among college students, who are frequently overloaded with activities and responsibilities. The greater your stress, the greater the toll it may take on your health and on your ability to achieve your goals. However, this doesn't mean you should try to get rid of *all* stress. Moderate stress is a productive risk that rewards you with motivation to do well on tests, finish assignments on time, and prepare for presentations.

MyStudentSuccess**Lab**
(www.mystudentsuccesslab.com) is an online solution designed to help you "Start Strong, Finish Stronger" by building skills for ongoing personal and professional development.

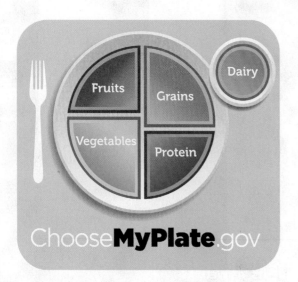

Your ability to manage stress depends in part on your understanding of how it affects you. Certain assessments look at your level of exposure to stressors. In the Get Practical exercise, you will fill one out that asks you how much a series of experiences have been part of your life recently. With the information it provides, you will have a better idea of how stressed you are and what factors cause the most stress for you.

Although you cannot always control what happens to you, you can control your response. One way to be in control is to use time management strategies. Another way to respond productively to stress is to be as physically and mentally healthy as you can. Although no one is able to make healthy choices all the time, consider what risks you are willing to take to earn the reward of a healthy body and mind.

Eat Well

Making intelligent choices about what you eat can lead to more energy, better general health, and an improved quality of life. However, this is easier said than done. College life can make it tough to eat right. Students have limited budgets, tend to eat on the run, build social events around food, and eat as a reaction to stress.

Healthy eating requires balance (varying your diet) and moderation (eating reasonable amounts). For guidance about the different types and amounts of food you should be eating, explore the information and helpful tools at www.choosemyplate.gov. The graphic, shown here, indicates an ideal balance of food groups. For example, half of your daily food intake should be fruits and vegetables—ideally, five servings a day.

Visit the Centers for Disease Control website at www.cdc.gov and use their BMI calculator to find out if you fall within a healthy range or would be considered overweight or obese. If you want to lose weight, set a reasonable goal and work toward it slowly. You may also want to consult health professionals, enroll in a reputable weight-loss program, and incorporate regular exercise into your life.

Get Exercise

Exercise is a key element of your health. The Mayo Clinic reports that risking the time and effort to exercise brings a variety of rewards including easing depression, warding off illnesses, reducing fatigue, and maintaining a healthy weight.[1] Dr. Mike Evans has a video on YouTube identifying 30 minutes of exercise a day as a more significant health intervention than any other. He asks a question: "Can you limit your sitting and sleeping to just 23½ hours a day?" When you think about it, that's a pretty minimal risk for a significant reward.[2]

Use the following ideas to help make exercise a priority, even in the busiest weeks:

- Walk to classes and meetings. Inside buildings, use the stairs.
- Use your school's fitness facilities.
- Ride your bike instead of driving.
- Play team recreational sports at school or in your community.
- Take walks or bike rides for study breaks.
- Find activities you can do outside of a club, such as running or pickup basketball.
- Work out with friends or family to combine socializing and exercise.

Remember that being healthy is part of your personal responsibility. Think preventatively about your well being and take charge of your choices.

Get Enough Sleep

College students are often sleep deprived. While research indicates that students need eight to nine hours of sleep a night to function well, studies show that students average only six to seven hours—and often get much less.[3] Inadequate sleep hinders your ability to concentrate, raises stress levels, and makes you more susceptible to illness and auto accidents. It also reduces your ability to learn and to remember what you study.

Students, overwhelmed with responsibilities, often feel they have no choice but to prioritize schoolwork over sleep. Some regularly stay up until the wee hours of the morning to study. However, if you choose the risk of sleeping instead of putting in a few more hours of studying, you may experience a greater reward at test time than if you had studied all night.

For the sake of your health and your GPA, find a way to get enough sleep. Look for tell-tale symptoms of sleep deprivation such as being groggy in the morning, dozing off during the day, or needing caffeine to make it through the day. Sleep expert Gregg D. Jacobs, Ph.D., has the following practical suggestions for improving sleep habits:[4]

- *Reduce consumption of alcohol and caffeine.* Caffeine may make you hungry (it drops your blood sugar level) or keep you awake, especially if you drink it late. Alcohol causes you to sleep lightly, making you feel less rested when you awaken.
- *Exercise regularly.* Regular exercise, especially in the afternoon or early evening, promotes sleep.
- *Take naps.* Taking short afternoon naps can reduce the effects of sleep deprivation.
- *Be consistent.* Try to establish somewhat regular times to wake up and go to bed.
- *Manage your sleep environment.* Wear something comfortable, turn down the lights, and keep the room cool. Use earplugs, soft music, or white noise if you're dealing with outside distractions.

Address Mental Health Issues

It is not enough to have a healthy body. Your well-being also depends on having a healthy mind. If you recognize yourself in any of the following descriptions, take practical steps to improve your health. Most student health centers and campus counseling centers provide both medical and psychological help or referrals for students with emotional disorders. Although asking for help may feel like a risk, most who do it find it is well worth the reward of feeling better and functioning more effectively.

Depression

Almost everyone has experienced sadness after setbacks such as breaking up with your partner or failing a course. However, a *depressive disorder* is an illness, not a temporary, pessimistic mental state that you can "snap out of." It is also fairly common among college students. Recent research reports that nearly half of surveyed students reported feelings of depression at some point, with over 30% saying that the level of depression made it difficult to function at times.[5] At its worst, depression can lead to suicidal thoughts and attempts.

Key 11.1 shows possible causes of depression as well as some typical symptoms, and offers coping strategies.

Try to find productive ways to reduce stress. This student has chosen to spend time outdoors, eat a healthful lunch, and connect with a friend on the phone.

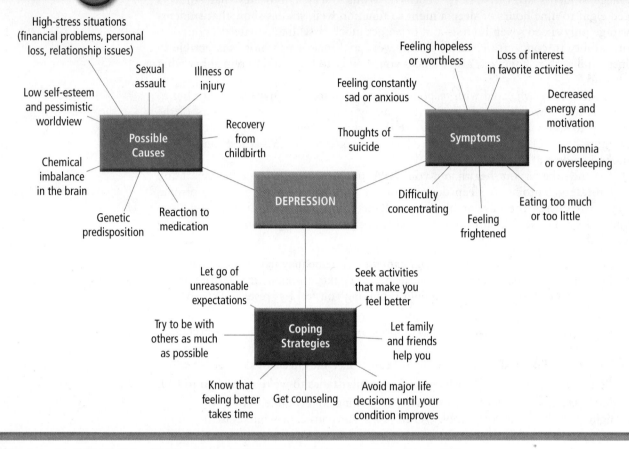

Source: *Depression,* National Institutes of Health publication 02-3561. Bethesda, MD: National Institutes of Health, 2002.

Eating disorders

Millions of people develop serious and sometimes life-threatening eating disorders every year, including anorexia nervosa, bulimia, and binge eating disorder. Negative effects of these disorders range from fertility and obesity issues to digestive tract and other organ damage, heart failure, and even death. There are three basic types of eating disorders:[6]

- *Anorexia nervosa.* People with anorexia nervosa restrict their eating and become dangerously underweight. They may also engage in over-exercising, vomiting, and abuse of diuretics and laxatives. Eventually, without proper nourishment, their internal organs begin to shut down, ending in death if no intervention occurs. Anorexia nervosa is often linked to excessive anxiety and perfectionism or the desire for control.

- *Bulimia nervosa.* People with bulimia engage in "binge episodes," which involve eating excessive amounts of foods and feeling out of control. Following the binge, the person feels remorseful and attempts to purge the calories through self-induced vomiting, laxative abuse, excessive exercise, or fasting. Bulimia is often linked to emotional distress that causes so much pain that an individual tries to "numb" the feeling by overeating.

- *Binge eating disorder.* Binge eating disorder is the most common eating disorder. People with this condition eat large amounts of food and feel out of control, similar to those with bulimia, but they do not purge after a binge episode. However, just like bulimics, they eat unusually fast, eat in secret, eat until they feel uncomfortably full, and feel ashamed of their eating behaviors.

get practical

COLLEGE STRESS EXPLORATION

All sorts of situations and experiences can cause stress during college. Furthermore, everyone has a unique response to any potential stressor. One way to assess your individual situation is to look at the different areas of your life, and rate how much stress you are experiencing in each at the current time. Use a scale from 1 to 10—1 being the lowest possible level of stress, and 10 being the highest possible.

____ 1. Increased independence and responsibility

____ 2. Family relationships

____ 3. Friend relationships

____ 4. Academic relationships (instructors, student peers, administration, etc.)

____ 5. Boyfriend/girlfriend/spouse relationships

____ 6. Managing time and schedule

____ 7. Managing money

____ 8. Performance on assignments

____ 9. Performance on tests

____ 10. Physical health and fitness

____ 11. Mental health and balance

____ 12. Academic planning (major, etc.)

____ 13. Career planning and vision for future

____ 14. Work situation, if you have a job on or off campus

____ 15. Current living situation (home with family, dorm, apartment with a friend, etc.)

Total your points here: _____

The lowest possible score is 15, and the highest possible is 150. The higher your score, the more stress you perceive you are experiencing currently. Things to think about:

■ Ponder what your total score says about your life at the moment. A score over 100 may indicate that reducing stress should be a top priority for you right now. A score under 50 may indicate that you are currently experiencing tolerable, and even productive, levels of stress.

■ Take a look at how you rated each item, and consider putting particular energy into the areas that you rated the highest. There are two ways to determine where your energy would serve you best: One, focus on any area that you rated a 7 or higher. Two, focus on the five areas that you rated highest, no matter what number you gave them.

School and community resources can help you manage whatever level of stress you are experiencing. On a separate sheet of paper or in a digital file, write down names, locations, hours, phone numbers, URLs, and any other pertinent information for the following resources:

■ Free counseling offered to students

■ Exercise facility

■ Sexual assault center

■ Other resource

Adapted in part from Kohn, P.M., K. Lafreniere, and M. Gurevich, "The Inventory of College Students' Recent Life Experiences: A Decontaminated Hassles Scale for a Special Population." *Journal of Behavioral Medicine*, vol. 13, no. 6, pp. 619–630. New York, NY: Springer Publishing, 1990.

Wellness and Stress Management

If you recognize yourself in any of these descriptions, risk asking for help from a counselor who can offer the reward of care and understanding. Contact your student health center or counseling center. For general advice about mental health issues, visit the Campus Mental Health: Know Your Rights! website found at www.bazelon.org. The right help can change—or, in some cases, even save—your life.

HOW CAN YOU MAKE EFFECTIVE
decisions about alcohol, tobacco, and drugs?

The stresses of college lead some students to experiment with alcohol, tobacco, and other potentially addictive substances. Although these substances may alleviate stress temporarily, they have potentially serious consequences and often derail you from your goals. As you read the information in this section, think about the effects of your actions on yourself and others. Measure the risk of substance use against the social risk of going against what others are doing, and decide which reward is more valuable to you. Continually look for ways to make positive, life-affirming choices.

You are responsible for analyzing the potential consequences of what you introduce into your body. Critical thinking questions can help you identify reasons for your choices and allow you to analyze potential effects of your actions. Ask questions like the following:

- Why do I want to do this?
- Am I doing this to escape from other problems?
- What positive and negative effects might my behavior have?
- Why do others want me to take drugs, and what do I really think of these people?
- How would my actions affect the people in my life?

Alcohol

Alcohol is a depressant and the most frequently abused drug on campus. Even a few drinks affect thinking and muscle coordination. Heavy drinking can damage the liver, digestive system, and brain cells, as well as impair the central nervous system. Prolonged use also leads to physical and emotional *addiction* (a compulsive need for a habit-forming substance). In fact, alcohol contributes to the deaths of 75,000 people every year through both alcohol-related illnesses and accidents involving drunk drivers.[7]

According to the Center for Disease Control (CDC), your tolerance and reaction to alcohol depend on a variety of factors including, but not limited to: age, gender, race or ethnicity, physical condition, the amount of food consumed before drinking, how quickly alcohol was consumed, use of drugs or prescription medications, and family history.[8] Key 11.2 shows the varying levels of drinking behaviors defined by the CDC.

Of all alcohol consumption, *binge drinking* is associated with the greatest problems, and is consistently an issue on college campuses, with over 42% of full-time students and over 35% of part-time students reporting a binge drinking episode in the month prior to the survey.[9] Students who binge drink are more likely to miss classes, perform poorly, experience physical problems (memory loss, headache, stomach issues), become depressed, and engage in unplanned or unsafe sex.[10] If you drink, think carefully about the effects on your health, safety, and academic performance.

Tobacco

In the United States, one in four men smoke, and one in five women smoke. Unfortunately, cigarette smoking still tops the list as the most preventable cause of death in the United States today, accounting for 438,000 deaths annually. That's like three jumbo jets filled to capacity crashing in the United States every single day, 365 days a year, killing everyone on board.[11]

Many students who use tobacco as a stress reliever become hooked on nicotine, a highly addictive drug found in all tobacco products. Nicotine's immediate effects may

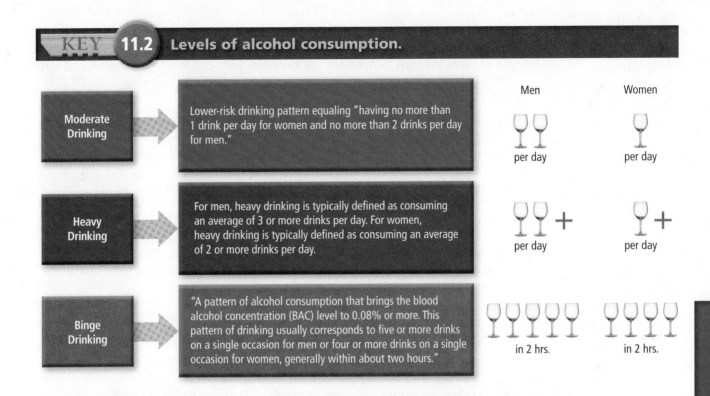

KEY **11.2** **Levels of alcohol consumption.**

Moderate Drinking	Lower-risk drinking pattern equaling "having no more than 1 drink per day for women and no more than 2 drinks per day for men."
Heavy Drinking	For men, heavy drinking is typically defined as consuming an average of 3 or more drinks per day. For women, heavy drinking is typically defined as consuming an average of 2 or more drinks per day.
Binge Drinking	"A pattern of alcohol consumption that brings the blood alcohol concentration (BAC) level to 0.08% or more. This pattern of drinking usually corresponds to five or more drinks on a single occasion for men or four or more drinks on a single occasion for women, generally within about two hours."

Source: Centers for Disease Control. "Alcohol and Public Health." October 14, 2011. Accessed on October 28, 2011, from http://www.cdc.gov/alcohol/index.htm

include an increase in blood pressure and heart rate, sweating, and throat irritation. Long-term effects may include high blood pressure, bronchitis and emphysema, stomach ulcers, heart disease, and cancer. Although advertisers try to convince you smoking is sexy, an estimated 1 billion people will die from tobacco-related illnesses worldwide in the 21st century.[12]

If you smoke regularly, you can quit by being motivated, persevering, and seeking help. The positive effects of quitting—increased life expectancy, lung capacity, and energy, better skin, and less body odor, as well as significant financial savings—may inspire any smoker to make a lifestyle change. If you're interested in quitting, investigate quitting resources at the Center for Disease Control (on their website, click on "S" to find "Smoking and Tobacco Use").

Drugs

College students may use drugs to relieve stress, to be accepted by peers, or just to try something new. In most cases, however, the negative consequences of drug use outweigh any temporary high. Drug use violates federal, state, and local laws, and you may be arrested, tried, and imprisoned for possessing even a small amount of drugs. You can jeopardize your reputation, your student status, and your ability to get a job if you are caught using drugs or if drug use impairs your performance. Finally, long-term drug use can damage your body and mind. Search at www.cdc.gov for information about the potential effects of different types of drugs.

Facing Addiction

If you think you may be addicted, seek help through counseling and medical centers, detoxification centers, and support groups. Because substances often cause physical changes and psychological dependence, habits are tough to break and quitting may involve a painful withdrawal. Asking for help isn't an admission of failure but a calculated risk that can earn you the reward of reclaiming your life.

Working through substance-abuse problems can lead to restored health and self-respect. Helpful resources can help you generate options and develop practical plans for recovery.

- *Counseling and medical care.* You can find help from school-based, private, government-sponsored, or workplace-sponsored resources in person or, in many cases, online. Ask your school's counseling or health center, your personal physician, or a local hospital for a referral.
- *Detoxification ("detox") centers.* If you have a severe addiction, you may need a controlled environment where you can separate yourself completely from drugs or alcohol, including the people and places associated with it.
- *Support groups.* Alcoholics Anonymous (AA) has led to other support groups for addicts such as Overeaters Anonymous (OA) and Narcotics Anonymous (NA). These groups are free, effective, anonymous, and meet in almost every city of the United States, almost every day of the week.

HOW CAN YOU MAKE EFFECTIVE
decisions about sex?

You choose what sexuality means to you and the role it plays in your life, and how you identify sexually is your personal business. However, the decisions you make go beyond the personal realm. Because sexual conduct can result in an unexpected pregnancy or passing on sexually transmitted infections (STIs), consequences can extend for years and can affect both the people involved in the act as well as their families.

Your success in school also depends on making choices that maintain health and safety—yours as well as those of others with whom you may be involved. Analyze sexual issues carefully. Look at potential effects of your choices, determine what rewards hold value for you, and consider what calculated risks can move you safely toward those rewards. Remember that sex needs to be a mutual decision. If you feel pressured and uncomfortable, the time is not right.

Birth Control

Using birth control is a choice that helps you decide when and if you want to be a parent. However, it is not for everyone. Evaluate the pros and cons of each option for yourself and your partner. Consider cost, reliability, comfort, and protection against sexually transmitted infections (STIs). Communicate with your partner, then make a choice together. For more information, check your library, the Internet, or a bookstore; talk to your doctor; or ask a counselor at the student health center or local Planned Parenthood office.

Sexually Transmitted Infections

STIs spread through sexual contact. This includes intercourse or other sexual activity that involves contact with the genitals. All STIs are highly contagious. The only birth control methods that offer protection are the male and female condoms (latex or polyurethane only), which prevent skin-to-skin contact. Have a doctor examine any irregularity or discomfort as soon as you detect it.

The most serious STI is AIDS (acquired immune deficiency syndrome), caused by the human immunodeficiency virus (HIV). AIDS has no cure and can result in death. Medical science continues to develop drugs to combat AIDS and related illnesses. Although the drugs can slow the progression of the infection and extend life expectancy, there is currently no known cure.

People acquire HIV through sexual relations, by sharing hypodermic needles for drug use, and by receiving infected blood transfusions. You cannot become infected unless one of those fluids is involved. Therefore, it is unlikely you can contract HIV from toilet seats, hugging, kissing, or sharing a glass. Other than not having sex at all, using condoms (latex only) is the best defense against AIDS. Avoid petroleum jelly, which can destroy latex. Be wary of "safe sex fatigue," where young and healthy people get tired of being vigilant about using condoms for every sexual encounter. Although some people dislike using condoms, it's a small price to pay for preserving your life.

To be safe, get an HIV test at your doctor's office or at a government-sponsored clinic. Your school's health department may also administer HIV tests, and home HIV tests are available over the counter. Consider requiring any of your sexual partners to be tested as well. If you are infected, inform all sexual partners and seek medical assistance. If you're interested in contacting support organizations in your area, call the National AIDS Hotline at 1-800-342-AIDS. Additionally, for more information on different types of STIs, look online at reliable sites such as www.cdc.gov or www.mayoclinic.com.

Personal Safety Strategies

Crime is a reality on campus as it is in any community. Alcohol and drug-related offenses may occur more frequently than other crimes on campus. College-age females are particularly vulnerable to sexual assault. Making intelligent choices is a crucial part of staying safe. Take these practical measures to prevent incidents that jeopardize your well-being.

Be aware of safety issues. Every college has its particular issues—problematic areas of the campus, particular celebrations that get out of hand, bad habits such as students propping open security doors. With awareness, you can steer clear of problems and even work to improve them.

Avoid situations that present clear dangers. Don't walk or exercise alone at night, especially in isolated areas. Don't work or study alone in a building. If a person looks suspicious, contact someone who can help.

Avoid drugs or overuse of alcohol. Anything that impairs judgment makes you vulnerable to assault. Avoid driving while impaired or riding with someone who has taken drugs or alcohol. Avoid attending large parties where people are binge drinking. It's too easy for rape to occur when someone is inebriated.

Avoid people who make you uneasy. If you feel threatened by anyone inside or outside of classes, tell an instructor or campus security. If you feel uncomfortable with someone, trust your intuition and get away from him or her. Stay alert and make no assumptions. Danger can lurk even with a friend whom you think you can trust.

Be wary of dangers online. Don't give out personal information online to people whom you don't know well. If you have a Facebook page or Instagram, be careful about the text and photos you post. If you feel that someone is harassing you by email or IM, contact an advisor or counselor (you may want to save the messages as proof of harassment).

Complete the following on paper or in digital format.

KNOW IT *Think Critically*

Move toward Better Health

Pick a behavior—eating, drinking, sleeping, sexual activity—that holds some kind of issue for you. Describe your behavior and your attitude toward what you do.

Example: *Issue:* binge drinking
Behavior: I binge drink probably once a week.
Attitude: I don't think it's any big deal. I like using it to escape.

Question to think about: Is it worth it?

Examine whether your behavior is a problem by noting positive and negative effects. To continue the example above:

Positive effects: I have fun with my friends. I feel confident, accepted, social.
Negative effects: I feel foggy the next day. I miss class. I'm irritable.

Based on the effects of your behavior, think about where you want to make a difference, and why. Then describe changes you could make by answering the following questions. For example, the binge drinker might consider investigating one new social activity that does not involve drinking.

1. How might you change your behavior?
2. How might you change your attitude?
3. What positive effects do you think these changes would have?

Commit to these actions to put positive change in motion. Describe your plan, including specific steps and a time frame.

WRITE IT *Communicate*

Managing stress. Look back at the Get Practical exercise on page 127 of this lesson. Note the stressors you have experienced in the past month. Identify the three that cause you the most significant stress at this point in time. Discuss each, giving an example of its effects. Finally, present any ideas you have for reducing and/or coping with these stressors in your life.

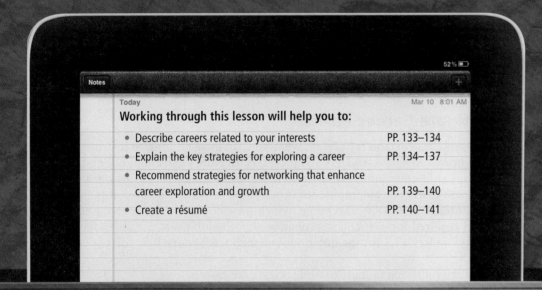

Careers and More

BUILDING A SUCCESSFUL FUTURE

THIS LESSON DEFINES *TRANSFERABLE SKILLS* AND TEACHES HOW SKILLS YOU BUILD IN SCHOOL SERVE YOU ON THE JOB. YOU WILL LEARN STRATEGIES FOR CONDUCTING AN EFFECTIVE JOB SEARCH AND HOW YOUR WORK THIS TERM WILL SUPPORT YOUR SUCCESS IN COLLEGE AND BEYOND.

52% 🔋

Notes ✛

Today   Mar 10   8:01 AM

Working through this lesson will help you to:

• Describe careers related to your interests   PP. 133–134

• Explain the key strategies for exploring a career   PP. 134–137

• Recommend strategies for networking that enhance
  career exploration and growth   PP. 139–140

• Create a résumé   PP. 140–141

HOW CAN YOU PREPARE
for career success?

College provides a once-in-a-lifetime opportunity to explore yourself and the careers available to you. The earlier you take the risk to consider career goals, the greater reward you can receive from your education and college resources, which can prepare you for work in both job-specific and general ways. Ideally, your career will reflect your values and talents and reward you with the income you need. Read on about more career preparation strategies including considering your personality and strengths, exploring majors, investigating career paths, building knowledge and experience, knowing what employers want, and creating a strategic plan.

Consider Your Personality and Strengths

Because who you are as a learner relates closely to who you are as a worker, results from learning assessments provide clues in the search for the right career. For example,

MyStudentSuccessLab
(www.mystudentsuccesslab.com)
is an online solution designed
to help you "Start Strong, Finish
Stronger" by building skills for
ongoing personal and
professional development.

Taking courses in an area of interest can help you see how well a job in this area might suit you. These students get hands-on experience in respiratory therapy as well as advice from an experienced instructor.

the Multiple Intelligences assessment points to information about your natural strengths and challenges, which can lead you to careers that involve these strengths. Look at Key 12.1 to see how those intelligences may link up with various careers.

Even the most ideal job involves some tasks outside of your comfort zone. Remember to approach the information in Key 12.1 as a guide, not a label. Your self-knowledge is a starting point for your goals about how you want to grow.

Finally, one other way to investigate how your personality and strengths may inform career choice is to take an inventory based on the Holland Theory. Theorizing that personality was related to career choice, psychologist John Holland came up with six different types that identify both personality and career areas: **Realistic**, **Investigative**, **Artistic**, **Social**, **Enterprising**, and **Conventional** (together known as **RIASEC**).[1] Holland developed two interest surveys that allow people to identify their order of preference for the six types and help them link their stronger types to career areas. Ask your career center about these surveys: the Vocational Preference Inventory (VPI®) or Self-Directed Search (SDS®).

Investigate Career Paths

Career possibilities extend far beyond what you can imagine. Talk to instructors, relatives, mentors, and fellow students about careers. Explore job listings, occupation lists, assessments, and other information at your school's career center. Check your library for books on careers or biographies of people who worked in fields that interest you. Visit websites such as O*NET Online, which provides information about education and skills required for particular occupations, on-the-job tasks, possible salaries, and more. Look at Key 12.2 for the questions you might ask yourself as you conduct your research.

Keep the following in mind as your investigate careers:

A wide array of job possibilities exists for most career fields. For example, the medical world consists of more than doctors and nurses. Administrators run hospitals, researchers test drugs, pharmacists prepare prescriptions, security experts ensure patient and visitor safety, and so on.

Within each job, there is a variety of tasks to perform. For instance, you may know that an instructor teaches, but you may not think about the fact that instructors may also write, research, study, design courses, give presentations, counsel, and coach. Take your career exploration beyond first impressions to get an accurate picture of the careers that interest you.

Some career areas are growing more than others. If you have an interest in a growing career area, statistically you will have a better chance of finding a job. According to government data, careers projected to grow through the year 2014 include nursing, teaching, general and operations managers, accountants, and more.[2] Look up the U.S. Bureau of Labor's Occupational Outlook Handbook for projected growth, as well as average salary information, in different fields.

MULTIPLE INTELLIGENCE	LOOK INTO A CAREER AS ...
Bodily-Kinesthetic	• Carpenter or draftsman • Physical therapist • Mechanical engineer • Dancer or actor • Exercise physiologist
Intrapersonal	• Research scientist • Computer engineer • Psychologist • Economist • Author
Interpersonal	• Social worker • PR or HR rep • Sociologist • Teacher • Nurse
Naturalistic	• Biochemical engineer • Natural scientist (geologist, ecologist, entomologist) • Paleontologist • Position with environmental group • Farmer or farm management
Musical	• Singer or voice coach • Music teacher • Record executive • Musician or conductor • Radio DJ or sound engineer
Logical-Mathematical	• Doctor or dentist • Accountant • Attorney • Chemist • Investment banker
Verbal-Linguistic	• Author or journalist • TV/radio producer • Literature or language teacher • Business executive • Copywriter or editor
Visual-Spatial	• Graphic artist or illustrator • Photographer • Architect or interior designer • Art museum curator • Art teacher • Set or retail stylist

Explore Majors

You probably have explored majors at other times during this course, perhaps as choosing a major relates to goal setting and self-knowledge. Look to previous ideas and work for guidance as you continue and extend your exploration.

What can I do in this area that I like and do well?	Do I respect the company or the industry? The product or service?
What are the educational requirements (certificates or degrees, courses)?	Does this company or industry accommodate special needs (childcare, sick days, flex time)?
What skills are necessary?	Do I need to belong to a union? What does union membership involve?
What wage or salary and benefits can I expect?	Are there opportunities near where I live (or want to live)?
What personality types are best suited to this kind of work?	What other expectations exist (travel, overtime, and so on)?
What are the prospects for moving up to higher-level positions?	Do I prefer the service or production end of this industry?

Focus on your interests and abilities. Countless sources of career advice make the point that pursuing a passion is a key element of career success. This doesn't mean that you'll love every aspect or every day of your job—no one does. However, you improve your chances of thriving if you spend the bulk of your job doing work that interests you and taps into your strengths.

Examine what your school offers. Even if you plan to transfer eventually, your school's major and certificate programs are an important aspect of your exploration. Look online and in the catalog to see what is offered. Meet with an advisor to discuss the options.

Consider career interests. If you are interested in one or more careers, investigate majors that may link to them—but don't narrow the field too much. An advisor can help you define which careers need specific majors and which are accessible from a broader range of educational backgrounds. For example, students going into medical professions usually need to major in a science or pre-med area, while students planning to pursue careers in business might major in anything from history to economics. Business owners are becoming more aware of how liberal arts majors bring value to the workplace through skills such as problem solving and writing.[3]

Build Knowledge and Experience

Even after comprehensive investigation, it's hard to choose the right path without knowledge or experience. Courses, internships, jobs, and volunteering are risks that promote those rewards.

Courses. Take a course or two in your areas of interest to determine if you like the material and excel in it. Find out what courses are required for a major in those areas. Check out your school's course catalogue for detailed information. Also, consider talking with the department chair, or an older student who has taken some of the courses, to gain more insight into the field.

Internships. An *internship*—a temporary work program in which a student can gain supervised practical experience in a particular professional field—gives you a chance to work in your chosen field to see how you like it. Your career center may list summer or year-round internship opportunities. For more comprehensive guides, check out reference books like those published by Vault, as well as Internet sources like Internships .com and Princeton Review.

Jobs. You may discover career opportunities while earning money during a part-time job. Someone who takes a legal proofreading job to make extra cash might discover an interest in law. Someone who answers phones for a newspaper company might be drawn into journalism.

Volunteering. Helping others in need offers rewards including an introduction to careers, experience, new contacts, and a positive impression on potential employers. Many schools sponsor volunteer groups or have committees that organize volunteering opportunities. The federal government encourages volunteerism through AmeriCorps, a federal volunteer clearinghouse, which awards its volunteers money to pay for tuition or student loans.

Service learning. The goal of service learning is to provide the community with service and give students knowledge gained from hands-on experience.[4] Students in service learning programs enroll in credit-bearing courses where service and related assignments are required. Taking the risk of service learning can reward you with a sense of civic responsibility, opportunity to apply what you learn in the classroom, and personal growth. If you are interested, talk to your advisor about whether your school offers service learning programs.

Know What Employers Want

If you want to enter the job market or are already in it, know that prospective employers look for particular skills and qualities that mark you as a promising candidate. Most employers require you to have a *skillset* (the knowledge and abilities needed to perform a specific job) that includes technical know-how, but in this rapidly-changing workplace, transferable skills may be even more crucial to your success.

Transferable skills

In the modern workplace, workers will hold an average of 11 jobs through their productive working years.[5] The high rate of job change means that abilities such as successful thinking and teamwork are crucial to workplace success and can transfer from one job or career to another. For example, you will need teamwork and writing skills for almost any job. Key 12.3 describes transferable skills that employers seek.

Emotional intelligence

Employers are also drawn to emotionally intelligent job candidates. Consider this scenario: You arrive at work distracted by a personal problem and tired from studying late the night before. Your supervisor is overloaded with a major project due that day. The person you work most closely with is coming in late due to a car problem. Everyone is stressed out. What does an emotionally intelligent person do?

- *Tune in to everyone's emotions first.* You: Tired and distracted. Your co-worker: Worried about the car and about being late. Your supervisor: Agitated about the project.
- *Pinpoint the thoughts that arise from these emotions.* People are likely to think that the deadline is in jeopardy.
- *Understand what the emotions are telling you.* Thinking that the deadline may not be met means that everyone is going to need an extra-focused and positive state of mind to get through the day and set aside distracted, negative thinking.

- *Manage the emotion with action.* You come up with a plan:

   1. Prioritize your task list so that you can concentrate on what is most pressing.
   2. Call your co-worker on his cell phone while he settles the car problem and let him know what's happening so he can prioritize tasks and support the supervisor when he arrives.
   3. Ask another co-worker to bring in a favorite mid-morning snack to keep everyone going during the long day ahead.

The current emphasis on teamwork has highlighted emotional intelligence in the workplace. The more adept you are at working with others, the more likely you are to succeed.

Create a Strategic Plan

After your exploration has led you to jobs or careers that interest you, get specific and create a plan for how you will pursue one or more of them. Establish the risks that make up this plan—whom you will talk to, what courses you will take, what skills you

KEY 12.3 **Employers look for candidates with these important skills.**

SKILL	WHY IS IT USEFUL?
Communication	Good listening, speaking, and writing skills are keys to working with others, as is being able to adjust to different communication styles.
Analytical thinking	Employees stand out when they can analyze choices and challenges, as well as assess the value of new ideas.
Creativity	The ability to come up with new concepts, plans, and products helps companies improve and innovate.
Practical thinking	No job gets done without employees who can think through a plan for achieving a goal, put it into action, and complete it successfully.
Teamwork	All workers interact with others on the job. Working well with others is essential for achieving workplace goals.
Goal setting	Teams fail if goals are unclear or unreasonable. Employees and companies benefit from setting realistic, specific goals, and achieving them reliably.
Cultural competence	The workplace is increasingly diverse. Employees are valued when they can work with, adjust to, and respect people from different backgrounds and cultures.
Leadership	The ability to influence and motivate others in a positive way earns respect and career advancement.
Positive attitude	Other employees will gladly work with, and often advance, someone who completes tasks with positive, upbeat energy.
Integrity	Acting with integrity at work enhances value. This includes communicating promptly, being truthful and honest, following rules, and giving proper notice.
Flexibility	The most valuable employees understand the constancy of change and have developed the skills to adapt to its challenge.
Continual learning	The most valuable employees take personal responsibility to stay current in their fields.

will work on, what jobs or internships you will investigate, and any other tasks. Be proactive in finding opportunities. But keep your plan flexible, seeing it as a structure to guide your actions, and knowing that there may be possibilities yet unknown to you.

With your knowledge of general workplace success strategies, you can search effectively for a job in a career area that works for you.

HOW CAN YOU CONDUCT
an effective job search?

Whether you are looking for a job now or planning ahead for a search closer to graduation, you have choices about how to proceed. In this challenging economy and struggling job market, finding the right job—or any job—may be tougher than you anticipated. Use resources available to you, know the basics about résumés and interviews, and plan strategically.

Use Available Resources

Use your school's career planning and placement office, your networking skills, classified ads, and online services to help you explore possibilities for career areas or specific jobs.

Your school's career planning and placement office

Generally, the career planning and placement office deals with post-graduation job opportunities, whereas the student employment office and financial aid office provide information about working during school. At either location—in person or online at the office's website—you might find job listings, interview sign-up sheets, and company contact information. The career office may hold informational workshops on different topics. Your school may also sponsor job or career fairs where you can meet potential employers and explore job opportunities. Get acquainted with the career office early in your college career.

Networking

Networking refers to the exchange of information or services among individuals, groups, or institutions. The most basic type of networking—talking to people about fields and jobs that interest you—is one of the most important job-hunting strategies. Networking *contacts* can answer questions regarding job hunting, job responsibilities and challenges, and salary expectations. Risk reaching out to friends and family members, instructors, administrators, counselors, alumni, employers, coworkers, and others for the reward of the help they can offer you.

Online social networking is another useful tool to help you in your job search. Tools like LinkedIn, Facebook, and Twitter allow members to connect with other individuals through groups, fan pages, and similar interests. During a job search, these sites can be used to meet people who work at companies you are interested in and showcase portfolio pieces. Businesses often search through LinkedIn profiles when they have job openings, so you never know who may contact you. However, online networking is no substitute for personal interaction—eventually you will have to talk to someone by phone or in person.

A word of caution: Your online presence is public. If you wouldn't want a potential employer (or your parents, instructor, or religious leader) to see something, don't

Take advantage of career fairs sponsored by your school or town. These career fair attendees pick up useful information and applications from a variety of employers.

Careers and More

post it. In fact, many employers review Facebook pages of applicants before inviting them for interviews.

Online services and classified ads

When jobs get advertised, they generate a lot of competition. However, it doesn't hurt to look at job advertisements. Although classified ads are still helpful for local possibilities, the Internet—with its enormous information storage capabilities and low cost—is a better location for job postings. Many employers post detailed job openings through online job boards. In addition to a job description and salary information, most online postings will contain company information and a link to where you can submit an application. To get the most out of your virtual resources:

- Join a business-focused social networking site, like LinkedIn, and look at jobs posted there. Network with your contacts to find out about upcoming and existing openings.
- Check the web pages of individual associations and companies, which may post job listings and descriptions.
- Look up career-focused and job listing websites such as CareerBuilder.com, Monster.com, America's Job Bank, BilingualCareer.com, JobBankUSA, or futurestep.com. Many sites offer resources on career areas, résumés, and online job searching in addition to job listings.
- Access job search databases such as the Career Placement Registry and U.S. Employment Opportunities.

If you apply for a position and nothing happens right away, follow up with a short email, or mail a hard copy version of your résumé with a note that you are still interested, or call and ask the status of the application process. Keep in mind that statistically, networking results in far more hires than online posting. Some experts recommend you spend no more than 10 to 20% of your time responding to online job sites.[6] You don't risk much with this activity, but your chances for reward are likewise low.

Use an Organized, Consistent Strategy

Organize your approach according to what you need to do and when you have to do it. Do you plan to make three phone calls per day? Will you fill out one job application each week? Keep a record—on 3-by-5 cards, in a computer file or smartphone, or in a notebook—of the following:

- People you contact plus contact information and method of contact (email, snail mail, phone)
- Companies to which you apply
- Jobs for which you apply, including those you rule out (for example, a job that becomes unavailable)
- Responses to communications (phone calls to you, interviews, written communications), information about the person who contacted you (name, title), and the time and dates of contact

Keeping accurate records allows you to both chart your progress and maintain a clear picture of the process. Your records help you follow up and stay in touch. If you don't get a job now but another opens up later at the same company, well-kept records will enable you to contact key personnel efficiently.

Your Résumé, Cover Letter, and Interview

"How-to" information about résumés, cover letters, and interviews fills entire books. To get you started, here are a few basic tips on giving yourself the best possible chance.

Cover letter and résumé

Cover letters and résumés are how you introduce yourself to prospective employers on paper so they will want to meet you in person. The purpose of the cover letter is to get the reader's attention so he or she will read your résumé. And the purpose of your résumé is to get the reader interested enough to call you in for an interview.

Keep your cover letter short and focused on the job and company you are interested in. A good cover letter usually covers four main points:

1. The position for which you are applying and how you learned about it
2. Why you are the best person for the job (your abilities)
3. Why you want to work for the employer
4. A call to action (how you plan to follow up)

Design your résumé neatly, using a current and acceptable format (books or your career office can show you some standard formats). Make sure the information is accurate and truthful. Proofread it for errors and have someone else proofread it as well. Type or print it on high-quality paper (a heavier bond paper than is used for ordinary copies). Include your cover letter on top of your résumé (but don't staple them together).

Prospective employers often use a computer to scan résumés, selecting the ones that contain *keywords* relating to the job opening or industry. Résumés without enough keywords probably won't even make it to the human resources desk. When you construct your résumé, make sure to include relevant keywords. For example, if you are seeking a computer-related job, list computer programs you use and other specific technical proficiencies. To figure out what keywords you need, look at the job descriptions and job postings and search online for examples of keywords related to your career interest.[7]

Interview

Be clean, neat, and appropriately dressed. Avoid tight or baggy clothing, extreme hairstyles, and flashy jewelry. Choose a nice pair of shoes—people notice (avoid spiky heels if you are a woman). You want interviewers to focus on you and your achievements, not your appearance.

Bring an extra copy of your résumé and any other materials that you want to show the interviewer, even if you sent a copy ahead of time. Avoid chewing gum and fidgeting. Don't text or check your Instagram—as a matter of fact, put all electronic devices away completely so you are not tempted to use them. Offer a confident handshake. Make eye contact. Show your integrity by speaking honestly about yourself. After the interview, no matter what the outcome, follow up right away with a formal but pleasant thank-you note.

Being on time to your interview makes a positive impression—and being late will almost certainly be held against you. If you are from a culture that does not consider being late a sign of disrespect, remember that your interviewer may not agree.

HOW CAN YOU CONTINUE TO GROW
as a risk taker and thinker?

You leave this course with far more than a final grade, a notebook or computer file full of work, and a credit hour or three on your transcript. You leave with a set of skills and attitudes that open the door to success in the 21st century.

Continue to Activate Your Successful Intelligence

Much as finding a job is the beginning of your career adventure, finishing this course is the beginning of your life as a calculated risk taker and successfully intelligent learner.

get analytical

To see how you use successful intelligence in your daily life, assess your perceived development on these motivating characteristics. Circle the number that best represents your answer, with 1 being "not at all like me" and 5 being "definitely like me."

1	2	3	4	5
Not at All Like Me	Somewhat Unlike Me	Not Sure	Somewhat Like Me	Definitely Like Me

1. I am able to translate ideas into action. 1 2 3 4 5

2. I am able to maintain confidence in myself. 1 2 3 4 5

3. I can stay on track toward a goal. 1 2 3 4 5

4. I complete tasks and have good follow-through. 1 2 3 4 5

5. I avoid procrastination. 1 2 3 4 5

6. I accept responsibility when I make a mistake. 1 2 3 4 5

7. I independently take responsibility for tasks. 1 2 3 4 5

8. I work hard to overcome personal difficulties. 1 2 3 4 5

9. I create an environment that helps me to concentrate on my goals. 1 2 3 4 5

10. I can delay gratification to receive the benefits. 1 2 3 4 5

If you completed this self-assessment at the beginning of the course, look back at your original scores. On a piece of paper or in a digital file, describe three changes over the course of the term that feel significant to you.

Finally, choose one self-activator that you feel still needs work. Analyze the specific reasons why it remains a challenge. For example, if you are still taking on too much work, is it because you want to please others? Write a one-paragraph analysis, and let this analysis guide you as you work to build your strength in this area.

How can you stay motivated to keep thinking and risking? Earlier in this course, you may have completed a self-assessment to examine your levels of development in some characteristics that promote action and productive risks. According to Sternberg, successfully intelligent people:[8]

1. *Translate thought into action.* Not only do they have good ideas; they are able to turn those ideas into practical actions that bring ideas to fruition.

2. *Have a reasonable level of self-confidence and a belief in their ability to accomplish their goals.* They believe in themselves enough to get through the tough times, while avoiding the kind of overconfidence that stalls learning and growth, and alienates others.

3. *Know when to persevere.* When the reward is worth the effort, they push past frustration and stay on course, confident that success is in their sights. They also recognize when they've hit a dead end and shift gears in response.

4. *Complete tasks and follow through.* With determination, they finish what they start. They also follow through to make sure loose ends are tied and the goal has been achieved.

5. *Don't procrastinate.* They are aware of the negative effects of putting things off, and they avoid it. They create schedules that allow them to accomplish what's important on time.

6. *Accept fair blame.* They strike a balance between never accepting blame and taking the blame for everything. If something is their fault, they accept responsibility.

7. *Are independent.* They can work on their own and think for themselves. They take responsibility for their own schedule and tasks.

8. *Seek to surmount personal difficulties.* They keep things in perspective, looking for ways to remedy personal problems and separate them from their professional lives.

9. *Focus and concentrate to achieve their goals.* They create an environment in which they can best avoid distraction and they focus steadily on their work.

10. *Have the ability to delay gratification.* They risk effort in the present for the reward of gratifying goal achievement in the future.

These characteristics are your personal motivational tools. Consult them when you need a way to get moving. You may even want to post them somewhere in your home, in the front of a notebook, or as a note in your smartphone. Use the "Get Analytical" exercise to see how you have developed your command of these characteristics over the course of the term.

Learn for Life with a Growth Mindset

Knowledge in many fields is doubling every two to three years, and your personal interests and needs are changing all the time. What you learn in college is just the beginning of what you need to learn throughout your life to succeed. With a growth mindset—the attitude that you can always grow and learn—you are as ready to achieve the goals you set out for yourself today as you are to achieve future goals you cannot yet anticipate.

Throughout this course, you have built your ability in each of the transferable skill areas you explored in Key 12.3. The attitudes and skills you acquired this term are your keys to success now and in the future. As you continue your education, you will further develop these tools that will benefit you in everything you do.

Cope with Change and Challenge

As a citizen of the 21st century, you will experience exciting changes as well as troubling ones. Changes such as job offers and job losses, scholarship offers, or failed courses will arise. Your ability to respond to change with risk taking aimed at a positive reward, especially if the change is unexpected and difficult, is crucial to your future success. The ability to "make lemonade from lemons" is the hallmark of people who know how to hang on to hope.

With successful intelligence, a growth mindset, and learned optimism, you will always have a new direction in which to grow. Your willingness to take calculated, productive risks will allow you to put these valuable tools to work and reward you with the achievement of your most valued goals. Risk being true to yourself, a respectful friend and family member, a focused student who believes in the power of learning, a productive employee, and a contributing member of society, to earn the ultimate reward of a meaningful life—a life that can change the world.

Complete the following on paper or in digital format.

KNOW IT *Think Critically*

Your Strategic Timeline

Considering your self-knowledge, experience, possible career paths, and understanding of the workplace, create a practical five-year timeline as a strategic plan to achieve a career goal. First, describe where you do want to be in five years. For each of the following time frames, write in the steps you think you will need to take toward that five-year goal. Include anything you envision in your path toward a career, such as steps related to declaring a major or a transfer to another school to pursue additional degrees.

- One month from now...
- Three months from now...
- Six months from now...
- One year from now...
- Two years from now...
- Three years from now...
- Four years from now...

Finally, create a timeline version of your plan, using a visual format you like and adding smaller goals as necessary. Keep your timeline where you can refer to it and revise it, since changes in the world and in your knowledge and experience may require adjustments in your plan.

WRITE IT *Communicate*

Create your personal mission. If you explored personal mission earlier in your course materials, look back at the description. Using Stephen Covey's personal mission definition (character, contributions, and values) as a guide, write your own personal mission statement that explains who you want to be (your character), what goals you want to achieve (your contributions), and the principles by which you want to live (your values). Consider this to be the statement by which you will live your life and accomplish your dreams. To generate ideas, you might imagine what your best friend would say at your retirement dinner.

CHAPTER 1

1. "Attitudes and Characteristics of Freshmen at 4-year Colleges, Fall 2007." *The Chronicle of Higher Education: 2008–9 Almanac,* vol. 55, issue 1, p.18. Data from "The American Freshman: National Norms for Fall 2007." University of California at Los Angeles Higher Education Research Institute.

2. Information in this section from the following sources: U.S. Census Bureau. "Average Earnings of Year-Round, Full-Time Workers by Educational Attainment: 2007." Current Population Reports, Series, P60-235, August 2008; U.S. Department of Labor, Bureau of Labor Statistics, Office of Employment and Unemployment Statistics. "Employment and Earnings." January 2005; Institute for Higher Education Policy. "Reaping the Benefits: Defining the Public and Private Value of Going to College." Washington, DC: The New Millennium Project on Higher Education Costs, Pricing, and Productivity, 1998.

3. Sternberg, Robert J. *Successful Intelligence: How Practical and Creative Intelligence Determine Success in Life.* New York: Plume, 1997, pp. 85–90; Dweck, Carol S. *Mindset: The New Psychology of Success.* New York: Random House, 2006, p. 5; and Jaeggi, Susanne, Martin Buschkuehl, John Jonides, and Walter J. Perrig, "Improving fluid intelligence with training on working memory," 2008, Proceedings of the National Acadamy of Sciences USA 105:6829–6833.

4. The Society for Neuroscience. *Brain Facts: A Primer on the Brain and Neurosystem.* Washington, DC: The Society for Neuroscience, 2008, pp. 34–35.

5. Sternberg, p. 12.

6. Dweck, Carol. *Mindset: The New Psychology of Success,* New York: Random House, Inc., 2006.

7. Dweck, *Mindset,* p. 16.

8. Ibid.

9. Center for Academic Integrity, "The Fundamental Values of Academic Integrity." October 1999. From http://www.academicintegrity.org/fundamental_values_project/pdf/FVProject.pdf

10. From "Facts About Plagiarism," 2007. From http://www.plagiarism.org/facts.html

11. Mayer, John D., Peter Salovey, and David R. Caruso. "Emotional Intelligence: New Ability or Eclectic Traits?" *American Psychologist,* vol. 63, no. 6, September 2008, p. 503.

12. Ibid., pp. 510–512.

13. Covey, Stephen. *The Seven Habits of Highly Effective People.* New York: Simon & Schuster, 1989, pp. 70–144, 309–318.

14. Based on Sternberg, pp. 251–268.

CHAPTER 2

1. Timm, Paul. *Successful Self-Management: A Psychologically Sound Approach to Personal Effectiveness.* Los Altos, CA: Crisp Publications, 1987, pp. 22–41.

2. Brody, Jane E. "At Every Age, Feeling the Effects of Too Little Sleep." *New York Times,* October 23, 2007. From http://www.nytimes.com/2007/10/23/health/23brod.html

3. Burka, Jane B., and Lenora M. Yuen. *Procrastination: Why You Do It, What to Do About It.* Reading, MA: Perseus Books, 1983, pp. 21–22.

4. Schwarz, Tony. "Four Destructive Myths Most Companies Still Live By." *Harvard Business Review,* November 1, 2011. From http://blogs.hbr.org/schwartz/2011/11/four-destructive-myths-most-co.html

5. "Takeaways and Quotes from Dr. John Medina's Brain Rules." Slideshare presentation, Slide 79. From http://www.presentationzen.com/presentationzen/2008/05/brain-rules-for.html

6. Schwartz.

CHAPTER 3

1. Hanson, Jim. "Your Money Personality: It's All In Your Head." University Credit Union, December 25, 2006. From http://hffo.cuna.org/012433/article/1440/html

2. Ibid.

3. "Attitudes and Characteristics of Freshmen at 4-Year Colleges, Fall 2007." Chronicle of Higher Education.

4. Tomsho, Robert. "The Best Ways to Get Loans for College Now." *The Wall Street Journal,* August 13, 2008, p. D1.

5. Supiano, Beckie. "In a Rocky Economy, 10 Steady Tips About Student Aid." The Chronicle of Higher Education, November 7, 2008. From http://chronicle.com/article/In-a-Rocky-Economy-10-Stea/1313

6. FinAid.org. "Defaulting on Student Loans." 2010. From http://www.finaid.org/loans/dcfault.phtml

7. Ryman, Anne. "Defaults on Student Loans Rising." *The Arizona Republic,* March 7, 2010. From http://www.azcentral.com/12news/news/articles/2010/03/07/20100307student-loan-defaults-CP.html

8. Woolsey, Ben, and Matt Schulz. "Credit Card Statistics, Industry Facts, Debt Statistics." CreditCards.com, January 15, 2010. From http://www.creditcards.com/credit-card-news/credit-card-industry-facts-personal-debt-statistics-1276.php#youngadults

9. "Sallie Mae's National Study of Usage Rates and Trends of Undergraduate Student Credit Card Use." April 2009. From https://www1.salliemae.com/about/news_info/newsreleases/041309.htm

10. Most items in bullet list based on Bowler, Michael. "Watch Out for Credit Card Traps." The Lucrative Investor, 2009. From http://www.thelucrativeinvestor.com/watch-credit-card-traps, and Arnold, Chris. "Credit Card Companies Abuse the Unwitting." NPR, November 6, 2007. From http://www.npr.org/templates/story/story.php?storyId=16035323

11. Curry, Pat. "How credit scores work, how a score is calculated." Bankrate.com, November 8, 2006. From http://www.bankrate.com/brm/news/credit-scoring/20031104a1.asp

12. The University of Arizona. "Young Adults Financial Capability: APLUS Arizona Pathways to Life Success for University Students Wave 2." September 2011, p. 29. From http://aplus.arizona.edu/Wave-2-Report.pdf

CHAPTER 4

1. Ruggiero, Vincent. *Beyond Feelings: A Guide to Critical Thinking,* 9th ed. New York: McGraw-Hill, 2012, p. 19.

2. Paul, Richard. "The Role of Questions in Thinking, Teaching, and Learning," 1995. Accessed April 2004 from http://www.criticalthinking.org/resources/articles/the-role-of-questions.shtml

3. Begley, Sharon. "Critical Thinking: Part Skill, Part Mindset and Totally Up to You." *Wall Street Journal,* October 20, 2006, p. B1.

4. Thomas, Matt. "What Is Higher-Order Thinking and Critical/Creative/Constructive Thinking?" (no date) Center for Studies in Higher-Order Literacy. From http://a-s.clayton.edu/tparks/What%20is%20Higher%20Order%20Thinking.doc

5. Cave, Charles. "Definitions of Creativity." August 1999. From http://members.optusnet.com.au/~charles57/Creative/Basics/definitions.htm

6. Gibson, Jennifer. "The Art of Medicine." *Brain Blogger,* October 31, 2010. From http://brainblogger.com/2010/10/31/the-art-of-medicine

7. Adapted from Tardif, T. Z., and R. J. Sternberg. "What Do We Know About Creativity?" *The Nature of Creativity,* R. J. Sternberg, ed. London: Cambridge University Press, 1988.

8. Sternberg, p. 212.

9. Cain, Susan. "The Rise of the New Groupthink." *New York Times,* January 13, 2012. From http://www.nytimes.com/2012/01/15/opinion/sunday/the-rise-of-the-new-groupthink.html?pagewanted=1&_r=1&smid=fb-nytimes

10. Ibid.

11. Michalko, Michael. "Twelve Things You Were Not Taught in School About Creative Thinking." *Psychology Today,* December 2, 2011. From http://www.psychologytoday.com/blog/creative-thinkering/201112/twelve-things-you-were-not-taught-in-school-about-creative-thinking

12. Ibid.

13. Lehrer, Jonah. "Groupthink." *The New Yorker,* January 30, 2012. From http://www.newyorker.com/reporting/2012/01/30/120130fa_fact_lehrer?currentPage=3

14. Ibid.

15. Sarah Lyman Kravits, 2012.

16. Lehrer, Jonah. *Imagine: How Creativity Works.* New York: Houghton Mifflin Harcourt, 2012, pp. 163–164.

17. Coon, Dennis. *Introduction to Psychology: Exploration and Application,* 6th ed. St. Paul: West, 1992, p. 295.

18. Cain.

19. Sternberg, p. 236.

20. Hayes, J.R. *Cognitive Psychology: Thinking and Creating.* Homewood, IL: Dorsey, 1978.

21. Sternberg, Robert J., and Elena L. Grigorenko. "Practical Intelligence and the Principal." Yale University: Publication Series No. 2, 2001, p. 5.

22. Rosenthal, Normal. "10 Ways to Enhance Your Emotional Intelligence." *Psychology Today,*

January 5, 2012. From http://www.psychologytoday.com/blog/your-mind-your-body/201201/10-ways-enhance-your-emotional-intelligence

23. Sternberg, pp. 251–269.

24. Schwartz, Barry. TED talk. From http://www.ted.com/talks/barry_schwartz_on_our_loss_of_wisdom.html

25. Sternberg, p. 128.

CHAPTER 5

1. Gardner, Howard. *Multiple Intelligences: New Horizons*. New York: Basic Books, 2006, p. 180.

2. Gardner, Howard. *Multiple Intelligences: The Theory in Practice*. New York: HarperCollins, 1993, pp. 5–49.

3. Gardner, *Multiple Intelligences: New Horizons*, p. 8.

4. Gardner, *Multiple Intelligences: The Theory in Practice*, p. 7.

5. Boeree, C. George. "Carl Jung." George Boeree personal website, 2006. From http://webspace.ship.edu/cgboer/jung/html

6. Waters, John K. "Broadband, Social Networks, and Mobility Have Spawned a New Kind of Learner." *The Journal*, December 13, 2011. From http://thejournal.com/Articles/2011/12/13/Broadband-Social-Networks-and-Mobility.aspx?Page=1

CHAPTER 6

1. Tugend, Alina. "Multitasking Can Make You Lose . . . Um . . . Focus." *The New York Times,* October 25, 2008.

2. System developed by Cornell professor Walter Pauk. See Pauk, Walter. *How to Study in College,* 10th ed. Boston: Houghton Mifflin, 2011, pp. 236–241.

3. Klein, Ezra. "Better Note-taking Through Technology." *The Washington Post,* May 16, 2011. From http://www.washingtonpost.com/blogs/ezra-klein/post/better-note-taking-through-technology/2011/05/09/AFMs8z4G_blog.html

CHAPTER 7

1. Robinson, Francis P. *Effective Behavior*. New York: Harper & Row, 1941.

2. Bauerlein, Mark. "Online Literacy is a Lesser Kind." The Chronicle of Higher Education, September 19, 2008. From http://chronicle.com/article/Online-Literacy-Is-a-Lesser/28307

3. Ibid.

CHAPTER 8

1. University of California–Irvine. "Short-term Stress Can Affect Learning And Memory." *ScienceDaily,* March 13, 2008. From http://www.sciencedaily.com/releases/2008/03/080311182434.htm

2. Bulletpoints from Petress, Kenneth C. "The Benefits of Group Study." *Education,* Vol 124, 2004. From http://www.questia.com/googleScholar.qst;jsessionid=L4TDXZJvQmb4whQFL7v1mjGfBgp4YGzjJyg0mL3g1SJKyjvXK4hN!-747430471!743789914?docId=5006987606

3. "Study Shows How Sleep Improves Memory." *Science Daily,* June 29, 2005 From http://www.sciencedaily.com/releases/2005/06/050629070337.htm

4. Speidel, Barbara J. "Overcoming Test Anxiety." Academic Success Center of Southwestern College. From http://www.swccd.edu/~asc/lrnglinks/test_anxiety.html

5. Gwynne, Peter. "The Write Way to Reduce Test Anxiety," Inside Science News Service, January 14, 2011. From http://www.usnews.com/science/articles/2011/01/14/the-write-way-to-reduce-test-anxiety

CHAPTER 9

1. "Conceptual Frameworks/Models, Guiding Values and Principles." National Center for Cultural Competence, 2002. From http://gucchd.georgetown.edu//nccc/framework.html

2. Information in the sections on the five stages of building competency is based on King, Mark A., Anthony Sims, and David Osher. "How Is Cultural Competence Integrated in Education?" Cultural Competence. From http://www.air.org/cecp/cultural/Q_integrated.htm#def

3. Team Technology. "The Basics of Team Building . . . and the Problem With Groups." 2001. From http://www.teamtechnology.co.uk/tt/t-articl/tb-basic.htm

CHAPTER 10

1. American Library Association. *Information Literacy Competency Standards for Higher Education.* Chicago, IL: The Association of College and Research Libraries, 2010, pp. 2–3.

2. Ibid.

3. Leibovich, Lori. "Choosing Quick Hits over the Card Catalog." *New York Times,* August 10, 2001, p. 1.

4. Robinson, Adam. *What Smart Students Know*. New York: Three Rivers Press, 1993, p. 82.

5. Gabriel, Trip. "Plagiarism Lines Blur for Students in Digital Age." *New York Times,* August 1, 2010. From http://www.nytimes.com/2010/08/02/education/02cheat.html?pagewanted=all

CHAPTER 11

1. Mayo Clinic. "Aerobic Exercise: Top 10 Reasons to Get Physical." Mayoclinic.com, 2012. From http://www.mayoclinic.com/health/aerobic-exercise/EP00002/NSECTIONGROUP=2

2. Evans, Mike. "23½ hours." *YouTube,* December 2, 2011. From http://www.youtube.com/watch?v=aUaInS6HIGo

3. CBS News. "Help for Sleep-Deprived Students." April 19, 2004. From http://www.cbsnews.com/stories/2004/04/19/health/main612476.shtml

4. Benson, Herbert, and Eileen M. Stuart, et al. *The Wellness Book.* New York: Simon & Schuster, 1992, p. 292; Jacobs, Gregg. "Life Style Practices That Can Improve Sleep (Parts 1 and 2)." *Talk About Sleep,* 2004. From http://www.talkaboutsleep.com/sleep-disorders/archives/insomnia_drjacobs_lifestyle_part1.htm and http://www.talkaboutsleep.com/sleep-disorders/archives/insomnia_drjacobs_lifestyle_practices_part2.htm

5. Briddon, Mike. "Struggling with Sadness: Depression among College Students Is on the Rise." Stressedoutnurses.com, April 22, 2008. From http://www.stressedoutnurses.com/2008/04/struggling-with-sadness-depression-among-college-students-is-on-the-rise

6. National Eating Disorders Association. "Learning Basic Terms and Information on a Variety of Eating Disorder Topics." 2010. From http://www.nationaleatingdisorders.org/information-resources/general-information.php#facts-statistics

7. "Alcohol Linked to 75,000 U.S. Deaths a Year." MSNBC, June 25, 2005. From http://www.msnbc.msn.com/id/6089353

8. Centers for Disease Control and Prevention. "Alcohol and Public Health: Frequently Asked Questions—How Does Alcohol Affect a Person?" October 28, 2011. From http://www.cdc.gov/alcohol/faqs.htm#howAlcoholAffect

9. Substance Abuse and Mental Health Services Administration. *Results from the 2010 National Survey on Drug Use and Health: Summary of National Findings.* NSDUH Series H-41, HHS Publication No. (SMA) 11-4658. Rockville, MD: Substance Abuse and Mental Health Services Administration, 2011. From http://www.samhsa.gov/data/NSDUH/2k10NSDUH/2k10Results.htm#Fig3-3

10. Seguine, Joel. "Students Report Negative Consequences of Binge Drinking in New Surey." The University Record, University of Michigan, October 25, 1999. From http://www.umich.edu/~urecord/9900/Oct25_99/7.htm

11. Martin, Terry. "Understanding Nicotine Addiction." About.com, September 19, 2011. From http://quitsmoking.about.com/od/nicotine/a/nicotineeffects.htm

12. Encyclopedia of Drugs and Addictive Substances. "Nicotine – What Kind of a Drug is it?" Gale Cengage, 2006. From http://www.enotes.com/drugs-substances-encyclopedia/nicotine

CHAPTER 12

1. Self-Directed Search, http://www.self-directed-search.com

2. Occupational Outlook Quarterly. "High-Paying Occupations with Many Job Openings, Projected 2004–14." Bureau of Labor Statistics, Spring 2006. From http://www.bls.gov/opub/ooq/2006/spring/oochart.pdf

3. May, Kevin. "Humanities and Liberal Arts majors Are Going into Business." *The BYU Daily Universe,* December 14, 2011. From http://universe.byu.edu/index.php/2011/12/14/humanities-and-liberal-arts-majors-are-going-into-business

4. National Service Learning Clearinghouse. "Service Learning Is . . ." May 2004. From http://www.servicelearning.org/article/archive/35

5. U.S. Department of Labor, Bureau of Labor Statistics. "Number of Jobs Held, Labor Market Activity, and Earnings Growth Among the Youngest Baby Boomers: Results from a Longitudinal Survey." News Release, September 10, 2010. From http://www.bls.gov/news.release/pdf/nlsoy.pdf

6. Adams, Susan. "Get a Job Using the Hidden Job Market." *Forbes,* July 5, 2011. Accessed on October 1, 2011, from http://www.forbes.com/sites/susanadams/2011/07/05/get-a-job-using-the-hidden-job-market

7. Job Interview and Career Guide. "Resume: Keywords for Resumes—Keywords List." December 8, 2009. From http://www.job-interview-site.com/resume-keywords-for-resumes-keywords-list.html

8. List and descriptions based on Sternberg, pp. 251–269.

Photo Credits: p. iii (top): Carol Carter; p. iii (botom): Sarah Lyman Kravits; p. xvi: Alex Slobodkin/E+/Getty Images; p. xvii (left): Pearson Education Inc.; p. xvii (right): Pearson Education Inc.; p. 2: Sarah Lyman Kravits; p. 3: Sarah Lyman Kravits; p. 5 (top): Orange Line Media/Shutterstock; p. 6: LifeBound, LLC; p. 14: Sarah Lyman Kravits; p. 16: LifeBound, LLC; p. 19: Kevin Eaves/Fotolia; p. 26: Paul Vasarhelyi/Shutterstock; p. 25: Mocker Bat/iStockphoto/360/Getty Images; p. 31: Sarah Lyman Kravits; p. 33: Shutterstock; p. 36: Rusya M/Fotolia; p. 38: Juniart/Fotolia; p. 42: LifeBound, LLC; p. 52: Sarah Lyman Kravits; p. 53: Reflektastudios/Fotolia; p. 58: Pixland/Thinkstock; p. 66 (top): LifeBound, LLC; p. 66 (botom): Ilolab/Shutterstock; p. 68: WavebreakmediaMicro/Fotolia; p. 78: LifeBound, LLC; p. 80: Andrew Johnson/Fotolia; p. 82: Pearson Education, Inc.; p. 84: LifeBound, LLC; p. 89: Blend Images/Shutterstock; p. 93: Sarah Lyman Kravits; p. 95: Sarah Lyman Kravits; p. 101: LifeBound, LLC; p. 102: JustinRossWard/Shutterstock; p. 103: Mangostock/Fotolia; p. 108: Riccardo Piccinini/Fotolia; p. 113: Sarah Lyman Kravits; p. 117: Kmit/Fotolia; p. 124: United States Department of Agriculture (USDA); p. 125: LifeBound, LLC; p. 130: iQoncept/Fotolia; p. 131: Fotolia; p. 134: Sarah Lyman Kravits; p. 137: Courtesy of LifeBound, LLC; p. 139: ZUMA Press, Inc./Alamy; p. 143: Leungchopan/Shutterstock.